A Philosophical Inquiry into Subject English and Creative Writing

While engaging with the current political-educational climate of England, this book offers a timely contribution to debates around questions of knowledge in relation to education and school-level English by drawing together theories of individual and disciplinary knowledge.

The book provides a philosophical conception of knowledge – as fundamentally embodied at the level of the individual, and a matter of cultural form at the level of shared or "common" knowledge – and an analysis of the implications of this for schooled English. The research draws from various related fields including literary criticism, philosophy (of knowledge and of symbolic form), and phenomenology. The book rethinks general notions of knowledge and lays out the problems that exist within knowledge and language systems in education, especially secondary and university levels.

This highly relevant and informative book offers an insightful resource for academics, researchers, and post-graduate students in the fields of education studies, educational policy and politics, philosophy of education, and literature studies.

Oli Belas is Senior Lecturer in the School of Education and English, University of Bedfordshire, UK.

Literature and Education
Series Editors: David Aldridge and Andrew Green

Editors' Introduction

Dr Johnson, in an essay in The Rambler (31 March 1750), acknowledges the potential powers of literature. Because of the imaginative hold they exert over readers, he suggests that literary works enjoy formidable didactic potential, and 'may perhaps be made of greater use than the solemnities of professed morality, and convey the knowledge of vice and virtue with more efficacy than axioms and definitions.'

The aim of the Routledge *Literature and Education* series is to address the multiple ways in which education and literature interact. Numerous texts exist that deal with literary issues for educational purposes, serving the schools and higher education markets. Within the academic field of educational studies, there are works on the value of literature for moral formation or for the broader humanistic development of students of all ages. Within literary studies, there is a range of works that discuss the ways in which authors, texts or literary movements address educational themes. However, comparatively little has been written that specifically explores the complex notions of how literary texts function educatively, or what happens to them once they are brought into educational spaces and used for educational purposes. Additionally, limited attention has been paid explicitly to the ways in which literature can be a resource for educational thought or can nurture and inspire educational change.

This series provides a space for these issues to be explored. It presents scholarship working at the intersection of literary and educational studies and seeks to define an important and emerging area of interdisciplinary enquiry. Titles in this series engage in significant ways with what happens when an intermediate space opens up between the study of literature and the study of education. The series proposes a broad understanding of literature and education that is not bound by particular national, pedagogical or political contexts, and titles address one or more of the following themes:

1. Literature as education

    This theme connects discussions within educational studies and literary studies about the extent to which literature can or ought to be considered as educational.

2. The co-construction of literature and education

    This theme addresses the various ways that the fields of literature and education have historically, theoretically and imaginatively served to co-construct one another, for example the relation of the literary canon to the literary curriculum, and the formation of literature as a school and university subject.

3. What literature can teach us about education

    This theme addresses the ways that educational questions have been explored by different writers, literary movements and genres, drawing on the combined theoretical and interpretive resources of literary and educational studies.

Our hope is that this series will encourage thinking about the relationship between literary texts, readers and educators, providing an opportunity for creativity, investigation and debate. By forging new interconnections between literary and educational studies, it is our aim to encourage and open up fruitful new areas of thought and practice through which readers will be inspired to reconsider their understanding of both literature and education.

Books in this series

George Orwell and Education
Learning, Commitment and Human Dependency
Christopher Hanley

Literature, Videogames and Learning
Andrew Burn

The New Newbolt Report
One Hundred Years of Teaching English in England
Andrew Green

Literature and Understanding
The Value of a Close Reading of Literary Texts
J. W. Phelan

James Joyce and Education
Schooling and the Social Imaginary in the Modernist Novel
Len Platt

A Philosophical Inquiry into Subject English and Creative Writing
Oli Belas

For more information about the series, please visit https://www.routledge.com/Literature-and-Education/book-series/LITED

A Philosophical Inquiry into Subject English and Creative Writing

Oli Belas

LONDON AND NEW YORK

First published 2023
by Routledge
4 Park Square, Milton Park, Abingdon, Oxon OX14 4RN

and by Routledge
605 Third Avenue, New York, NY 10158

Routledge is an imprint of the Taylor & Francis Group, an informa business

© 2023 Oli Belas

The right of Oli Belas to be identified as author of this work has been asserted in accordance with sections 77 and 78 of the Copyright, Designs and Patents Act 1988.

All rights reserved. No part of this book may be reprinted or reproduced or utilised in any form or by any electronic, mechanical, or other means, now known or hereafter invented, including photocopying and recording, or in any information storage or retrieval system, without permission in writing from the publishers.

Trademark notice: Product or corporate names may be trademarks or registered trademarks, and are used only for identification and explanation without intent to infringe.

British Library Cataloguing-in-Publication Data
A catalogue record for this book is available from the British Library

Library of Congress Cataloging-in-Publication Data
Names: Belas, Oli, author.
Title: A philosophical inquiry into subject English and creative writing / edited by Oli Belas.
Description: Abingdon, Oxon ; New York, NY : Routledge, 2023. | Series: Literature and education | Includes bibliographical references and index. Identifiers: LCCN 2022025232 (print) | LCCN 2022025233 (ebook) | ISBN 9780367487362 (hardback) | ISBN 9781032374581 (paperback) | ISBN 9781003042617 (ebook)
Subjects: LCSH: English philology--Study and teaching--Great Britain. | Creative writing--Study and teaching--Great Britain. | Knowledge, Theory of--Philosophy--Great Britain.
Classification: LCC PE68.G5 B45 2023 (print) | LCC PE68.G5 (ebook) | DDC 420/.710941--dc23/eng/20220907
LC record available at https://lccn.loc.gov/2022025232
LC ebook record available at https://lccn.loc.gov/2022025233

ISBN: 978-0-367-48736-2 (hbk)
ISBN: 978-1-032-37458-1 (pbk)
ISBN: 978-1-003-04261-7 (ebk)

DOI: 10.4324/9781003042617

Typeset in Bembo
by KnowledgeWorks Global Ltd.

Contents

Series Editor Introduction   viii
Acknowledgements   x

PART I
Aims and Scope of the Book   1

1   Writing in, about, and from the Classroom   3
2   Mapping the Terrain of Schooled English and Creative Writing   12

PART II
Problems of Knowledge   29

3   Problems of Individual Knowledge   31
4   Problems of Curricular and Disciplinary Knowledge: The Curious Case of School English   59
5   Reading/Writing and a (Very) Rough Sketch of Revised English Studies (Coda to Part II)   88

PART III
Writing Beyond the English Studies Classroom   107

6   Thinking as a Kind of Writing, Writing as a Kind of Philosophy; or, On Lightbulb Moments   109

Index   143

Series Editor Introduction

As is fitting for a series that explores the interaction between literature and education, we have occasionally had cause to comment on the ways in which series authors' work exemplifies the pedagogical principles they are exploring in the work of others. This has never been truer than in the case of the present book, in which Oliver Belas self-consciously and reflexively (to paraphrase his own expression) "commits" an act of creative writing.

Anticipating Belas' reminder of the etymology of the word "essay," the work you are about to read essays a great deal in a way that is "personal, exploratory, confessional, revelatory." Belas throughout the following pages, displaying a breadth, clarity, and confidence in scholarship that are truly impressive, is reaching for new forms of writing and of expression that supplement the traditional "expository essay" with creative attempts to distort and expand the conventions of academic writing. The result is often subtle, witty, and surprising. We have found the book to be as entertaining as it is informative.

As with other texts in the *Literature and Education* series, this book enriches our view of literary studies by combining it with insights drawn from philosophy of education. This interaction offers new insights into notions of "writing" as Belas expounds an original argument around the nature and aims of English on the school curriculum. Perhaps the most attention-grabbing contribution is the argument that school English does not conform to the "knowledge rich" or "powerful knowledge" paradigm into which many contemporary policymakers and curriculum influencers would like to force it. But that is not the extent of the book's contribution to debates surrounding the nature of knowledge. Belas' eventual conclusion is that English fits such paradigms no more nor less than any other curriculum subject. His highly scholarly and tightly reasoned thinking on the place and nature of "knowledge" in education extends beyond his consideration of curricular English and challenges our thinking and our broader consideration of knowledge and the expression of learning across a range of subject areas. Philosophers of education and those interested in curriculum thought in the broadest sense will learn much from Belas' masterful treatment of the philosophical literature on "tacit" knowledge and the interplay of propositions, concepts, and embodiment.

Belas does not shy away from the controversial implications of his thesis. Anyone who aspires to English education undoubtedly wants to encourage their students to read and to "know" the texts they have read. But Belas' highly nuanced treatment of claims to literary knowledge and the ways in which such knowledge might be "framed" and "packaged" introduces a note of caution into the contemporary "knowledge rich" environment of schooled English. One much-lauded and influential new school, under the explicit influence of E. D. Hirsch, requires students to read only from an authorized list of important cultural products and provides "knowledge organizers" (like some species of dystopian educational personal shoppers/life gurus) to guide their engagement with and interpretation of those texts. There is, of course, a politics to such practices. Belas urges that school English should reposition students within the pedagogical hierarch as the producers of literary texts, as reader-writers who "inhabit" the way of being of a writer.

Belas' commitment to social justice in the curriculum and his willingness to pursue the implications of his argument lead to the bold assertion – surprising and refreshing for a writer on schooled English – that academic writing has very few important conventions or structures. This book therefore offers an extension of important contemporary raciolinguistic work on the political history and colonial implications of "Standard English" as a form of speech[1] – extending this to a warning about teacherly attempts to promote "Standard English." Belas' work goes on to suggest that in the contemporary world of academia there may be a variety of written forms and a range of "languages" within which students might be allowed and encouraged to produce their work.

We hope that readers will enjoy engaging with Belas' writing, which he presents as an enticement into a certain way of doing philosophy or to encourage an essay in thought through the reading encounter.

David Aldridge and Andrew Green

Note

1. I. Cushing and J. Snell, "The (White) Ears of Ofsted: A Raciolinguistic Perspective on the Listening Practices of the Schools Inspectorate," *Language in Society* (2021) (on early view at the time of publication).

Acknowledgements

As well as to those mentioned in Chapter 1, thanks are due to my colleagues in the School of Education and English at the University of Bedfordshire – not least to Andy Goodwyn, who (along with Michael Faherty and Phil Wright) took a punt on me in late 2017; to Cassie and J (the WAGs); to HT; to Anna and Billy; to Ralph and Julia; to the students, past and present, I've been lucky enough to work with; and to my parents- and brother-in-law, Linda, Murray, and Graham. My thanks, finally, to Andrew Green and David Aldridge, series editors for this book, for encouraging me to submit a proposal, and for their patience, support, and enthusiasm for the book as it developed.

Part I

Aims and Scope of the Book

Chapter 1

Writing in, about, and from the Classroom

Motivation and Focus of the Book

In this book, my focus moves back and forth – no doubt a little awkwardly – between subject-specific and more general concerns regarding language, knowledge, and education. My subject-specific concerns are with English, primarily Literature and Creative Writing. Throughout the book, I capitalize "English Literature" and "Creative Writing" when referring to the schooled subjects; and by "schooled," I mean simply the subjects as they've taken and changed shape in formal educational contexts. When "English literature" and "creative writing" appear (lower-case l, c, w), I'm referring, respectively, to literatures in English, and to a generalized activity of writing: neither relies on formal educational contexts for their particular characters. The difference between creative and other forms or modes of writing doesn't inhere in a special meaning we can ascribe to the word "creative" (a freighted term in educational discourse – policy- and practice-related, research-based[1]): creative writing is simply a mode in which the writing itself is the centre of interest. Notes left on fridges sometimes are and sometimes aren't creative. As Richard Rorty suggests – an idea with which I'm bookending the present work – some writing wishes it were, and some wishes it weren't, writing.[2] Though literature in English far predates schooled English Literature, the latter has never existed outside of a pedagogical logic; it is a product of state-controlled mass schooling, and, because of this, certainly was and quite possibly is as much a mechanism of control as of liberation.[3] In England, curricular content and assessment fall under central government control, and the punitive accountability and performance metrics by which most schools are bound put a great deal of downwards pressure on the post-Romantic ideals of personal growth and self-realization through literature that have enjoyed mainstream success since the later 1960s.[4] This is a pressure felt today by many of England's English teachers, among whom post-Romantic ideals are not uncommon,[5] but it's also one which may be challenged, as John Yandell suggests, from within the classroom space.[6] The politics and disciplinary identity of English Literature will be considered briefly in the next chapter and in greater detail in Chapters 5 and 6.

DOI: 10.4324/9781003042617-2

4 Aims and Scope of the Book

This book is motivated by a desire for what I call a "writerly turn" in schooled English. But, as I explain in the next chapter, that desire doesn't involve a rejection of all forms and traditions of English other than Creative Writing; nor does it entail a jettisoning of critical essayism. If the writerly turn I advocate did require such rejection and jettisoning, the book would end here. What is called for is a recalibration of, or reorientation with respect to, the writerliness of the subject (the Barthesian echo is addressed in Chapter 2). That – as I'll repeat in the next chapter – is an unashamedly weak thesis, as positive theses go. But I've come to be a little wary of positive theses in the competitive mode, of arguments that need to win. While some of the philosophical work takes place at a relatively high level of generality (this is especially the case in Chapter 3), my examples and cases are drawn mostly from England and America; and, in the main, my comments on government policy come from a place of sadness regarding curriculum design, anger regarding cultural and identity politics.[7] But where I critically engage at length with other academics – with, for example, Neil Gascoigne and Tim Thornton in Chapter 3; Robert Eaglestone in Chapters 4 and 5; Michael Young in Chapter 4 – the aim hasn't been to disprove, discredit, or rubbish their work. I only engage with their work because it has significantly shaped my own thinking, and because I agree with much of what they say. My disagreements are, in most cases, relatively fine-grained, and I give what space I do to articulating them because figuring out those disagreements has been instructive for me, and because those with whom I'm in dialogue deserve sustained, critical attention. In the chapters that follow, then, I've set out to be critical but not dismissive, exploratory as much as thetic.

Writing Out

Though this book has very little to say about pedagogy – it wasn't conceived as a *How to Teach…* project – late in its writing, I realized a simple yet essential connection between it and my teaching. As much as the views expressed herein find their way into my teaching, so too have they been shaped by, and are the results of, discussions had in the classroom and other marginal spaces – marginal in the dual sense of denigrated, devalued, or simply ignored, but sites from which mainstream discourses and dominant ideas might (perhaps) be challenged.[8] My own relationship to philosophy and academic writing has shifted and been recalibrated by the students I've worked with at the University of Bedfordshire, by my experiences teaching at secondary and university levels, and by my experiences teaching across university Education and English programmes. Students who, in the last two academic years, have taken second- and third-year classes in educational philosophy, and first- and second-year classes in sociolinguistics, and those who've been stuck with me as their Dissertation supervisor this last academic year (2021–22) – all have affected my thinking and writing on, in, and about academia in ways they almost certainly don't realize. They have changed the way I live and move in academic spaces.

Before joining, in January 2018, what's now the University of Bedfordshire's School of Education and English, I was a secondary English Literature, Language, and (briefly – see the next chapter) Creative Writing teacher. Those experiences have, of course, also left their mark on this book. The cohort of students with whom I worked between 2012 and 2016, the years during which they were studying for their GCSE and A Level qualifications (ISCED 2 and 3), is the cohort I often think of as having taught me how to (try to) *be* a teacher. Lewis Richmond – his complex relationships with formal education, language, and identity and their push-pull effect on one another; and his willingness to talk with me about these – has steered my own work in recent years (as with the students at Bedfordshire, I suspect more than he realizes – or realized until I sent him these lines). I'm not using "complex" as a codeword; it's not a euphemism for "bright kid, shame about the grades." Lewis did very well at school (by any metric the school would have used), even better at university. All the while, he remained committed (ostensibly (he talked about it) and performatively (he lived it)) to his Multicultural London English. I say his relationship with formal education, language, and identity (and their intersectionality) is complex simply because it's just that; these are entangled lines of flight that occupy Lewis's innovative performance art and poetry. Lewis has recently taken up a job as Resident Poet in a school in east London: "As quickly as I tried to escape I've found myself back in school," he wrote me (in the series of messages which began when I asked if I could include him in this book). After reading an early draft of this chapter, he wrote me again (the following was split across two messages): "It brings to mind that my resistance to the strict conformity to genre (and perhaps conformity in general lol) was always kinda there but very much cultivated" at school (despite the restrictions of the curriculum, we were able to find space for Lewis's experimentalism). "And now all these years later that's one of the main traits of my creative writing" – playing at the boundaries of form, tradition, and genre – "and a subject your book talks about." The discussions, in Chapters 5 and 6, of academic linguistic convention are in no small measure Lewis's.

This book was completed at a time when my friend and colleague Neil Hopkins and I were rethinking how we do and teach philosophy.[9] Our approach is, we hope, aligned with what is often called a decolonized approach. Neil and I are allied to that movement. I only hesitate to call what we have done and are attempting to do "decolonizing" because I'm mindful of the concerns some scholars have raised *on the sides of anticolonialism and antiracism* regarding the language and mainstreaming of decolonization.[10] Perhaps a decentring or de- and re-territorializing approach would best describe what we're trying to do.[11] Our approach to teaching, and whatever we might call that approach, aside, this book bears more than a trace of my friendship with Neil, and of our friendship with Lewis Stockwell.[12]

It bears the impress, too, of conversations with: Judith Suissa (about, among other things, antiracism, antisexism, academic freedom), Marys Richardson and Healy, John White, and other members of the Philosophy of Education Society of Great Britain; Jim Clack and Uvanney Maylor, both colleagues at the University of Bedfordshire. Jim and I lived down the road from one another for several years, and realized we were probably becoming friends just as he was preparing to leave Walthamstow for Brighton. He and I have worked together to try to revise our modules and our teaching in a broadly critical-pedagogical spirit.[13]

Significant others who've directly influenced the shape and grain of this book: Tim Jarvis, Liliana Carstea, Doug Cowie, and Katie Prangle (many, many conversations about reading, writing, music, film, teaching, sensibility, the elusiveness of "academic standards," the Ray Dudley Way...); Eva Aldea and Marcus Cheadle (many, many conversations about reading, writing, music, film, teaching, sensibility, bread, salt beef, dogs, becoming-animal/becoming-human/becoming-stronk...); Tim Armstrong and Bob Eaglestone (respectively my PhD supervisor and advisor; there are few obvious connections between my PhD and this book, though the latter swims in the former's wake); Erin and Trevor Buchmann; my parents (conversations, among others, had during the journey between Bedford and Walthamstow); my brothers; Peter Goh; my wife Sarah, who loves me and loves English and gives no shits about academic philosophy and will probably never read this book.

It's conventional to include acknowledgements early in an academic book, before the first chapter. But I make these acknowledgements here because the individuals, groups, and contexts I've mentioned have directly shaped this book. Methodologically, this is a work of writing out; to be precise, of writing out from the classroom. As with my use above of "marginal," there's a dual sense to my use of "writing out from...": Rachel Sagner Buurma and Laura Heffernen's book *The Teaching Archive* argues that what's characteristic of English Literature – a subject, remember, that has never existed outside a pedagogical logic – is that its knowledge is made in and disseminated centrifugally from the classroom, understood as a laboratory space.[14] Their book is a series of case studies which, drawing on archival research, demonstrate the ways in which signal moments in literary criticism and scholarship are the products of classroom practice – this in contrast to views of the classroom as a marginal space in which knowledge already formed is disseminated "down" from the teacher to students, a space of secondary importance which pulls the scholar away from the real work of research (knowledge production). Perhaps it's no surprise that a scholarly work interested in tracing histories of the co-creation of literary knowledge is itself a collaborative work; the authors make the point that every sentence of *The Teaching Archive* has been written collaboratively (it isn't a compilation of individually written chapters).[15]

What's true for Buurma and Heffernen of English may (that is, *can*; perhaps, *should*) also be true of philosophy, conceived and practised in a certain way. We have examples of collaborative and decentred philosophy, philosophy *as* pedagogy (and not merely something to be "delivered" via pedagogic technique) in the works of Cornel West and bell hooks, and, more recently, in the public philosophy of Myisha Cherry.[16]

I have my own recent experience of philosophy in the Buurma-Heffernen mode. The curriculum for the second-year philosophy module mentioned above is decided by the students, who nominate the topics to be addressed. This year (academic year 2021–22), those students, week after week, did profound, original philosophical work, very often by grounding their comments in lived experience (the decision to share personal experience with the class is itself a philosophical and brave move). The module's aim has been to co-create something closer to an epistemically just educational space, to make the class a work of standpoint epistemology in action.

In one session, early in the semester, I was referring to John White's work on curriculum design. A series of excellent questions (*what would John White say about...*) followed. I answered as best I could. Eventually, I said, "Maybe I'll just ask John White." John wrote a 1500-word essay, addressed to the students taking the class, in which he explained his views; he and I then video-recorded a conversation, based on that piece, which I shared with the class. He posted his essay, headed with a note explaining why it'd come about, to ResearchGate.[17] Three things strike me about this episode. First, the beauty of giving and receiving another's writing as a gift and gesture of recognition.[18] Second, the exchange – both direct and indirect – between me, the students, and John was not only (or even primarily) about the communication and clarification ("delivery") of philosophical ideas ("curricular content"); rather, the exchange and the gestures of gift-giving and -receiving were themselves philosophical: philosophy as a mode of living, an orientation the students have themselves recognized in their feedback (roughly, "philosophy is everywhere"). Third, the gift John wrote was produced as a response to questions from me, prompted by questions and comments that occurred to the students, who were themselves speaking from particular positions, and whose questions were spurred by what I was saying John had said or might say. And around and around we went: philosophy made in the classroom.

The first sense in which this book writes out from the classroom, then, is simple enough: the final shape of the book was forged in the classroom. Though this is not a pedagogical guide, it is, in many ways, dispatches from the classroom, a tortuous lab report.

Marginal Spaces

In *The Practice of Everyday Life*, Michel de Certeau distinguishes between *space*, which he likens to interpretative and creative acts, and *place*, that which is produced by design, and by certain ways, styles, and habits of dwelling. De Certeau's space is, perhaps counter-intuitively, temporal: space (like literature, it's worth saying, in Derrida's view[19]) happens; and, when it does, it punctures the administrative dream of place. Contrast the administrative fantasy of the school as an ordered and orderly *place* – mapped not only by floor plans, but also timetables, dress and conduct codes (for staff and students), and so on – with students' tactical subversions of that orderliness (strict adherence to the one-way system in order to be late for lessons; strategic use of surveillance blind-spots; reinterpretation of uniform codes…[20]). De Certeau considers the ways in which walking can confound the mapping of place, and can reterritorialize and ironize it. By walking, he claims, *place* becomes re-articulated or mobilized as *space*. If "place" is ordered, regulated, "proper," then "*space is a practiced place.* Thus," he writes, "the street geometrically defined by urban planning is transformed into a space by walkers. In the same way, an act of reading is the space produced by the practices of a particular place."[21]

As well, then, as positioning the classroom as a centre of knowledge co-production, the second sense in which this book writes out from the classroom is that it's been written outside of or beyond the classroom imagined as an orderly, regulated place, and through marginal (informal, unplanned) conversations had in marginal (academically devalued; unschooled, though not unregulated) spaces: stolen moments in my office, at home, on walks (long or short, solo or accompanied, with or without music or podcasts), in the pub, at the gym, on park benches, on drives between home in Walthamstow and work in Bedford… The book has emerged from numerous unplanned walks in the spirit of de Certeau. I don't think there's anything new about this as a matter of fact: many books have been written in many places-and-spaces. But here I want to claim as a methodology the marginal practices that have produced this book: at some point, I became aware that the conversational and perambulatory meanderings I've mentioned were a large part of how the book was being written; once aware, I went with it, embraced it. Why wouldn't I, given this book's – like so much work in the academic humanities since the pragmatist, existential, and phenomenological turns – concern with experience?

A final thought on walking-writing. I love to walk (in the usual sense), and I know myself well enough to know that, as I tire, I become less sure-footed; I have to look and take care where I plant my feet. As time's gone on, I've attempted, more and more, to walk with one foot in and one out of strictly schooled discourse, to stop practising academic discourse as place and to remap it, through my own writing attempts, as a space of possibility.

Synopsis of the Book

Having given, in this chapter, a brief, personal account of the motivation for and development of this book, in Chapter 2, I give reasons for suggesting that schooled English be recentred around writing practices. It is, to an extent, a synopsis of the chapters that follow, and in which more theoretically detailed analyses are developed. In Chapter 2, I consider (briefly) the history of English as a schooled subject, and its use by governments – from the nineteenth century to the present day – as a mode of aesthetic and civic education. I consider, too, the brief career of A Level Creative Writing in England, discontinued for being overly skills-oriented and insufficiently knowledge-based. The knowledge/skills opposition is rejected in Chapter 3, which develops a general theory of personal knowledge as consisting always in embodied, practical skill.

Though Chapter 3 works at a high level of generality, its relevance to the book's subject-specific concerns lays in the claim that problems of knowledge turn out, often, to be problems of language – the raw material of our subject-centred inquiry. In that chapter, I aim to address some familiar binary oppositions: practical and theoretical knowledge; knowledge and skills; explicit and tacit knowledge; knowing-how and knowing-that. The central argument can be stated simply: at the level of the individual, there's no knowledge that's not practical; knowledge can't be prised apart into theoretical and practical components; individual knowledge *is* skill (or, sometimes, "knowing-how"). One reason for the length of Chapter 3 is that while its main claims can be stated succinctly, its justifications cannot. Another reason for giving the question *what is knowledge?* such prominence is that whenever knowledge is invoked in conversations about education – particularly policy-focussed conversations – we find ourselves swimming in the crosscurrents of politics and philosophy.[22] All too often, there is little clarity as to what *knowledge* is supposed to mean or do beyond conferring prestige: knowledge good; skills – not bad exactly, they just need to know their place. But as Christopher Winch and John Gingell suggest, if "the idea that pupils being educated should end up [knowing] more at the end of the process than they did at the beginning" is, for many, a given, then broad-level questions about knowledge "must be central concerns for any theory of education."[23]

In Chapter 4, I explore questions of disciplinary knowledge and identity, focussing in particular on Michael Young's theory of powerful knowledge. There, I argue that different subjects don't map to or consist in different types of personal knowledge (since all personal knowledge is embodied practical skill). Talk of disciplinary *knowledge* is misleading, as it can encourage just such a misstep (from different subjects to different "types" of knowledge); instead, we do better to talk of disciplinary identity, which can be easily defined as follows: disciplines are what their practitioners do. The only questions, then, following from this definition, are: who's to count as a practitioner, on what basis, and according to whose authority? Chapter 3 aims to dissolve the apparent difference between theoretical and practical personal knowledge, so that in Chapter 4 we can dismiss the idea that different subject-areas map to, draw on, or exploit different types of knowledge: they can't do this if there are no different types of knowledge. Subject or disciplinary identity, then, cannot be predicated on an idea that there is a "type" of knowledge appropriate to or characteristic of that subject.

Chapter 5 is a coda of sorts: from an analysis of the criticism/scholarship debate that continues in literature studies, via a discussion of aesthetic experience, I return to the rationale for the writerly turn I advocate for English studies; and in doing so, the subject-specific concerns of the book come to an end. In the final chapter, I consider the significance of writing to higher education generally. There, I offer a modest defence of discipline, while calling for a more flexible understanding of academic writing, one that has little concern for academic standards and conventions so-called (there are, I argue, very few of these, and they are, in the main, poorly defined).

Note for readers unfamiliar with England's system of Key Stages (KS): Primary education covers ages 5–11 and KS1-2; secondary, ages 11–16 (KS3-4) and 16–18 (KS5); further education (FE), ages 16 and above, and generally KS4-5. KS4 culminates in national exams (GCSEs, usually taken when students are 15 or 16 years old); these are equivalent to the International Standard Classification for Education (ISCED) level 2. In England, A Levels are usually taken for the first time when students are 17 or 18; they are equivalent to ISCED level 3.

Notes

1. See, for example, Anna Craft, *Creativity in Schools: Tensions and Dilemmas* (Abingdon: Routledge, 2005); Ian Munday, "Creativity: Performativity's Poison or its Antidote?" *Cambridge Journal of Education* 44(3) (2014), pp.319–322, and "A Creative Education for the Day After Tomorrow," *Journal of Philosophy of Education* 50(1) (2016), pp.49–61.
2. Richard Rorty, "Philosophy as a Kind of Writing: An Essay on Derrida," *New Literary History* 10(1) (1978), pp.141–160.
3. Oliver Belas and Neil Hopkins, "Subject English as Citizenship Education," *British Educational Research Journal* 45(2) (2019), pp.320–339; Simon Gibbons, "W(h)ither the radicals?" *English in Education* 50(1) (2016), pp.35–43; Ian Hunter, *Culture and Government: The Emergence of Literary Education* (Basingstoke: Macmillan, 1988).
4. The post-Romantic emancipatory and self-expressive view of schooled English secured mainstream status in the wake of the 1966 Dartmouth Conference and John Dixon's summary of that event, *Growth through English: Set in the perspectives of the seventies* (Oxford: Oxford University Press, 1975).
5. Andy Goodwyn, "The State of English: NATE's Annual Survey," *Teaching English* 24 (2020), pp.29–32.
6. John Yandell, "Classrooms as Sites of Curriculum Delivery or Meaning-Making: Whose Knowledge Counts?" *Forum* 56(1), pp.147–155; see also Gibbons, "W(h)ither the radicals?"
7. See Myisha Cherry's work on the philosophy of anger: *The Case for Rage: Why Anger is Essential to Anti-Racist Struggle* (New York: Oxford University Press, 2021); "The Errors and Limitations of Our 'Anger-Evaluating' Ways," in Cherry and Owen Flanagan (eds), *The Moral Psychology of Anger* (London: Rowman and Littlefield, 2018), pp.49–65.
8. Echoes here of Deleuze's concept of the minoritarian: see relevant entries in Adrian Parr (ed.), *The Deleuze Dictionary*, Rev. Ed. (Edinburgh: Edinburgh University Press, 2010).

9. Neil lives and works in the Deweyan democratic spirit. See his "Creating Sites of Community Education and Democracy: Henry Morris and the Cambridgeshire Village Colleges. A Reflection 90 Years on from Their Inception," *British Educational Research Journal* 46(5) (2020), pp.1099–1110 (DOI: <https://doi.org/10.1002/berj.3615>), and *Democratic Socialism and Education: New Perspectives on Policy and Practice* (Switzerland: Springer, 2019).
10. See, for example, Olúfẹ́mi Táíwò, "Rethinking the Decolonization Trope in Philosophy," *The Southern Journal of Philosophy*, Spindel Supplement, 57 (2019), pp.135–159; Eve Tuck and K. Wayne Yang, "Decolonization Is Not a Metaphor," *Decolonization: Indigeneity, Education, and Society* 1(1) (2012), pp.1–40.
11. One can never de- without – even briefly – re-territorializing (see Parr, *Deleuze Dictionary*).
12. See our (short-lived) podcast, *Ed. Space*, <https://anchor.fm/oliver-belas> (accessed 30 November 2021).
13. See Jim Clack's "Can We Fix Education? Living Emancipatory Pedagogy in Higher Education," *Teaching in Higher Education* (2019), DOI:10.1080/13562517.2019.1704724.
14. Rachel Sagner Buurma and Laura Heffernen, *The Teaching Archive: A New History for Literary Study* (Chicago: University of Chicago Press, 2021).
15. Buurma and Heffernen, *The Teaching Archive*, note "On Authorship" (ix): "We have written every line of this book together, and we have elected to list authorship alphabetically. This author order represents neither a hierarchy nor a division of labor."
16. bell hooks's Teaching Trilogy, *Teaching to Transgress: Education as the Practice of Freedom* (New York: Routledge, 1994), *Teaching Community: A Pedagogy of Hope* (New York: Routledge, 2003), *Teaching Critical Thinking: Practical Wisdom* (New York: Routledge, 2010); hooks and Cornel West, *Breaking Bread: Insurgent Black Intellectual Life* (New York: Routledge, 2017); Myisha Cherry, *Unmuted: Conversations on Prejudice, Oppression, and Social Justice* (New York: Oxford University Press, 2019) (see also Cherry's *UnMute Podcast*, from which this book comes: <https://unmutetalk.podbean.com/> and <https://www.myishacherry.org/the-unmute-podcast-2/> (accessed 30 November 2021).
17. John White and Oliver Belas, "The School Curriculum and its Aims: Official, Real and Desirable," October 2021, <https://www.researchgate.net/publication/355575768_The_school_curriculum_and_its_aims_official_real_and_desirable> (accessed 30 November 2021).
18. John asked to be kept in the loop as to how the module goes. At the time of writing, there are three weeks left. One student asked, mid semester, "how will we feed back to John White?" In the end, the students agreed that they'd feed back to me directly (they didn't want me to leave the room – "there's enough of us here who'll tell you what we really think!"), that I would knock their and my thoughts into a piece of writing, and that I'd send it to them, allowing time for comment, approval, and so on.
19. Jacques Derrida, "'This Strange Institution Called Literature': An Interview with Jacques Derrida," in *Acts of Literature*, ed. Derek Attridge (London: Routledge, 1992), pp.33–75.
20. Dick Hebdige, *Subculture: The Meaning of Style* (London: Routledge, 1979).
21. Michel de Certeau, *The Practice of Everyday Life*, trans. Steven Randall (Berkeley: University of California Press, 1984), p.117.
22. For a sense of this, see my "Education, Knowledge, and Symbolic Form," *Oxford Review of Education* 44(3) (2018), pp.291–306 (DOI: 10.1080/03054985.2017.1389711).
23. Christopher Winch and John Gingell, "Knowledge," in *Philosophy of Education: The Key Concepts*, 2nd Ed. (Oxon: Routledge, 2008), p.109.

Chapter 2

Mapping the Terrain of Schooled English and Creative Writing

The Turn to Writing

Writing is overlooked in schooled English – English Literature especially – and it would be a good idea if this were not the case. A model of schooled English that centred creative writing practices would be preferable to the current dominant model that takes literary criticism as primarily a special kind of *reading* and a version of literary criticism as *the* way to do schooled English Literature. Nor would it be a bad idea to recentre writing as practice – as both a mode of thinking and a form of thought – in education generally.

These – to echo comments made in Chapter 1 – are the unashamedly weak central theses of this book. Weak because "good idea" and "not a bad idea" are about as far as I'm prepared to push things. There are no arguments in what follows against critical writing in general, certainly not against literary criticism and critical essayism; if there were, these would be arguments against this very book. In Chapters 4 and 5, I consider what I think a misguided argument – which isn't new but has made a relatively recent comeback – over the appropriate, best, or most authentic way of doing literature study. That argument asks us to choose between literary criticism (usually some version of close reading) and scholarship (literary history, biography, theory …). I don't come down on either side of that debate, though I do reject the argument that close reading is somehow, as if "by nature," more aesthetically attuned than literary-theoretical and-or historical approaches.[1] So long as there are literary scholars and critics producing literary history, theory, and criticism, schooled English would do well to teach versions of each of these and to do so explicitly – to foreground, that is, the different ways into (methods for) literature study available to us.

The reasons I reject the argument that close reading is more aesthetically responsive than other literary-critical methods are teased out across Chapters 4 and 5. But in brief: there are many ways in and by which we might articulate our responses to literary texts, many resources we might draw upon. Context – that most familiar and vague catch-all – can never be bracketed out of our responses or our explanations of those responses; so the idea that,

DOI: 10.4324/9781003042617-3

as a matter of methodological principle, we wouldn't draw on the resources of history, biography, theory, philosophy, and so on is perverse (and, in a strict sense, impossible). We might not call attention to the ways in which we contextualize our readings, but contextualize them we inevitably will: there are, as I will insist throughout Part II, no ways of knowing that aren't framed.[2] There is, to be sure, something akin to magic in our most profound encounters with literature (and with other artforms, other aesthetic encounters); but that magic is the spark produced by the crossing of two live wires, or by flint striking flint. The spark *is* the aesthetic "content": it isn't "in" the text, but rather emerges between text and reader(s) (aesthetic experiences may be individual or group experiences).[3] Giving voice to aesthetic encounters isn't, then, a matter of "putting into words" the aesthetic "content" of the text. Artworks may trigger profound aesthetic experiences; but this is not the same as saying that the artworks "have" an aesthetic "content." There is no such content – no inside correlated to the outward appearance of the text, no depth correlated to its cosmetic surface, no "true" or "deeper" meaning correlated to its apparent or surface meaning.[4] There is, then, nothing "behind" literary criticism, in the way we may imagine "real" events to be behind the empirical research report, and to or in place of which the report points or stands.[5] In literary criticism, the work – the knowing – is "in" the writing. Better: it *is* the writing.

So, to repeat, my suggestion that a more creative-writing-centred model of schooled English would be a good idea doesn't entail a rejection of (more or less "traditional") literary criticism. It involves adjusting how we think about literary criticism – and, by extension, how we think about schooled essayism (the expository essay as a central tool of educational assessment) more generally (this is the focus of this book's final chapter). Recentring writing doesn't mean making education all about writing. My focus here is on the re- more than the centring. "Good" writing doesn't happen and can't be taught in the way that flatpack furniture can be assembled. So yes, writing should be brought back into the frame and into sharper focus. But recentring writing also means a recalibration of so-called "academic standards" – of what might count as "good," "permissible," "effective" academic writing; of the linguistic resources that might feed and even rejuvenate academic writing.[6]

The first reason, then, for suggesting it would be a good idea to centre creative writing practices in schooled English is that literary criticism is a fundamentally creative *and* writerly mode. This isn't, first, to presuppose a hard boundary between reading and writing, and, second, to come down on the side of writing to the exclusion of reading. It *is* to take for granted the idea that the special sorts of critical reading privileged not only in schooled English but also other academic humanities – History, Philosophy, and so on – are always articulated as special sorts of writing, and, too, that any sort of critical writing is always-already a type of reading. Even when the mode of communication is speech rather than script, the sorts of questions that tend to be posed in the English classroom – questions of the "what do you think of...?" and "how do you respond to...?" variety – ask for performances closer in many ways to writing than to spontaneous, casual talk. We ask students to stake claims and explain them, to get their stories straight as to why they think what they think. We ask them, that is, not only to answer the questions posed, but to narrate the *whys* of their *whats*. That these answers are sought in front of others and in classroom environments gives them a semi-permanence: we're asking students to go on the record with, and thereby underwrite, their answers. To say, then, that literary criticism is a fundamentally creative *and* writerly mode is an attempt to foreground the method by which critical readings are articulated. Here and throughout this book, "writerly" and "readerly" bear the trace of Barthes: I take it for granted, first, that no reading – the special sorts of close critical reading associated with schooled English Literature – takes place outside of or separate from a writing; and, second, that reading is not a matter of deciphering "hidden" yet determinate meanings "in" the text.[7] Once again: (critical) reading takes place as a writing of sorts; to set something down in writing is to offer some kind of a reading.

The second reason for suggesting a turn towards writing is that it's an oddity of schooled English that it marginalizes the practice and, therefore, direct experience of the very things it's supposed to be about. Once upon a time, I thought this a new-ish sort of argument; not entirely original, but one that challenged the presuppositions upon which more than a century of schooled English (in England at least) has been based. But as D.G. Myers has shown, there was a time in the later nineteenth century when university English in the United States sought to establish Creative Writing as the means for recuperating an already lost rationale for literature study – namely, that the best reason for studying literature was that more might be produced.[8]

Close reading, histories of which usually start in the early twentieth century with I.A. Richards, emerged as a way of training future teachers of a then-fledgling subject to be better readers. The point of criticism, for Richards, is "to discriminate between experiences and to evaluate them."[9] Presumably by this, he meant *aesthetic* experiences, though R.G. Collingwood accused Richards's methods of being too psychological and mechanistic ever to be truly aesthetic.[10] Regardless of Collingwood's sideswipes, and as we'll explore further in Chapter 5, the idea that close reading hooks us up to the aesthetic like no other method of critical reading persists in more and less prescriptive forms. Notwithstanding the concerns of some that schooled English is being reduced to (in particular) history, in England – where curricula, exams, and final awards are centrally controlled and administrated – there's a consensus between educator-critics and the exam boards that whole-text understanding, articulated through close critical analysis, is the most effective way of reading literature.[11] Franco Moretti's distant reading is hardly about to take off in schools, colleges, and universities:[12] close reading of one sort or another is still the thing. Indeed, so deeply embedded in the close reading tradition (broadly conceived) is the culture of Anglophone schooled English that alternative orientations sometimes seem unthinkable. Internecine arguments are more likely to be over which species of close textual analysis is best than over the dominance of the critical-cum-expository-essayistic paradigm itself.[13] And while the deep rootedness and familiarity of that paradigm are precisely what makes it *feel* like the natural mode for doing English, the widespread, tacit acceptance of this state of affairs is a funny thing, given both the supposed subject-matter of English Literature (literary texts) and the post-Romantic attitude that has characterized schooled English, particularly since Dixon's personal growth model.[14]

In terms of subject-matter: *if* the point of English is to understand what makes texts work — and it's by no means clear or obvious that this is *necessarily* the point — then why not analyze texts with a view to making your own? Analysis wouldn't be the endpoint, but, rather, a first methodological step toward one's own original writing. (This isn't to suggest that one couldn't possibly undertake creative writing projects without formal analysis of other inspiration or stimulus texts).

As for the post-Romantic attitude that shapes thinking around English education, this takes us from the second to a third reason for suggesting schooled English be recentred around creative writing practices.

English Now and Then: Aesthetic Education as Civic Education

If the point of schooled English is Romanticist self-development and -expression, individual moral-aesthetic growth — and it's not a given that *this* is *the* point, either — then no one writerly form or genre intrinsically enables this better, "more," or more naturally than any other. There's a western essayistic tradition that tends to be traced from Montaigne, and which is profoundly personal, exploratory, confessional, revelatory.[15] But the expository academic essay, framed primarily as a means by which "understanding" is demonstrated and assessed, is likely to limit the essay's apparent scope or actual appeal as a mode and form of (self-)expression and, in the case of schooled English, aesthetic exploration. In a report for the Edexcel exam board, A Level English Literature examiners give examples of the sorts of analyses and comments that were more or less successful: "students who recognized *x* and understood the ways in which ... tended to do better on this part of the exam," that sort of thing.[16] Such gestures signal that there *are* ways of reading texts, if not quite rightly or wrongly then at least better or worse (presumption, in the spirit of Barthes, of the readerly text?). Let me say, briefly and without space to spell out an argument, that it *is* possible to distinguish more and less *convincing* readings of texts in ways that are relatively non-authoritarian *and* relatively non-problematic.[17] This doesn't much matter here. What does is, first, that if the essay is conceived or perceived as a vehicle for the reproduction of readings already made, then much assaying is likely to go out of the essay. Second, one is reminded of Ian Hunter's point, made in his landmark *Culture and Government: The Emergence of Literary Education*, that the emergence of close reading in the early twentieth century marks not only a beginning – of schooled English in a form that remains familiar – but also the culmination of a governmental logic in which aesthetic training, moral instruction, and civic management are interlaced. As Hunter points out, although "Romantic aesthetic education" has influenced current thinking around schooled English, its thrust was never towards the general or the democratic, but rather the particular and the individual. Modern literary education, Hunter argues, is Romantic in its aesthetic drive, but deeply un-Romantic because its "aesthetic imperative is deployed as a discipline in the government of populations," not the autopoietic revelation of the authentic individual.[18] Hunter's claim is that government-administered aesthetic education, via schooled English especially, is a mechanism of discipline and control: it may teach us not only, in the spirit of Richards, how to discern between aesthetic experiences; it may school us in *what* aesthetic experiences we should be having, in what aesthetic experiences count, as such, at all.

The implications of Hunter's insight are significant. Consider recent calls to decolonize and diversify school curricula. One version of the diversify argument is a call for wider representation along the various axes of identity. There are good reasons for such a call, though the point isn't to stop at the claim that there should be more minoritized authors on the curriculum. Charles Mills often turns to Black- *and* white-authored literature as a source of insight into structural racism.[19] He argues that society's systemic inequalities are constitutive of social worlds; the social may be non-physical but it *is* real, material: we live (in) the social. Mills is therefore able (without resorting to biological essentialism) to treat literature as a rich source of alternative epistemologies. Lack of curricular diversity, then, isn't simply a failure of representation and-or recognition, an issue of who's included in and who's excluded from the curriculum; it's also a signal that certain standpoints and experiences will be centred and licensed to speak, while others won't.[20]

These aren't "merely theoretical" concerns. In both England and America, central government has made several recent interventions aimed at preventing antiracist and anticolonial conversations from taking place in educational settings. In England, these include:

- threatening to withdraw state funding from museums if "controversial" artefacts were removed from display (for critics of the government, "controversial" was code for "colonial" and "colonialist");
- stipulating that school reading materials must not come from "organizations," including and especially anti-capitalist groups, "that take extreme political stances on matters";

- Kemi Badenoch (Minister for Women and Equality at the time of writing) stating that the government "stand[s] unequivocally against critical race theory," and that the discourse is as "a dangerous and divisive ideology that should not be adopted in educational theory";
- Badenoch, in the same parliamentary address, declaring that she and the government "do not want teachers to teach their white pupils about white privilege and inherited racial guilt. Let me be clear," she continued, "that any school that teaches those elements of critical race theory as fact, or that promotes partisan political views such as defunding the police without offering a balanced treatment of opposing views, is breaking the law";
- a government-commissioned report on race, published in March 2021, concluding that, while racism existed at an interpersonal level (some individuals have racist beliefs; some individuals experience racism), there's no evidence of structural racism or race-related inequality in England. In a notorious passage on education from the report's introduction, we're told that:

Neither the banning of White authors or token expressions of Black achievement will help to broaden young minds. We have argued against bringing down statues, instead, we want all children to reclaim their British heritage. We want to create a teaching resource that looks at the influence of the UK, particularly during the Empire period. We want to see how Britishness influenced the Commonwealth and local communities, and how the Commonwealth and local communities influenced what we now know as modern Britain. One great example would be a dictionary or lexicon of well known British words which are Indian in origin. There is a new story about the Caribbean experience which speaks to the slave period not only being about profit and suffering but how culturally African people transformed themselves into a re-modelled African/Britain.[21]

This is a confused and confusing bit of writing (forget, for now, the grammatical non-parallelism of "African/Britain" and the genuinely devastating impact of that on the sense of the sentence). It's hard to find examples of white authors and their work being banned from England's school curricula, other than, perhaps, the removal of Steinbeck's *Of Mice and Men* and Harper Lee's *To Kill a Mockingbird* in the mid-twenty-teens, several years before this report was published. Those texts were removed by then Education Secretary Michael Gove – not, so the received wisdom goes, because they were written by white but, rather, American – that is, not British – authors.[22] Many will agree that tokenism is no good – this is one of the antiracist criticisms of Black History Month (October in the UK): set aside the implications that Black histories occupy a separate cultural space from others, that they are (as indicated by the marked form, "*Black* history") outside the main stream of "proper" or "normal" history, and that 11 months of the year are, if not white, then certainly non-Black history months. The extracurricular spaces (assemblies, home-room or tutor periods, and so on) to which Black History Month is often restricted can mean that Black histories, to the extent that they're discussed at all, are kept *in* schools yet *off* the curriculum: Black History Month "celebrations" can all too easily be acts of containment and control, of cultural-historical incarceration (again, *pace* Foucault), rather than of recognition.[23] Why bringing down statues *cannot* be an act of cultural assertion and (in the spirit of the government report on racism) reclamation is anyone's guess, as is the logical connection between the first and second sentences of the passage cited above. The lexicon of Indian loan words that *would* be a "great idea" already exists: no doubt the authors of the report would be delighted with Yule and Burnell's late-nineteenth-century *Hobson-Jobson*, which everywhere bears the trace of colonialism and imperialism but never discusses it and which presupposes the sort of narrative of benign progress via the spread of "western" modernity which the government report wishes to "reclaim."[24] Finally, given the other government interventions listed above, I suppose the happy histories of slavery and colonialism recommended by the report could become just about the only ones permissible in schools. It's worth, on that front, saying that the UK government's various statements on race, culture, and colonialism run counter to recommendations made by Remi Joseph-Salisbury and the Runnymede Trust (a UK race-equality and race-relations thinktank) in 2020.[25] Joseph-Salisbury's report, *Race and Racism in English Secondary Schools*, "calls for anti-racism to be placed at the centre of our education systems. This should be reflected in policies, in the curriculum, in the racial demographic of the teaching force, and in the competencies" – what the report calls the "racial literacy" – "of teachers."[26]

Interestingly, around the time when the UK government was making the moves listed above, the USA's then-President Donald Trump passed Executive Order 13950, "Combating Race and Sex Stereotyping." Trump, like Badenoch, described critical race theory as divisive, as well as, along with diversity training, un-American. EO13950 – revoked in January 2021 by President Joe Biden – was seen by many as an anti-equity move, aimed particularly at critical race theory, associated discourses, activism, and activists. Kimberlé Crenshaw pointed out in an episode of her podcast, *Intersectionality Matters*, that according to EO13950, she and her co-hosts would be able to discuss critical race theory on the podcast but not in the lecture hall or seminar room.[27]

By casting critical race theorists and antiracist activists as ideological extremists, the UK and USA governments position themselves as non-ideological and therefore "reasonable"; as offering simple truths, unfiltered through ideological lenses. The government simply tells it like it is. By attempting to police what conversations can and can't be had in school classrooms, government is attempting to intervene in and to stipulate what does and doesn't count as knowledge; it is attempting to construct and shore up orders of acceptable knowledge, even as its non-ideological self-presentation is an apparent rejection of the idea that knowledge is socially constructed; and it's doing this in a way that could make it harder for teachers to say that this is what's happening, because to do so could become personally and professionally risky.

Let me be clear: I don't assume that teachers and students are not ever having these risky conversations – my own experiences as well as those of other teachers close to me say otherwise; and John Yandell writes of the subversive and liberatory practices that go on in the English classroom *despite* ever-shrinking curricular possibilities.[28] My concern is that the opportunities for these conversations will be reduced by the constant tightening of political-institutional screws we've witnessed in recent years. Read this political climate alongside generally restrictive assessment regimes and narrowed curricular scope; and read it – particularly, tellingly – alongside that passing comment about "white authors" in the government's race report. Hard not to think, with Hunter, that in the era of mass state schooling, aesthetic education through literature is understood by government agencies as a mechanism not of liberation but of control: a way of shaping citizens and a national identitarian narrative.

While the UK government's recent noises around race and education are a living example of Jacques Rancière's observation that politics always has an aesthetics, and aesthetic a politics, this is not a new turn.[29] If anything, schooled English's implication in the government's anxieties about civic control and national identity-building is literary education being put to its original ideological use. The emergence of state education in England in the later nineteenth century was bound up in political concerns over the rise of the working-class electorate: how to educate in order to contain them and maintain the institutional status quo amid sociopolitical change. As Robert Lowe (at the Education Office between 1859 and 1864) put it, state-controlled education of the masses was "a question of self-preservation" and "preservation of the institutions of the country"; the lower classes, now that they had the franchise, must be educated to "appreciate and defer to a higher cultivation when they meet it," in order to "be able properly and intelligently to discharge the duties devolving on them."[30] For Lowe, English literature and language were of primary importance; they were constitutive of a national cultural identity. England's literature, said Lowe, is "unparalleled in the world," and yet, of "our great classical authors," a young man at university "knows nothing [...]; and the consequence is that our style is impoverished, and the noble old language of our forefathers drops out of use."[31] Lowe's view was shared by Joseph Angus, examiner in English (its language, literature, and history) at the then-new University of London. Angus declared English Literature "the reflection of the national life, an exhibition of the principles to which we owe our freedom and progress: a voice of experience speaking for all time."[32] Both Lowe and Angus exemplify a "political tradition" of educational thinking about English, one in which text selection is aimed at inculcating "certain desired values" in students (specifically in young men).[33] Literature was used as a form of moral and civic education, as a "civilizing" tool, not only at home but also abroad, out in the Empire and among the colonies.[34]

History delights in irony: a subject which has come to think of itself as anti-authoritarian and emancipatory, chiefly on a post-Romantic model,[35] has its roots in governmental techniques and strategies of civic control. Things can change, of course. Schooled English need not be now what it once was. Recent research carried out by England's National Association for the Teaching of English (NATE) suggests that a broadly post-Romantic, emancipatory-cum-personal-growth model of schooled English continues to shape teachers' sense of purpose. But that same research suggests, too, that teachers do indeed feel the squeeze of the political and curricular structures within which they and their students work. Not uncommonly, teachers feel sustained by their relationships with their subject and their students, but are enervated by the political-institutional demands of schooling.[36] As Mark Fisher has argued, the late-capitalist logic (what Fisher calls capitalist realism) of which education is a function is radically depersonalized and decentred, infinitely malleable and absorbent. Individual intention is nullified by the demands of The System, which, in Fisher's view, is algorithmically rational, an intentional but non-sentient aether (as in John Carpenter's *The Fog*); it functions like the viral aliens in Octavia Butler's novel *Clay's Ark*, evolutionarily "programmed" to reproduce and whose human victims self-consciously experience their own loss of agency.[37]

Fisher's is not an entirely pessimistic view, however. Resistance is not entirely futile, but it requires, he writes, a future orientation, a striving towards new possibilities as well as an account of past and present grievances. He calls for a repoliticization of the cultural sphere: forms of analysis and activism that foreground the ideological work of governments' post- or non-ideological posturing, which "transform the taken for granted into the up-for-grabs."[38]

Fisher writes on a grand political scale; this book does not. I don't think, not for a moment, that my suggestion of a writerly shift in schooled English is a general sociopolitical remedy. But I do think that if the emancipatory potential of schooled English is to be realized, then one way of moving closer to that realization is to make the subject's disciplinary history part of its schooled subject-matter. It's not enough to question and-or broaden the range of "permissible" readings afforded by or within a particular paradigm and its associated methodologies. We need, too, to be willing to challenge paradigms and methodologies themselves. This doesn't entail – as I've already said – throwing out literary criticism and close reading altogether. It simply requires making those forms and methods part of the subject-matter. It means turning a critical eye onto the ways received methods are rationalized, and on how they've come to be formed; onto, that is, the method*ologies* as well as the methods. (As Michael Monahan has said with respect to the academic philosophical canon, we needn't insist on not reading Plato, Aristotle, Kant, and the usual philosophical suspects; we simply need to ask why we might want or need to study them and to be willing to make space for other texts, voices, perspectives.[39]) A willingness to engage in methodological critique means a willingness to think about the linguistic conventions that go with or govern certain methods. Space is needed in which "academic conventions," so-called, can be interrogated and questioned: can be transformed, that is, from a taken-for-granted into an up-for-grabs.

The Space and Place of Creative Writing[40]

To understand how creative writing practices fit into this picture, consider the brief history of A Level (or high-school) Creative Writing in England:

> During development of subject content, it became clear that for AS and A Levels in creative writing and health and social care, it has not been possible to draft subject content in accordance with the department's guidance and Ofqual's principles for reformed AS and A Levels. As a result, these subjects will not be developed further.
>
> The DfE's guidance and Ofqual's principles required reformed A-levels to avoid overlap with other subjects, have clearly defined and rigorous content, and be right for progression to Higher Education. It was concluded to be problematic that there are connections between Creative Writing and English, and that Creative Writing is (or could be construed to be) more skills based than knowledge based. Ultimately, this prevented AQA from reforming this qualification.

In England, A Levels are normally taken over a period of two academic years. In the 2013–14 academic year, A Level Creative Writing ran for the first time. By spring 2015 – months, that is, before the first national cohort of Creative Writing A Level students had completed the course – the national government had announced its plans to discontinue Creative Writing and a number of other "non-academic" – or "non-knowledge-based" – courses.

The first of the quotations above is the Department for Education (DfE) announcement of the end of Creative Writing; the second is the notification published by the AQA, the exam board that supported the Creative Writing A Level.[41] These announcements were published between approval and publication by the Quality Assurance Agency (QAA) – the body responsible for monitoring standards in HE – of the Benchmark Statement for Creative Writing in UK universities. Whereas the QAA Benchmark Statement for English defines English as "a core academic subject" "compris[ed]" of the "three complementary strands" of English Literature, English Language, and Creative Writing, the separate statement dedicated to Creative Writing states that, "[i]n the UK, the formal methods of teaching that first began to develop in relation to Creative Writing in the 1970s have now established it as an academic subject in its own right, methodologically independent of English or other 'parent' subjects."[42] A little later, we're told that "Creative Writing contributes significantly to related subjects such as English Literature and Language, Drama, Media, Journalism, Film Studies and Theatre Studies. [...] As a subject, [Creative Writing] is naturally interdisciplinary."[43] Where Creative Writing is first presented or fashioned as an essential component of the corporate body that is English, now it's a discrete subject with perhaps only a family resemblance to several others, English first listed, but not necessarily foremost, among them.

At the very moment, then, when the *difference* of Creative Writing is being formally asserted in Higher Education, the subject is being erased from secondary and further education. This happened at a time when government spokespersons made a big deal about the importance of "knowledge-rich" over and above a "skills-centred" education – a difference which, as we'll find in Part II, holds no logical water. Here, for example, is Nick Gibb (Minister of State for School Standards between 2010 and 2012, then 2015 until 2021) claiming that a "good education"

> is dependent upon, and impossible without, a fundamental basis of knowledge about the subject in question. Put simply, a commitment to social justice requires us to place knowledge at the heart of our education system. *And this is not a statement of opinion – it is a fact established by decades of research by cognitive scientists* [...].
>
> It is an unfortunate fact, however, that many modern conceptions of education either ignore the importance of knowledge, or actively deride it. During the 1960s, it became fashionable amongst educationists to dismiss the accumulation of knowledge as a joyless anachronism: rote learning of unconnected facts, inflicted upon bored and unwilling pupils. School curricula were increasingly rewritten to focus not upon subject content, but upon skills and dispositions. [...]
>
> It always saddens me to see thrilling content of education, be it timeless literature, scientific wonders, or great historical events, being relegated to a backseat, so that these comparatively joyless "skills" and "processes" can come to the fore.[44]

Benchmark statements, policy documents, course specifications, curriculum outlines, and the like are often read as stylistically neutral, strategically bland even. Yet these texts do not "merely" reflect, state, point; their language doesn't carve nature at the joints. They also discursively produce the very thing at which they appear merely to be pointing.[45] Such documents are roadmap texts, and one of the many remarkable things about maps is that, despite their obvious textuality and symbolism, we so often forget or overlook their obvious textuality and symbolism. One thinks of a reliable map realistically or faithfully representing the mapped terrain. Yet this is surely wrong. Maps don't depict objects and places themselves, but rather the spatial *relations* between them. As Peter Whitfield points out, the Renaissance-era map is a "newly created" text that's mistaken for unproblematically mirroring the world, rather than reconfiguring our relation to it.[46] Similarly, what we might call the internal *coherence* of the map itself gets mistaken for the *correspondence* between text and thing. Maps appear to pre- and pro-scribe possibility; they open and foreclose certain interpretative possibilities (which routes might we take over this terrain?). They produce discursive, imaginary *spaces*; they don't mirror *places*. While English and Creative Writing are constituted and emerge in very different ways in the Benchmark Statements, Creative Writing at secondary level has been removed from the disciplinary map altogether. "Secondary English," "English" in HE, "Creative Writing" – these name the *productive mappings* of very different terrains, and these mappings are indicative of very different educational concerns over the nature of knowledge (the central concerns of Chapters 3 and 4). I am, then, accusing Nick Gibb, the DfE, and other government mouthpieces not of telling it like it is, but of committing acts of creative writing.

The disciplinary borders of Creative Writing, especially in the UK, and the subject's relationship to knowledge are also being repeatedly re-negotiated and re-mapped from within the academy and "inside" the discipline. Andrew Cowan of the University of East Anglia, the UK "home" of university Creative Writing, is resistant to the theorization of Creative Writing – that is, theory drawing on language "outside" of Creative Writing (sociology, philosophy, and so on).[47] Yet he produces, in the very articulation of that resistance, a theoretically inflected anti-theory theory that seeks to defend both the uniqueness of Creative Writing and its standard pedagogical practices, principally the workshop. (This concern over Creative Writing's borders and disciplinary purity parallels the criticism/scholarship argument that persists in English Literature studies (see Chapter 5).) Part of Cowan's defence of Creative Writing rests on the opposition of literary practice and literary knowledge. Neither term is defined, though what he appears to mean by literary practice emerges in the course of analysis and argument more clearly than what he means by literary knowledge. Interestingly, while the educational politics of Cowan and Gibb, not to mention the DfE, are clearly opposed, all deploy the opposition of knowledge to skills and-or practice in order to advance or rationalize their arguments. A practice-based general theory of knowledge is the focus of Part II, in particular Chapter 3. Here, a few words on knowledge and practice in relation to Creative Writing and English.

One of the tropes running through Michel de Certeau's *The Practice of Everyday Life* is narrativity, both the strategic, normative narratives that structure public culture – what he calls "the scriptural economy" – and the narratological tactics by which norms are resisted, turned back on themselves, ironized. One such narratological tactic de Certeau considers is the walk. By walking, he claims, *place* becomes re-articulated or reconstituted as *space* (place, remember, is ordered, mapped, located; space is mobile and mutable, a product of practice).[48] The productivist model of knowing favoured in this book, and developed in Part II, is not unique to Creative Writing; and nor is Creative Writing intrinsically more spatial than "platial," in de Certeau's sense, more innovative or imaginative than other versions of schooled English. As Tim Jarvis points out in a response to Cowan, unquestioning loyalty to workshop-based pedagogy may well encourage a consensus view of writing ("good," "bad," and everything in between) that is inimical to experiment and exploration.[49] The line of argument in this book, then, isn't: creativity is good; English Language and Literature aren't creative, Creative Writing is; therefore the latter should be the model for all schooled English. Creativity is a freighted term, and it's perfectly possible to do well on a Creative Writing course without being original or innovative (and in saying this I'm saying nothing of how to determine the measures by which judgements of originality and innovation are to be made). The real interest at the centre of this book isn't a positive thesis regarding school and language arts, but, simply, a genuine interest, an open and ongoing fascination, with our complex relationship with language.

Schooled English in all its forms takes language for granted, pre-supposes its availability. This book does little to challenge that. But it does, as we'll find in the final chapter, ask that space be made for greater variety of styles and registers, both in schooled English particularly and academic writing generally. Because of the book's subject-specific interests in English Studies, I do focus primarily on the essay and essayism. I'd like to say, however, that by the time you read this a number of the modules on which I teach will have been revised to allow for a variety of forms of writing ("traditional" academic and-or journalistic essays; artefactual submissions (fine-or-visual art, film, and so on); photojournalistic pieces; Creative Writing and-or reimaginative submissions; podcasts …). Several colleagues and I had been considering such revisions to our modules anyhow; but the decision to go ahead with them was finally made, for me, when my friend Erin Buchmann spoke to some of our students about her and her regional Education Board's work alongside Indigenous communities in Northern Ontario. Just one part of that work – framed by concerns over educational justice and equity, and what Miranda Fricker has termed "epistemic injustice" – has been to broaden the range of both the systems of knowledge recognized in schooling and the forms that high-school students' projects can take. The hope is that students will feel greater affinity with their work; that they will find greater scope for self-exploration and -expression and for pursuing issues that matter to them.

The writerly shift I advocate is a call for students to be able to dwell and play in language and for academic writing to be enriched from below. As mentioned in Chapter 1, my own recent experiences in the university classroom have profoundly shaped and reshaped my pedagogical and writerly relationships with academic philosophy and the academic humanities more broadly; they have directed and redirected the course of this book, which has become, in the spirit of Rachel Sagner Buurma and Laura Heffernen's *The Teaching Archive*, an exercise in writing out from the classroom.[50]

Notes

1. See, for example, Joseph North, *Literary Criticism: A Concise Political History* (Cambridge, MA: Harvard University Press, 2017). For a challenge to such either-or disciplinary formulations, see the section in the Introduction called "Disciplinary History Against the Divide," in Rachel Sagner Buurma and Laura Heffernen, *The Teaching Archive: A New History for Literary Study* (Chicago: University of Chicago Press, 2021), pp.6–13.
2. Funny how things work out, and how confirmation bias shapes things: I've long stood by the idea that all knowledge is epistemically framed. But I was reminded, weeks before submission of the typescript of this book, that this is the starting point for Michel Foucault's entire project, announced in his 1970 lecture "The Order of Discourse," trans. Ian McLeod, in Robert Young (ed.), *Untying the Text: A Post-Structuralist Reader* (Boston, MASS: Routledge & Kegan Paul, 1981), pp.51–78.
3. For examples of this sort of a model in educational philosophy, see David Aldridge, "Religious Education's Double Hermeneutic," *British Journal of Religious Education* 40(3) (2018), pp.245–256, and Paul Standish, on whom Aldridge draws, "Impudent Practices," *Ethics and Education* 9(3) (2014), pp.251–263.
4. There's a sort of residual Deleuzianism to these claims. Residual because I've been affected in significant ways by my very unscholarly and piecemeal reading of Deleuze and by indirect encounters with him – primarily through conversations with Eva Aldea and Tim Jarvis. Eva, a good lapsed Deleuzian, makes me think I'm maybe a closet or natural Deleuzian.
5. I explore this further in Chapter 6, where I consider Rorty's ideas about writing that does and doesn't wish it were writing.
6. See Chapter 6.
7. Roland Barthes, *S/Z: An Essay*, trans. Richard Miller (New York: Hill and Wang, 1974).
8. D.G. Myers, "The Rise of Creative Writing," *The Journal of the History of Ideas* 54(2) (1993), pp.277–297.
9. I.A. Richards, *Principles of Literary Criticism* (1924; London: Routledge, 1989), p.vii.
10. R.G. Collingwood, *The Principles of Art* (1938; Oxford: Oxford University Press, 1958), pp.35, 262–264.
11. In a recent educational pamphlet, written for the Philosophy of Education Society of Great Britain, Robert Eaglestone warns against the dangers of reducing literature study to an "ersatz history"; and here he's in unison with one of England's major exam boards, Edexcel, which emphasizes in its 2017 examiners report the importance of close textual analysis over generalized historical or biographical context. Eaglestone, *"Powerful Knowledge," "Cultural Literacy," and the Study of Literature in Schools, IMPACT* 26 (PESGB/Wiley Online Library: <https://onlinelibrary.wiley.com/doi/epdf/10.1111/2048-416X.2020.12006.x> (accessed 01 October 2021)), p.27; Pearson Edexcel, "Examiners' Report June 2019: GCE English Literature 9ET0 02," and "Examiners' Report June 2017: GCE English Literature 9ET0 03" (Pearson Education Ltd).
12. Franco Moretti, *Distant Reading* (London: Verso, 2013).
13. This paradigm looks like a textbook case of Foucauldian discursive formation. See Foucault, "The Order of Discourse."
14. John Dixon, *Growth through English: Set in the perspectives of the seventies* (Oxford: Oxford University Press, 1975).
15. Michel de Montaigne, *The Complete Essays*, trans. M.A. Screech (London: Penguin, 1993); see also Brian Dillon, *Essayism* (London: Fitzcarraldo Editions, 2017).
16. Pearson Edexcel, "Examiners' Report June 2017: GCE English Literature 9ET0 03."

17 There isn't space for explication of this claim. The roots of it, though, can be discerned in my reading of Brandom: see Part II.
18 Ian Hunter, *Culture and Government: The Emergence of Literary Education* (Basingstoke: Macmillan, 1988), p.5.
19 Charles W. Mills, *Blackness visible: Essays on philosophy and race* (Ithaca: Cornell University Press, 2015).
20 On this, see my and Neil Hopkins's "Subject English as Citizenship Education," *British Educational Research Journal* 45(2) (2019), pp.320–339. In that piece, we use the example of Sam Selvon's *The Lonely Londoners* (1956; London: Penguin, 2006), the only text by a Black author on a cluster of novels thematized by the exam board (Edexcel) as Colonisation and its Aftermath. In general, I stand by the arguments developed in that paper – indeed, some of those arguments are reworked in this chapter. What Neil and I don't consider in that piece, however, is the fact that minoritized writers do appear elsewhere on the Edexcel syllabus. The exam board has, it seems, been careful not to position Black writers as writing (or "having" to write) only about race and racism, women writers about sex, gender, and sexism, and so on. However, it does lead to a strange situation in which Twain's *Huckleberry Finn* is studied under the theme "Colonisation and Its Aftermath," but Morrison's *Beloved* isn't.
21 Commission on Race and Ethnic Disparities, *Commission on Race and Ethnic Disparities: The Report*, <https://www.gov.uk/government/publications/the-report-of-the-commission-on-race-and-ethnic-disparities> (accessed 28 November 2021), p.8. See also my "The Government's Creeping Authoritarianism," PESGB Blog (22 March 2021), <https://www.philosophy-of-education.org/the-governments-creeping-authoritarianism/> (accessed 37 June 2021). See also Busby, "Schools in England Told Not to Use Material from Anti-Capitalist Groups," *The Guardian* (27 September 2020), <https://www.theguardian.com/education/2020/sep/27/uk-schools-told-not-to-use-anti-capitalist-material-in-teaching>; Kimberlé Crenshaw, *Intersectionality Matters* (podcast), The African American Policy Forum, "Episode 31. Truth Be Told Remi: The Destructiveness of Donald Trump's Equity Gag Order & What Biden Must Do Now," <https://soundcloud.com/intersectionality-matters/31-truthbetold-the-destructiveness-of-trumps-equity-gag-order-what-biden-must-do-now>; Joseph-Salisbury, *Race and Racism in English Secondary Schools*, The Runnymede Trust (2020), <https://www.runnymedetrust.org/projects-and-publications/education/racism-in-secondary-schools.html>; Hansard, "Black History Month," Volume 682: Debated on Tuesday 20 October 2020, *UK Parliament*, <https://hansard.parliament.uk/Commons/2020-10-20/debates/5B0E393E-8778-4973-B318-C17797DFBB22/BlackHistoryMonth?highlight=critical%20race%20theory#contribution-C8980402-C448-4265-B82A-F3A465E34808>; Jessica Murray, "Teaching White Privilege as Uncontested Fact is Illegal, Minister Says," *The Guardian* (20 October 2020), <https://www.theguardian.com/world/2020/oct/20/teaching-white-privilege-is-a-fact-breaks-the-law-minister-says>; Peter Stubley, "Museums Risk Funding Cuts if They Remove Controversial Objects, Culture Secretary Warns," *Independent* (27 September 2020), <https://www.independent.co.uk/news/uk/politics/statues-british-museum-government-funding-black-lives-matter-oliver-dowden-b651318.html>; *US Dpt. of Labor* (n.d.), "President Biden Revokes Executive Order 13950," <https://www.dol.gov/agencies/ofccp/executive-order-13950>. All online sources accessed 01 March.
22 Richard Adams, "Michael Gove Hits Back in Row Over GCSE Syllabus," *The Guardian* (27 May 2014), <https://www.theguardian.com/politics/2014/may/27/michael-gove-denies-ban-of-american-novels-from-gcse> (accessed 28 November 2021).

23 Although, on the limits and dangers of a politics of recognition, see Glen Sean Coutlhard, *Red Skin White Masks: Rejecting the Colonial Politics of Recognition* (Minneapolis: University of Minnesota Press, 2014).
24 Henry Yule and A.C. Burnell, *Hobson-Jobson: A Glossary of Colloquial Anglo-Indian Words and Phrases, and of Kindred Terms, Etymological, Historical, Geographical and Discursive*, 2nd Ed., William Crooke (ed.) (1886; London: John Murray, 1903). Full text available via Project Gutenberg, <https://www.gutenberg.org/cache/epub/58529/pg58529-images.html> (accessed 29 November 2021).
25 Joseph-Salisbury, *Race and Racism in English Secondary Schools*, The Runnymede Trust (2020), <https://www.runnymedetrust.org/projects-and-publications/education/racism-in-secondary-schools.html> (accessed 29 November 2021).
26 This quote from the summary on the report's landing page (see n.25).
27 See Jacey Fortin, "Critical Race Theory: A Brief History," *The New York Times* (8 November 2021), <https://www.nytimes.com/article/what-is-critical-race-theory.html> (I include this because Fortin reads CRT off against recent political events in the US); David Smith, "How Did Republicans Turn Critical Race Theory into a Winning Electoral Issue?" *The Guardian* (3 November 2021), <https://www.theguardian.com/us-news/2021/nov/03/republicans-critical-race-theory-winning-electoral-issue>; Julia Carrie Wong, "The Fight to Whitewash US History: 'A Drop of Poison is All You Need'," *The Guardian* (25 May 2021), <https://www.theguardian.com/world/2021/may/25/critical-race-theory-us-history-1619-project>. For Memorandum M-20-34, in which CRT and diversity training are called divisive and un-American, see <https://www.google.com/url?sa=t&rct=j&q=&esrc=s&source=web&cd=&ved=2ahUKEwjrhvD-Mnb70AhVKhP0HHapgC2UQFnoECAwQAQ&url=https%3A%2F%2Fwww.whitehouse.gov%2Fwp-content%2Fuploads%2F2020%2F09%2FM-20-34.pdf&usg=AOvVaw3eBLDiKwvwzFsx3SNc8rI8>. Kimberlé Crenshaw, *Intersectionality Matters* (podcast), The African American Policy Forum, "Episode 31. Truth Be Told Remi: The Destructiveness of Donald Trump's Equity Gag Order & What Biden Must Do Now," <https://soundcloud.com/intersectionality-matters/31-truthbetold-the-destructiveness-of-trumps-equity-gag-order-what-biden-must-do-now>. All sources accessed 29 November 2021.
28 John Yandell, "Classrooms as Sites of Curriculum Delivery or Meaning-Making: Whose Knowledge Counts?" *Forum* 56(1), pp.147–155.
29 Jacques Rancière, *The Politics of Aesthetics*, Gabriel Rockhill (ed. and trans.) (London: Bloomsbury, 2004).
30 Robert Lowe, *Primary and Classical Education: An Address. Delivered before the Philosophical Institution of Edinburgh on Friday, November 1, 1867* (Edinburgh: Edmonston and Douglas, 1867). Available online through the Wellcome Library, <https://dlcs.io/pdf/wellcome/pdf-item/b21964798/0> (accessed 18 May 2018), pp.9, 32, 8.
31 Lowe *Primary and Classical Education* (26).
32 Andrew Sanders, *The Short Oxford history of English literature*, 3rd Ed. (Oxford: Oxford University Press, 2004), p.8.
33 Richard Beach and Thomas Swiss, "Literary Theories and Teaching of English Language Arts," in Diane Lapp and Douglas Fisher (eds), *Handbook of Research on Teaching the English Language Arts*, 3rd Ed. (London: Routledge, 2011), accessed online via Credo Reference, <http://0-search.credoreference.com.brum.beds.ac.uk/content/entry/routengart/literary_theories_and_teaching_of_english_language_arts/0?institutionId=210> (accessed 29 November 2021); James Marshall, "Research on Response to Literature," in Michael L. Kamil, Peter B. Mosenthal, P. David Pearson, Rebecca Barr (eds), *Handbook of Reading Research* Vol. III (New York: Routledge, 2009), pp.382–402.

28 Aims and Scope of the Book

34 Gauri Viswanathan, *Masks of conquest: Literary study and British rule in India* (New York: Columbia University Press, 1989); Robert Eaglestone, "What do We Teach when We Teach Literature?" *The Use of English* 67(3) (2016), pp.4–12.
35 Hunter, *Culture and Government*; Dixon, *Growth Through English*.
36 Andy Goodwyn, "The State of English: NATE's Annual Survey," *Teaching English* 24 (2020), pp.29–32.
37 Mark Fisher, *Capitalist Realism: Is There No Alternative?* (Ropley, Hants: Zero Books, 2009), pp.69–70; John Carpenter (dir.), *The Fog* (1980); Octavia E. Butler, *Clay's Ark* (1985; VGSF-Victor Gollancz, 1991).
38 Fisher, *Capitalist Realism* (78).
39 Michael J. Monahan, Editor's Introduction to the supplement on the Spindel Conference, *The Southern Journal of Philosophy* 57 (2019), pp.5–15.
40 This section draws on my article "Creative Writing: Mapping the Subject," *Use of English* 68(4), pp.45–53.
41 DfE, "Additional reformed GCSE and A Level subject content consultation [2015]," <http://dera.ioe.ac.uk/24261/1/Additional-reformed-GCSE-and-A-level-subject-content-consultation.pdf>, and NAWE, AQA's notice of the discontinuation of the Creative Writing A Level, <http://www.nawe.co.uk/DB/nawe-news/creative-writing-a-level.html> (both accessed 17 February 2017).
42 QAA, *Subject Benchmark Statement: English* [2015], <http://www.qaa.ac.uk/en/Publications/Documents/SBS-English-15.pdf>, (§1.3, p.5); QAA, *Subject Benchmark Statement: Creative Writing* [2016], <http://www.qaa.ac.uk/en/Publications/Documents/SBS-Creative-Writing-16.pdf>, 2.1/p.6 (accessed 23 July 2021). QAA's Creative Writing benchmark statement was updated in 2019. References are to the original document, but all quotations can be found in the newer version (available at <https://www.google.com/url?sa=t&rct=j&q=&esrc=s&source=web&cd=&ved=2ahUKEwiqo-qIodP3AhV-gP0HHYaxC3wQFnoECAoQAQ&url=https%3A%2F%2Fwww.qaa.ac.uk%2Fdocs%2Fqaa%2Fsubject-benchmark-statements%2Fsubject-benchmark-statement-creative-writing.pdf%3Fsfvrsn%3D2fe2cb81_4&usg=AOvVaw3T5FM9Oi19yvLWi5QCXiV5> (accessed 09 May 2022)).
43 QAA, *Subject Benchmark Statement: Creative Writing* [2016] (§2.11, p.7).
44 Nick Gibb, "Nick Gibb: What is a Good Education in the 21st Century?" Gov.uk, <https://www.gov.uk/government/speeches/what-is-a-good-education-in-the-21st-century> (accessed 18 February 2021, emphasis added).
45 Again, one thinks of Foucault, "The Order of Discourse."
46 Peter Whitfield, *Mapping the World: A History of Exploration* (London: The Folio Society, 2000), p.14.
47 Andrew Cowan, "Blind Spots: What Creative Writing Doesn't Know," *TEXT* 15.1 (2011), <http://www.textjournal.com.au/april11/cowan.htm> (accessed 23 July 2020).
48 Michel de Certeau, *The Practice of Everyday Life*, trans. Steven Randall (Berkeley: University of California Press, 1984), p.117. See Chapter 1.
49 Tim Jarvis, "'Pleasure balks, bliss appears' or 'The apparatus shines like a blade': Towards a Theory of a Progressive Reading Praxis in Creative Writing Pedagogy," *TEXT* 15.2 (2011), <http://www.textjournal.com.au/oct11/jarvis.htm#smi2r>; see further responses, Lucy Neave, "Teaching Writing Process," *TEXT* 16.1 (2012), <http://www.textjournal.com.au/april12/neave.htm>, Cowan, "A Life Event, a Life Event: The Workshop that Works," *TEXT* 16.1 (2012), <http://www.textjournal.com.au/april12/cowan.htm#wan2r> (all accessed 17 February 2020).
50 Buurma and Heffernan, *The Teaching Archive*.

Part II
Problems of Knowledge

Chapter 3
Problems of Individual Knowledge[1]

Introduction

The words knowledge and skill are often used as if they name distinct domains, states, or capacities – sometimes an opposed, sometimes a complementary pair; but nearly always distinct. (We encountered an example of this in Chapter 2, with the announcement that A Level Creative Writing would be discontinued, and the exam board's suspicion that the government considered the course skills-oriented rather than knowledge-based.) While England's National Curriculum framework contains 167 mentions of "knowledge" and 100 of "skills," it has only twelve instances of the collocation "knowledge and skills" and three of "knowledge, skills and understanding," that last bundle seeming to stand for the general curricular aims of schooling (what else would those aims be?). But whether there is meant to be some clear semantic difference between, for example, pupils' "language skills" and "knowledge of language" is less certain.[2]

If there is *any* kind of implied distinction between knowledge, skill, and understanding in the National Curriculum document, it's probably something like this: knowledge is the foundation on which skills and understanding rest; it's best represented by propositions that say something about how the world just is, and which are true independently of anyone's feelings about them (the propositions) or it (the world). Skill is the ability to apply knowledge to a particular task, problem, or situation. Understanding is the ability to integrate knowledge and skill into broader contexts of action and complexes of information: the ability, perhaps, to take knowledge and skills beyond the situations in which they were learned and contexts to which they were first applied – and to improvise. But that explanation risks circling back to skill, so that we end up with a definition that is, in fact, no definition at all: skill is the ability to put knowledge into action; understanding is the increasingly deft and flexible – skilful – deployment of skill. According to this view, whatever skill is, understanding is merely "skills-plus."

Pinpointing differences of political meaning between knowledge, skill, and understanding is largely guesswork, because we don't have much to go

DOI: 10.4324/9781003042617-5

on: the ways in which knowledge, skill, and understanding are parcelled out or bundled up in curriculum documents; the ways in which those words are invoked in various statements made by policymakers and commentators. Curriculum documents and political speeches are not works of philosophy (though they inevitably imply some (more or less consistent) philosophical presumptions), so attacking them as if they are would be disingenuous, were it not for the politicization of knowledge and skill, and the privileging of the former over the latter. When a Schools Minister contrasts "joyless 'skills'" unfavourably with the "thrilling content of" a "knowledge-based curriculum" – note where scare quotes do and do not occur in those quotes – we're meant to nod along with the common-sense distinction between and privileging of the rich contents of knowledge over the empty form of skills.[3] Because such statements are not in the genre of philosophy, one seldom comes across any attempt at formal definition; knowledge, skills, and understanding are just chucked about as if obviously or "transparently" meaningful. One of the starting assumptions of this chapter is that they are not.

A reason for thinking that knowledge is presumed to be the foundation of skills and understanding is that, by force of linguistic habit, it's nearly always mentioned first when it's not mentioned in isolation. But there are other indications of the political move towards, or subscription to, a view of knowledge proper as foundational: the relatively widespread idea that broad curricula can be built around some kind of "core" knowledge; the purchase that E.D. Hirsch's work on core knowledge and cultural literacy enjoys, both in the USA and in England; the influence, and controversy, of Michael Young's conception of "powerful knowledge"; the pushback, in England especially, against the apparent skills-obsessiveness of educational policymakers in the late 1990s and early 2000s; the comforting idea that knowledge consists of independently true, easily articulable propositions (facts).[4]

There's more to be said about the epistemic and disciplinary aspects of curriculum design, and some of it will be said in the next chapter. Here, my concern is less with the epistemic than with the epistemological, with, that is, a general theory or philosophy of knowledge; and my aim is to convince you that individual or personal knowledge can't be cashed out in the opposing terms of the practical and the theoretical, knowledge and skill, the codifiable and the tacit, the explicit and the implicit. When our focus is what the individual knows, knowledge and skill can't be prised apart. There is no personal knowledge that is not practical in some way. Or, in traditional philosophese: there's no hard line between the epistemological and the ontological; certainly, the latter is neither reducible to nor dependent upon the former. (Here, *personal* means simply the knowledge that any particular person might have; it doesn't mean knowledge of the self.)

Articulating a general philosophy of knowledge matters to this book and to educational philosophy broadly, because challenging the theoretical/practical binary lays bare the moral and ideological uses to which words like knowledge and skills have been put. Not that talk about skills and knowledge in educational contexts *shouldn't* be ideologically or morally framed; rather, such talk can't *not* be. Such framing should, therefore, be made explicit, and not passed off as "good common sense shared by all reasonable people (folks like us)." The general theory outlined in this chapter makes all personal knowledge acquisition a matter of skill development, and it rejects attempts to map different "types" of knowledge to different subject-areas or disciplines (an issue to be pursued in Chapter 4).

The idea that different subjects require different "types" of knowledge confuses the basic phenomenological condition of being a knower with different disciplinary practices. This chapter sets the stage for the broad argument running through the next: subject-areas or disciplines (particle physics and bike-riding, say) are distinguished by being different practices focussed on or immersed in different subject-matters, not by being rooted sometimes in skill, sometimes in knowledge. This is no more mysterious than saying that while the drummer, bassist, keys, and horn player in a jazz quartet have a common subject-matter, at the same time each is involved in a distinct practice (drumming, bass-ing...); no more mysterious than saying that the particle physicist and stunt-rider know (how to do) different things.

Knowing-How and -That; Knowing Tacitly and Explicitly

The distinction between knowing-that and knowing-how is most closely associated with Gilbert Ryle, who, in the second chapter of *The Concept of Mind*, argues that practical knowledge (knowing-how) can't be reduced to theoretical or propositional knowledge (knowing-that). The Cartesian "intellectualist legend" that Ryle rejects claims that being knowledgeable or skilled consists first in doing "a bit of theory and then [...] a bit of practice." Skilful acts are, on this model, the result of the body following the executive commands of the mind. But this model, Ryle claims, is fallacious, as it leads logically to an infinite regress. If we think what's actually happening when I kick a ball is that my body is realizing the propositional rules, or theory, for ball-kicking, and that these are necessarily prior to the act itself, then – says the Rylean critique – we need to assume that the rules or theory are generated by some prior rules or theory, which are themselves generated by prior rules or theory, which are themselves generated by ... As Ryle puts it, "if, for any operation to be intelligently executed, a prior theoretical operation had first to be performed and performed intelligently, it would be a logical impossibility for anyone ever to break into the circle." Practical capacity, knowing-how, comes first: "Efficient practice precedes the theory of it; methodologies presuppose the application of the methods." Or, to draw a parallel with Hilary Putnam's philosophy of language, if meaning "is a coarse grid laid over use," then for Ryle and anti-intellectualists like him, theory is a gloss on practice – an explicatory mechanism or overlay, not a prior condition or cause.[5]

If you're buying what Ryle's selling, a consequence of his critique of the "intellectualist legend" *should* be that we give up all talk of knowing-that as if it were a type or domain of knowledge quite distinct from knowing-how. The intellectualists, writes Ryle, have "misconstrued the type-distinction between disposition and exercise into its mythical bifurcation of unwitnessable causes and their witnessable physical effects" (34); *intelligent* and *intellectual* have been elided, or confused, such that we often talk as if a knowledgeable act has "special antecedents," when in fact it "has a special procedure or manner" (32). All knowledgeable performances, or what we might call demonstrations of knowledge, are, for Ryle, practical matters.

The familiar Rylean story is worth a quick retelling for two reasons. First, it sets the stage for a problem to be addressed in Chapter 4: while Ryle sets up the knowing-that and knowing-how distinction in order to collapse it, some commentators — with whom this book is otherwise broadly aligned — wish to leave each pin standing in its own lane. They reinstate and reinforce the distinction, then argue something like this: there *are* different types of knowledge, all equally valid, authentic, useful, desirable; different subjects may — often do — promote, demand, or embody either one knowledge-type more than the other; English Literature — along with other cognate arts-humanities subjects — is primarily a matter of knowing-how.[6] Some commentators fall into the trap of reinforcing the distinction between knowing-how and knowing-that in order to make a case for the equal status of the former in relation to the latter. For Ryle, no such case needs to be made; personal knowledge *is* practical knowledge first and foremost. Second, to the extent that educational policy does treat knowledge and skills as distinct — whether discrete and opposed forms of knowing, or two parts of a cluster of competencies — it tends to presume, as mentioned above, the self-evidently practical and physical character of skills on the one hand, the rational, intellectual character of knowledge on the other. Where focus on skills rather than knowledge is cited as a problem, the concern seems to be that while skills are admirable, and can be appreciated and observed, they do not have "objectively" verifiable "content" and cannot be easily or reliably measured because the sort of knowledge they are is neither easily nor fully codifiable.[7] If this is right, then policymakers' interest (often stated, rarely explicated) in knowledge-rich over and above skills-based curricula have something to do with the problems of tacit knowledge.

Tacit knowledge — best-known by Michael Polanyi's slogan, "we know more than we can tell" — is often contrasted with explicit knowledge.[8] Because this opposition is, it will turn out, destined to break down, the problems bearing on tacit and explicit knowledge cannot be disentangled from the problems of knowledge in general. Take the following passage, excerpted from a reference-work entry on epistemology:

> Knowledge can be either explicit or tacit. Explicit knowledge is self-conscious in that the knower is aware of the relevant state of knowledge,

whereas tacit knowledge is implicit, hidden from self-consciousness. Much of our knowledge is tacit: it is genuine but we are unaware of the relevant states of knowledge, even if we can achieve awareness upon suitable reflection. In this regard, knowledge resembles many of our psychological states. The existence of a psychological state in a person does not require the person's awareness of that state, although it may require the person's awareness of an object of that state (such as what is sensed or perceived).[9]

Ryle claims that knowledgeable acts count as such because they indicate general propensities or dispositions rather than states. John Coltrane was (and is) a great saxophone player because of what he did and how he did it time and time again, not because he once sounded good by fluke or only once happened to impress (and possibly confound) folk with his musicianship. Musicians know how to play when they aren't playing as well as when they are. A musician might have an off day here and there, but not so many that we'd say "they don't know how to do it anymore." Or, if they did have a long run of off days, then we might indeed be led to say "they've lost it" – in which case, we *would* be saying something along the lines of "they no longer know how to play." But this, in Ryle's terms, is to say they've lost a propensity, disposition, or ability they once had, not that they are no longer in a knowing or capable state. My being angry now may have nothing to do with whether I'm fairly described as a generally angry person; if I *am* fairly described this way, then my current angry state is just one example, one more bit of evidence, of my general (pre-)disposition. But although someone may characteristically be a good musician, and another may characteristically be happy or angry, we wouldn't say of the musician that they were often in a state of being-able-to-play well, on the same model of the one who's often in a state of anger. (Of course, it may be that the musician finds being in certain emotional states are more or less conducive to better playing.) Likewise, we probably wouldn't say that so-and-so "really knows how to be angry," outside of irony-laced conversations about the often spectacular nature of their outbursts. Someone commonly described as knowledgeable by others is not in and out of states of being knowledgeable; they may or may not, however, be in a situation *now* that allows or invites them to demonstrate their knowledge, which, moreover, they may be able to demonstrate while in any of a range of psychological or emotional states. It makes little sense, then, to say either that knowledge *is* itself a state, or that it's *like* a psychological state, and that tacit knowledge consists in our being unaware of our knowledgeable states.

If knowledge is not a state, then nor is it clear that the criterion of taciturnity of tacit knowledge is self-unawareness, -unconsciousness, or the hiddenness of our knowledge from ourselves. The excerpt above does allow that one might become aware of one's tacit knowledge after the fact and "upon suitable reflection." This perhaps gets us a little nearer the mark, for it suggests that tacit knowledge is hidden from our own self-view in the moment of the knowledgeable act, though it need not remain hidden afterwards. But this raises questions: if the knowledge is identifiable as such, even retrospectively, then in what sense is it tacit? If the knowledge which is supposedly "there" (where?) can't be identified as such, in what sense is it knowledge?

These are the two prongs of the tacit knowledge problem which Neil Gascoigne and Tim Thornton address in their book *Tacit Knowledge*. They set out to define and carve a space for an idea of tacit knowledge that makes good on its dual status as both tacit and knowledge. Distinct from what they call the Principles of Codifiability and Inarticulacy – which state, respectively, that "[a]ll knowledge can be fully articulated, or codified, in context-independent terms," and that "[t]here can be knowledge that cannot be articulated" – Gascoigne and Thornton posit the Principle of Articulacy: "All knowledge can be articulated, either in context-independent terms (i.e. it can be codified) or in context-dependent terms." Context-dependency is their mark of taciturnity, for it's propitious context that allows tacit knowledge to speak, and they offer the following definition: tacit knowledge is "context-dependent but conceptually structured practical or personal knowledge" (*TK*, 4, 5, 167).

Gascoigne and Thornton want to preserve Ryle's insight that knowing-how (practical knowledge) is logically prior to knowing-that (knowledge fully codifiable in linguistic or propositional form). They also want to preserve the "close connection" that Ryles establishes "between practical knowledge and ability" (*TK*, 81). However, they concede two points to Ryle's neo-intellectualist critics: first, "there is no general semantic marker for practical knowledge": that is, speaking in terms of knowing *how* to do something is not always indicative of practical ability; we may have either theoretical or practical know-how or both (I can know *how* to carry out mental arithmetic; and-or I can know *how* to perform a box-jump from a standing start). "Second, practical knowledge has a conceptually structured content that can be articulated 'from within.' To that extent," Gascoigne and Thornton say, "practical knowledge is more like theoretical knowledge or knowledge-that than might at first be thought. So if tacit knowledge is construed as practical knowledge there is, nevertheless, a content known" (*TK*, 81). Gascoigne and Thornton's intellectualist concessions are a reminder that knowing-that and knowing-how are not synonymous with, respectively, theoretical and practical knowledge; and that Ryle's intention is not to name metaphysically existent entities (different types of knowledge), but to diagnose and correct our bad linguistic habits and lay bare the ways these shape our understanding of self and world.

Imagine, in the context of a philosophy lecture, a tutor outlining a particular theory (call it T_1), and following that outline with "I *know that* a counterargument might run as follows ..." (call the counterargument T_2). Perhaps the lecturer's knowledge-that derives from her having read (and remembered and understood) a version or versions of T_2. (If T_2 is a summary of several more or less complementary accounts, then her having understood it is a function of her knowing how to map various points of con- and di-vergence and of her being able to assimilate the several particular accounts to a more general one.) Or her knowledge of T_2 might derive from her being able to anticipate certain interlocking objections to T_1, to read those likely objections "off against" or "into" T_1. Or it might be that T_1 is in fact the position to which the lecturer objects, and that T_2 is her (or closer to her) position. The theories she's sketching might be the particular arguments of particular thinkers, or they might be generalized positions (schools or clusters of thought). None of these possibilities matters for now; what *does*, in this case, is that knowledge framed or presented in terms of knowledge-that doesn't track with theoretical knowledge alone, because, at the personal level, there is no such knowledge *alone*. Having knowledge of theory (or philosophy) is not the same as having theoretical knowledge, in the sense that the theoretical/practical distinction is often thrown about. In our imagined case, the theoretical/practical distinction dissolves, because the lecturer's knowledge-that is a function of her ability to philosophize: her knowledge of philosophy *is* her knowing how to do it. (To anticipate a theme of the following chapter, notice, too, that to say *she can do philosophy* is to identify her as belonging to a particular discursive practice and community (without specifying what doing philosophy actually involves).)

We can also imagine instances in which know-how talk might be used, but which are not practical in the way practical knowledge is typically pictured – instances that aren't of the bike-riding or basketball-playing sort, easily observable and appreciable by onlookers in terms of physical movement. Classic ratiocinative mystery stories typically dramatize such instances when, in a moment of revelation, the detective suddenly knows *how* the crime was committed. The detective's moment of revelation is of the same character as Wittgenstein's agent who, faced with some problem (arithmetic, say), suddenly exclaims "now I know how to go on."[10] In such moments, once again, the practical/theoretical distinction melts away, because, though the activity in which the detective is absorbed is intellectual and imaginative, nevertheless, as in the case of the philosophy lecturer, it *is* an activity. Better, a cluster of activities: inferring, projecting, deducing (though doubtless some will be keen to point out that deduction is *not* in fact Sherlock's default mode of reasoning) – in short, any number of intellectual-imaginative doings that amount to the detective's *solving the crime* (which is only ever a blood-soaked puzzle waiting to be pieced together).

Though Gascoigne and Thornton are right to block the presumed synonymy between knowledge-that and theoretical knowledge, knowledge-how and practical knowledge, it's not clear that a hard border can be set up between practical and theoretical knowledge. Take the example (to which we'll return) of the expert sports coach who knows *how* to coach others to a level of athletic competence far exceeding their own. Here, we have an instance of know-how apparently *not* accompanied by what we might think of as parallel or complementary practical ability, and yet we must surely think of the coach's ability as a coach in terms of practical knowledge and expertise. If there is no hard border between theoretical and practical knowledge, then it may be a mistake to think (in cases like that of the expert sports coach) that theoretical know-how is characterized by lacking a parallel, equivalent, or complementary practical know-how.[11] Such a deficit view is mistaken, because equivalence, parallelism, and complementarity (of, for example, knowing how to talk about boxing and being able to box) are the wrong currencies in which to cash out the relationship between so-called *theoretical* and *practical* know-how: while it may seem obvious to organize theoretical and practical know-how into mutually co-implicating pairs (theoretical and practical knowledge of the same *x*), nothing necessitates this. We do better to think of boxing and coaching boxing as distinct activities or abilities with a common subject-matter or interest. If we think in these terms, then the coach who coaches "beyond" their own sporting ability is neither mysterious nor particularly interesting (there is no contradiction or tension between being a "failed" boxer yet a "great" coach), while the idea that they could *theoretically* coach beyond their own coaching ability is meaningless.

(Tacit) Knowledge and Conceptuality

We'll step back into the ring shortly; for now, back to Gascoigne and Thornton's definition of tacit knowledge: context-dependent, conceptually structured personal or practical knowledge. For knowledge to count as knowledge proper, it must be knowledge *of* something; to be able to say that any person has *knowledge of ...* is to imply or presuppose that whatever knowledge they have is conceptual; and if we can't say, at least in part, just *what* a person has knowledge *of*, then we can't say that they have knowledge at all (*TK*, 77, Ch. 2, *passim*). Stipulating tacit knowledge's conceptual structure, then, ensures in principle that it can properly be considered knowledge. By virtue of its having a conceptual component, tacit knowledge still "answer[s] to standards independent of the subject" or knower (*TK*, 7). But this brings us back to the problem, outlined above, of how such knowledge can sensibly be called *tacit*.

For Gascoigne and Thornton, remember, tacit knowledge is "context-dependent but conceptually structured practical or personal knowledge." Mid-way through and late in the book, they further qualify their definition of personal-practical knowledge, as we've already heard, as having "conceptually structured content that can be articulated 'from within'" (*TK*, 81, 67). The idea is that knowledge's taciturnity is not its ineffability: if knowledge is knowledge, then it always says or answers to something, though it might not say much. Tacit knowledge is tacit inasmuch as it can't be fully expressed or demonstrated by, in, or through words; some practical demonstration or skilled performance is also required. Taciturnity, then, identifies the context-dependency, or the situatedness, of personal-practical knowledge, and the paradigm abstract image of tacit knowledge is some knower successfully executing a skilled performance accompanied by a suitable demonstrative: **This** *is how you x*. While Gascoigne and Thornton agree with Ryle that "[i]ntelligent practice is not a stepchild of theory,"[12] and thus with the claim that, whatever practical knowledge is, it's not first "to do a bit of theory and then to do a bit of practice," it *is*, they maintain, a matter of being able both to execute some skilled performance *and* to do some verbal pointing (very likely at one's self): the two modes of expression or demonstration must run in tandem. The one is not the source or cause of the other, but there's no *practical* knowledge where there is not some skilled performance, and no practical *knowledge* where there's no conceptual "content."

While firmly on the side of Ryle, intellectualist concessions notwithstanding, Gascoigne and Thornton are less impressed by Heidegger-inflected versions of tacit knowledge or the sort exemplified by Hubert Dreyfus and his philosophy of skilled or fluid coping.[13] Their rejection of Dreyfus's phenomenology is rooted in a critique of his non-conceptualism, his idea that both our most basic and most advanced modes of being are so fluent that they cannot be conceptual.

The usual philosophical quibble, though: what conceptual means isn't self-evident, and this has led to some ultimately dead-end confrontations, notably between Dreyfus and John McDowell. Working within a Kantian framework, McDowell argues that mindedness is always-already conceptual. Dreyfus, by apparent contrast, wants to promote a picture of knowledge as skilled embodied act, in which intentional but non-conceptual action is prior to conceptual mindedness.[14] McDowell agrees with Dreyfus that the so-called "myth of the mental" as primary or primordial should be rejected, *if* that myth is taken to be a story of a foundational third-person awareness of our own first-person doings; if, that is, the characteristic mark of the mental, or mindedness, is supposed to be self-reflective detachment – a "stepping outside" and "monitoring" of one's self.[15]

Kant himself had something to say about first- and third-person awareness:

> The **I think** must **be able** to accompany all my representations; for otherwise something would be represented in me that could not be thought at all, which is as much as to say that the representation would either be impossible or else at least would be nothing for me. [...] But this representation is an act of **spontaneity** [...]. **I** call it the **pure apperception**, [...] since it is that self-consciousness which, because it produces the representation **I think**, which must be able to accompany all others and which in all consciousness is one and the same [....] For the manifold representations which are given in a certain intuition would not all together be **my** representations if they did not all together belong to a self-consciousness; i.e., as my representations (*even if I am not conscious of them as such*) they must yet necessarily be in accord with the condition under which alone they **can** stand together in a universal self-consciousness [...].[16]

In other words, the self-reflective "I think" is the effect of, or is predicated upon, there already being a unified thinking subject capable of spontaneity – of deliberate or intentional, though not necessarily self-monitoring, responses to an environment that means (something) for the individual person.

Dreyfus's chariness of McDowell's use of conceptuality is not entirely unwarranted. In *Mind and World*, McDowell *does* claim that it's only by virtue of experience being conceptual through and through that self-reflection or -consciousness is possible: "it is essential to conceptual capacities [...] that they can be exploited in active thinking, thinking that is open to reflection about its own rational credentials." Since making that claim, however, McDowell has also said that there is little purchase in the twinned ideas that, "if mindedness informs an experience, the subject has a detached contemplative relation to the world she experiences, and that if mindedness informs an action, the agent has a detached monitoring relation to what she is doing." This clarification is crucial: for McDowell, as for Kant, spontaneity is a feature of mindedness; and our ability to reflect on ourselves and our actions is a *consequence of*, and *not the causal grounds for*, conceptuality.

Mind-detachment is *not*, then, what McDowell means by claiming that "mindedness" and thus conceptuality are "pervasive. [...] We should not pretend to find a detached self in all our experiencing and acting," which would amount not to mind-pervasiveness but to a "Myth of Mind as Detached."[17]

One might wonder, though, how McDowell makes the case for pervasive conceptuality, given his acceptance that mindedness does not inhere in self-reflection or -consciousness, detached third-person monitorings of our first-person activities. The short answer to how – or why – McDowell insists on the always-already conceptual structure of experience and knowledge is simply this: that our experiences are always-already conceptual is a logical antecedent of our knowing, more often than not, how to go on. Knowing how to go on indicates our involvement with a conceptual, because meaningful, world, whether or not we have proper names for those meaningful bits of the world. In situations where and when we don't know how to go on, pervasive conceptuality is often still proven, for such not-knowing indicates a "gap," "break," or mistake in conceptual circuitry. Being lost involves being mistaken about where you thought you were, relative to other landmarks, and so is still conceptual; it doesn't mean absolute disorientation, a radical not knowing who, what, and where you are.[18] Taking a candy pencil or *trompe l'oeil* painting of a violin for the thing copied, impersonated, or represented is a category mistake that is easily fixed, but is only possible on the basis of conceptuality (knowing what candy, paintings, pencils, and violins are). Further illustration may be useful.

Take the often-cited test case of colour recognition. No matter how large a person's colour vocabulary, her sensitivity to chromatic differences will likely outstrip it. But being unable to affix a unique name to a particular shade occurrence is not an instance of non-conceptual experience, for our always-already operative concepts of colour and shade allow for such situation-specific demonstrative utterances as: (i) "*that* shade of *x*"; (ii) "*this*, rather than *that*, shade of *x*"; or (iii) "*that* ... is the same shade of *x* as ...."[19] Such utterances, McDowell contends (and Gascoigne and Thornton agree) are enough to prove that conceptuality is operative. Spoken or written language, then, appears to be a useful index of the conceptual; but it doesn't matter very much whether our linguistic pointing involves correct (conventional) use of a proper noun ("the object coloured *Skobeloff*"; "the object coloured *hex #007474*"), a definite description ("the object with the colour composition 0% red, 45.5% green, and 45.5% blue in RGB colour space; and 100% cyan, 0% magenta, 0% yellow, and 54.5% black in CMYK colour space"), or a suitable demonstrative ("*that* shade of greeny-blue"). Conceptuality is also temporal; it must "persist into the future, if only for a short time," so that "it can be used also in thoughts about what is by then past, if only the recent past" (see demonstrative (iii) above).[20] Conceptuality can't get off the ground without presumptions of repetition, duration through time, consistency, and commonality.

So while it does not entail mind-detachment, pervasive conceptuality does, for McDowell, guard against the reductive naturalism that runs alongside the Myth of the Given — roughly, the idea that we can have direct, unmediated contact with the world and, therefore, knowledge of it[21] — which "we can avoid," he writes, "if we hold that in the experiencing itself, capacities that belong to their subject's rationality are in play." If our responses to sensory experience are thought to be non-conceptual and a matter of disposition only, then, argues McDowell, "the experience itself goes missing." Machines and automata are predisposed to respond in this way or that to certain stimuli; we would not, in McDowell's story, want to say they had experiences, which are marked as such by the understanding's being "already inextricably implicated in the deliverances of sensibility themselves. Experiences are, in part, impressions made by the world on our sense, products of receptivity; but those impressions themselves already have conceptual content," in the sense that experiences, when we respond to them by knowing how to go on, are always-already meaningful to us. The always-already conceptual nature of experience is what, logically, enables self-reflection. But, once again, this is not a basic condition of conceptuality. Rather, in circular fashion, it is because we do, more often than not, know how to go on that it doesn't make sense to McDowell to say that experience is not conceptual. Experience is always-already conceptual, in the sense that experiences can stand as reasons for spontaneous action or judgement. And it is this faculty of spontaneity, or judgement, that marks us as sapient — as knowers. McDowell's assumption is that we cope fluidly with our world, yes, but this is by virtue of the world being meaningful or significant for us; therefore, experience, fluid coping — call it what you will — is conceptual: "Having things appear to one in a certain way is," as McDowell puts it, "already itself a mode of actual operation of conceptual capacities."[22]

Conceptuality, then, runs all the way up and down our skilled, deliberative acts, and there is nothing incompatible between Dreyfus's idea of fluid coping and McDowell's arguments for pervasive conceptuality. Indeed, where fluid coping results from practiced repetition,[23] McDowellian conceptuality is surely involved: without it, repeated actions would count only as reflex motions and twitches – they would be "'mere' neurology," as Gascoigne and Thornton put it (*TK*, 108).

Knowledge Thick and Thin: Context and-or Background

In order to explain the non-conceptual domain of skilled acting, some phenomenology-inflected accounts draw on the idea of a so-called Background. In its Heideggerian version, the Background is usefully simple and frustratingly complex, as it seems to be a catch-all term for something like: that which is presupposed but which is unanalyzable and-or unsayable; all that is taken for granted when, as is always necessarily the case, we're forced to start *in medias res*. Useful, then, to have a term that helps us avoid such unwieldy constructions; frustrating, because Background at times appears to be both everything and nothing.

In Heideggerian Background talk – and Dreyfus's version especially – Gascoigne and Thornton find "both knowing *how* and knowing *that*" conceived as being "founded on a sort of *ur*-knowing how, which comprises the background" (*TK*, 47). But "no such (putatively explanatory) domain" as this so-called Background is needed, they argue, not least because of the (by now) familiar basic problem: if the Background and its contents are inarticulable, then they can make no contribution to knowledge; if they aren't, then they can offer nothing to our understanding of knowledge's taciturnity: instead, "it is Foreground all the way (which is to say, there's neither foreground nor background)" (*TK*, 132).

As Dreyfus notes, however, what is often called Background in anglophone philosophy has no fixed term in Heidegger other than Dasein's basic *Being-in-the-World* – the way Dasein orients itself towards and within *its* world, and by which Dasein's world emerges, or is disclosed, for it *as significant*.[24] If this is right, then, perhaps surprisingly given McDowell's professed Kantianism and Heidegger's professed anti-Kantianism,[25] there may not be very much that separates McDowell's version of conceptuality from Heidegger's notion of Being-in-the-world.

McDowell assumes that the always-already-known and always-already-articulable are correlative of the "distinctive self-knowledge of an agent," which consists not only in "knowledge of *what* she is doing, but also knowledge of *why* she is doing it." It "does not matter" that answering these *What?* and *Why?* questions "will break the flow" of activity; what's important is that our answering these questions – which, normally, we can – "gives expression to something [we] already knew when [we were] acting in flow."[26] This is similar to Heidegger's formulation of Dasein as a context constituted by and constitutive of always-already familiar involvements.[27] Both McDowell and the Heidegger of *Being and Time* presuppose an always-already familiar and meaningful world, in which, just as Gascoigne and Thornton say, nothing is in principle "hidden." The spatial and visual language is a little misleading, however, for the fact that something is not hidden does not mean we are looking at or for it, nor that we are bound to notice it. All we're really talking about here is whether or not certain features of a more or less familiar environment do or don't come – not into view, but simply into focus; whether or not we attend to them or they grab our attention.

There is another way of formulating Background. Wittgenstein offers an idea of a background that is *not* a matter solely of personal capacity ((tacit) knowledge, neurology, whatever); nor is it a matter of tactile non-linguistic engagement (the background abilities that, for Dreyfus, must be presupposed in order to explain skilled bike-riding, skiing, pool-playing, and so on); nor is it a matter of having-to-hand all those propositions one knows oneself to believe true (could one ever have all such propositions simultaneously "in mind"; do – and could – I ever know all that I believe to be true or false?). According to Wittgenstein, all utterances mean what they mean in relation to some context or cultural frame: "When we first begin to *believe* anything, what we believe is not a single proposition, it is a whole system of propositions."[28] The philosopher's standard trick, for example, of testing or exemplifying ideas against or through simple declaratives (*the cat sat on the mat*; *I perceive a table* ...) is one in which culture and context are not bracketed out, but simply taken for granted – transparency or self-evidentiality is nothing more, but also nothing less, than the presumption of shared familiarity. There is nothing wrong with this *I-perceive-a-table* method, *per se*; we have to start testing and exemplifying from somewhere. But we can never reach a point of absolute objective bedrock, a truly external and perspectiveless perspective. There is no view from nowhere.[29] As Wittgenstein put it: "It is so difficult to find the *beginning*. Or, better: it is difficult to begin at the beginning. And not try to go further back" (*OC*, 471). The mistake is to confuse presumed shared familiarity – "common ground" – with absolute or metaphysical objectivity. Again, our explanations, tests, and practices must begin from somewhere (*in medias res*, as mentioned above), and there is potentially no end to the demand for reasons grounding these explanations, tests, and practices; we can always ask *yes, but why?* just one more time, "[a]s if giving grounds did not come to an end sometime. But the end," says Wittgenstein, "is not an ungrounded presupposition: it is an ungrounded way of acting" (*OC*, 110).

Wittgenstein realizes that we are acculturated in ways that are not empirically testable, because certain presuppositions, beliefs, and values form the all-but-imperceptible systems which make it possible for our overt, deliberative, self-conscious acts to show up as meaningful (good, bad; true, false ...). This system is "inherited," and it is this which forms a type of "background":

> I did not get my picture of the world by satisfying myself of its correctness; nor do I have it because I am satisfied of its correctness. No; it is the inherited background against which I distinguish between true and false. (*OC*, 94)

One could not plot all the propositions within this system, nor could one map its outer limits – in part because, whatever cultural "game" we are playing, "the game can be learned [...] without learning any explicit rules" (acculturation again) (*OC*, 95); in part because our cultural frames or systems are "not so much the point of departure, as the element[s] in which arguments have their life" (*OC*, 105); in part because what is here a principle grounding belief and action may there be a claim to be tested (*OC*, 98); and, finally, in part because both frame and picture, ground and edifice, may change over time:

> the river-bed of thought may shift. But I distinguish between the movement of the waters on the river-bed and the shift of the bed itself; though there is not a sharp division of the one from the other. [...]
> And the bank of the river consists partly of hard rock, subject to no alteration or only to an imperceptible one, partly of sand, which now in one place now in another gets washed away or deposited.[30]

There are parallels between Wittgenstein's insight that no statement can be meaningful outside of some broader system of meanings (the language game), and the Derridean maxim that there is nothing outside the text.[31] But neither Derrida nor Wittgenstein need be read as advocating some kind of frictionless textuality; rather, both claim that there is no such thing as context-free knowledge, only modes of saying and doing that are so familiar their frames of reference have become imperceptible, or, more crudely, forgotten:[32] the frames of reference are not hidden, we may simply have stopped, for the most part, noticing them. This is so even in the most paradigmatic cases of apparently context-free, independently verifiable propositions, such as those of arithmetic.

As McDowell argues, there are no context-, value- or perspective-free vantage points: there is no view from outside. In the case of arithmetic, the objective truth of the system is not secured from a vantage point outside the system; claims to the system's objectivity presuppose the system's coherence – we are, as it were, already "in" an arithmetical world in which shared practices make common responses likely, and judgements of right and wrong predictable and explicable *in relation to the system*. This doesn't cast doubt on the objectivity or coherence of arithmetic, nor, McDowell stresses, on the possibility "that the correctness [of an arithmetical] move [...] can be proved";[33] it simply makes such truths system-relative and dependent upon those working "in" the system knowing how to speak a shared language and knowing how to go on.[34]

I suggested earlier that there isn't much that's incompossible between McDowell's pervasive conceptuality and Heidegger's *Being-in-the-World*; the latter is conceptual to the extent that it presupposes a world of meaningful tactile encounters which, moment to moment, may or may not "catch" our attention. What Heidegger shares with Kant and Kantians like McDowell is the presumption that persons are deeply embedded, either in *the* world (Kant) or their world*s* (Heidegger). What Wittgenstein adds to the mix is the idea that saying is a form of acting, and that questions of language cannot, ultimately, be dissociated from questions of culture, value, knowledge, belief – of what Stanley Cavell calls "the whirl of organism," Wittgenstein "forms of life."[35] As well as being embedded in a world of tangible stuff, we are also enmeshed in linguistic milieux.

There is, then, no sharp line between background and context; but we may wish to distinguish between the knower as a context – no knower, nothing known – and the linguistic or discursive milieux as contexts in which knowers move and play. Jimmie Rodgers was the flesh-and-blood context which made a particular, distinctive style of folk yodelling possible; no Jimmie Rodgers, no unique Jimmie-Rodgers-yodelling-know-how. But if the topic of conversation is Jimmie Rodgers (and his yodelling-know-how), then nothing is known without some referential and discursive space to which the interlocutors can "point" and which they can inhabit: Jimmie Rodgers now as subject-matter. Here, *context* is something like Wittgenstein's ungrounded way of acting: the presupposed common ground necessary for the conversation to get started in the first place and to have any sort of coherence *is* Wittgenstein's presumptions of inherited backgrounds and systems of meaning. The common ground may or may not stretch that far, of course: of two interlocutors, both might be able to have a sustained conversation about the songs of Jimmie Rodgers, though perhaps only one knows how to place him in a broader history of American folk music.[36] Pervasive conceptuality, *pace* McDowell, presumes that there are no ways of knowing, and no forms of knowledge, that are not context-dependent in the dual sense of requiring a person-who-knows and a linguistic or discursive frame within which knowledge coheres. Conceptuality *is* contextuality; and context is, in Wittgenstein's sense, background. Sometimes context is "thin": it goes unnoticed; we don't feel its envelope. Sometimes it is "thick," and we feel ourselves bump up against it.

(Tacit) Knowledge and Language

Wittgenstein's idea of *background* – the idea that discursive frame or milieu is what enables knowledge of ... to cohere as such – suggests that conceptuality and language are more or less synonymous. Based on the Principle of Articulacy, the claim that all knowledge is (to some degree) articulable seems to be the claim that knowledge can (to some degree) be put into words. If so, then *articulable* is roughly synonymous with *expressible*, *effable*; and yet *articulation* might answer not only to tacit *knowledge's* condition of linguistic expression, but also to *tacit* knowledge's condition that linguistic expression be distinct from, yet joined to and interact with – be *articulated* with – practical performance: the common-or-garden example of skilled bike-riding, say, combined with the demonstrative "**This** is how you ride a bike."

But the demonstrative "**This** is how to ride a bike" doesn't encode the knowledge of how to ride a bike (nor do Gascoigne and Thornton suggest it does). Rather, it acts as or stands in the place of a partial linguistic description of that knowledge. *Description* is being used broadly here; it may be no more than a date-, time-, and place-stamped signpost to the bike-riding performance, a way of pointing to an example of bike-riding and subscribing to it as an instance of bike-riding made good. The example might be what I myself am doing now; it might be what someone else just over there is doing now; it might be film footage of me, or someone else, riding a bike. Whatever it is, the example stands as some kind of a model of the referred-to thing.[37]

So the demand that tacit knowledge be articulable seems to be the demand that it can be put *into* words. Or better, that it can be put *under* some linguistic description. Better, because the latter turn of phrase avoids suggesting that knowing how to *x* can be translated into some other medium or mode. To say we can offer partial linguistic descriptions of bike-riding is quite different to saying bike-riding can be "put into words": what would the latter mean? What do we ever put into words other than words?

If conceptuality runs all the way through experience, as McDowell suggests, and does not preclude what Dreyfus calls fluid coping, then what is the relationship between conceptuality and language? Are they synonymous; or is conceptuality prior to language, that *something* which makes linguistic expression possible? If *conceptual* has a Kantian flavour, then we might think in terms of sensory experience being shaped by the categories or concepts of our perceptual apparatus; in the terms, that is, of Kant's famous slogan, which summarizes the interdependency of intuition and understanding: "Without sensibility no object would be given to us, and without understanding none would be thought. Thoughts without content are empty, intuitions without concepts are blind."[38] Conceptual structure, on this model, is something like a neuro-psychical agency, which allows experiences to become meaningful and is prior to or separate from our linguistic powers. There are some who may well accept this view of the tacit as the dimension of Kantian conceptuality, the realm of the faculty of the understanding – the ground beneath which we can dig no deeper.[39] Others, of course, will not. For Robert Brandom, conceptuality and propositionality are more or less synonymous, because knowledge can't be identified as such outside of a socially constituted space (background, milieu) in which reasoning (in linguistic form) can take place.[40]

Nor is the model of the tacit Kantian conceptual structure what Gascoigne and Thornton have in mind: the tacit dimension cannot, in their story, be the realm of "sub-personal" mechanics and autonomous, non-experiential cognitive processes: tacit knowledge *is* a distinct mode of knowing, synaptic activity is not; they're interested when and why the lightbulb flashes, not the wiring which makes that possible.

The sub-personal account – which presents not tacit knowledge, *per se*, as a distinct form or mode of knowing, but, rather, presents our neurocognitive makeup as the tacit grounds of all personal knowledge – is an account of knowledge as the epiphenomena of our biology. This account is, at root, a Kantian story, in which conceptualism is the autonomous faculty of the understanding, which gives meaning to sensibility (still, for Kant, an element of mindedness). A third story is the one rejected by Ryle in *The Concept of Mind*: the idea that knowledge is conceptually structured at a "deep" level, that our skilful copings can be thought of as encoding propositions, perhaps even executive commands.[41] This story takes knowledge to be structured like a language: it tells us that the "inside" of knowledge is propositional. A fourth story sees linguistic descriptions of knowledge as either sitting alongside or pointing the way to practical know-how, but keeps the two separate: the description under which the skilled act is put may draw attention, without being essential, to that act. This story gives us an explanatory framework for the first and second: it tells us that Kant and those who follow him use language as perhaps the only available, or most efficient, explicatory mechanism for pointing to non-linguistic structures and phenomena. But, to underscore a point made above, these non-linguistic structures and phenomena are *not* put "into" words; rather, they're put "under" partial linguistic descriptions.

How, then, might conceptuality be distinct from articulability? If articulability *is* linguistic, are we to imagine language as referring only to spoken and scribed instances of natural language, or can the very idea of a language expand and contract? Can we think of distinct, formal, or semi-formal languages as operating both "within," and being parasitic upon, natural language (the languages of philosophy, physics, sociology …), but also in non-verbal modes (the languages of music, cinema, weightlifting …)?

The short answer, which owes a great deal to Nelson Goodman, to the last question is *yes*. Forget, for now, knowledge in the form of talking-about some subject. Instead, take as a paradigmatic, seemingly obvious case of *doing* the example of boxing, and the famous boxing scene in Charlie Chaplin's film *City Lights*.[42]

The Chaplin character, needing to make a quick buck, agrees to take the fall in a staged bout. But when his would-be opponent ducks out to avoid being collared for some never-disclosed crime, the protagonist is thrown into a "real" fight.

In the arena and inside the ring, on fight night, we have a coherent linguistic world in which there are permissible and impermissible moves. But we also have a character who doesn't speak the language of boxing, who doesn't know (at least not always) when he's breaking the rules, when he's no longer speaking the language; who knows neither how to negotiate nor make his way through the world into which he's been thrust: after entering the ring, Chaplin's unwilling and unwitting fighter holds the ropes open so his cornermen can enter (things should be the other way around); when his opponent moves to touch gloves (the typical gesture of good sportspersonship and a promise to play by the rules), Chaplin's character goes to shake hands, and then attempts to shake the hand of every man in the ring; he kicks, runs, and hides from, and launches himself at his opponent; he shields behind the referee, popping out to get in several opportunistic haymakers. Briefly, it looks like he might win the fight (though unconventionally, unsportingly). But Chaplin's character cannot be said to know how to box, barely that he knows he's supposed to be boxing. He understands neither the physical frames around him nor the linguistic frames they signify and are signified by. He is not at home in this milieu. Though Chaplin's character and his opponent occupy the same physical space, they have little or no common ground; they do not, in the ring, speak the same language. (And if the jokes in this scene land, moreover, it is because we the audience may be outside the ring but not outside the world of boxing; we can inhabit that discursive space comfortably enough to know what Chaplin's character does not, and to recognize that he does not know what he does not know.)

That knowledge can be identified as such – that we can point to it – is to presuppose its belonging to some meaningful context or background, *pace* Wittgenstein. Knowledge of any sort, then, presupposes some sort of symbolic systematization, and so might be linguistic in the broadest possible sense implied by Wittgenstein and explored in detail by Goodman: we can indeed talk about the languages of music, boxing, cinema, and so on. If our earlier talk of discursive or *linguistic* frames and milieux seemed to privilege spoken and-or written language, perhaps we might now speak more broadly of *symbolic* worlds and frames.[43]

On the view being urged here, language is a function – in the same way that for McDowell, as for Kant, the introspective "I think" is a function – of knowledge, not its "base." Mindedness is not constituted by internally "held" propositionally structured descriptions or pictures of the world, but emerges from what Merleau-Ponty calls "the dialectic of milieu and action."[44] As Charles Taylor writes, "understanding and know-how [...] [are] not 'within' me in a kind of picture"; they are "in the interaction" *between* me and my world.[45] We see this with pre-verbal children, whose repeated deliberate and deliberative acts signify conceptualized engagements with their environments,[46] and whose ability to go on successfully exemplifies knowledge as being conceptual without being propositionally or linguistically structured "at base." Propositionality is neither the ground of knowledge nor is it synonymous with conceptuality. The corporeal person is the ground of possibility of conceptuality, knowledge, and, further "up" the chain (as it were), propositionality. Knowledge *is* symbolically organized (conceptual), though it need not take spoken- or written-linguistic form.

Contributory and Interactional Expertise

In the *City Lights* example, boxing is offered as a seemingly paradigmatic example of so-called "practical" knowledge (or lack thereof). Let's return to our earlier example of the expert boxing coach and their expert student, and let's assume that while the student continues to make progress under the coach's guidance, the latter could not face the student in the ring (let's say that in our imagined example, the student is already fighting to a level the coach never reached). One way of framing the differences between these two is to say that the protégé has practical ability, or know-how, where the coach has theoretical knowledge or expertise: but this was rejected, on the grounds that the coach is a coach first and foremost, not a boxer, and has practical coaching knowledge. To say that the boxing coach has (only) theoretical knowledge of boxing is to misidentify the knowledge-of that gives the coach her identity as a coach.

Another way of framing this example is to see the coach's ability as secondary to the pupil's: this perhaps seems to be the direction we've been moving in when I've suggested that to talk about weightlifting, say, is no longer to do any weightlifting. The theoretical knowledge seems to be dependent or parasitic upon the associated practice, because a theory must be a theory-*of* something.[47]

If we are tempted to view the differences between the sorts of knowledge that the boxer and the coach possess along these lines, then we might be tempted to borrow from Harry Collins, and to say that the boxer's knowledge is "contributory," the coach's "interactional"; the first because the boxer's expertise allows her to participate in the ring, the latter because the coach's expertise allows her to speak authoritatively about boxing without having to box.[48]

Collins and his colleagues first developed the idea of interactional expertise as a way of persuading

> sociologists of a "relativist" or "social constructivist" bent to take expertise seriously – to treat it as something *real*. The rhetorical trick was to persuade such sociologists to reflect upon their own expertises. Sociologists of scientific knowledge (such as myself), must have some understanding of the particular science they are going to observe and analyse in their field studies.[49]

In subsequent defences and refinements, Collins has stressed the importance of not over-democratizing interactional expertise;[50] we do not *become* interactional experts during long and involved discussions down the pub simply by virtue of our having had those long and involved discussions (though interactional experts may, of course, demonstrate their know-how in various settings, pubs included). Interactional experts have real, specialist knowledge.

The distinction between contributory and interactional expertise may be useful when drawing lines between the expert field scientist and the historian or sociologist of science. However, if the conceptual nature of any ability is *in*, and not *behind*, the executed action, as both Taylor and McDowell suggest, then what according to one story is interactional expertise is also, according to another, contributory. There is nothing in Collins's account that conflicts with this; what needs to be noticed is that interactional and contributory knowledge are themselves context- or frame-dependent (in the ways outlined above). In the field of experimental science, the sociologist of science may have interactional scientific knowledge or expertise, while in the field of sociology of science he has contributory knowledge or expertise. And, of course, the sociologist of science may also be an experimental scientist, and therefore have contributory expertise across fields (an example of which Collins makes use). To think of a non-boxer who is an expert coach as having interactional expertise in relation to the sport may not be wrong; it is simply to choose to view things strictly from "within" the symbolic world of boxing, not of coaching. In the latter symbolic world, the coach has contributory expertise. Not all great boxers will, upon retirement, become coaches, of course. And of those who do, not all will become great coaches, though they may be able to give a perspicacious account of what makes a great coach. In this instance, the boxer has interactional knowledge or expertise when it comes to coaching.[51]

Things are further complicated because Collins tries to draw a line between language and practice, even as he recognizes this is not always possible, nor something we can necessarily make sense of:

> Natural language is an interesting case of a skill because to master interactional expertise in a language is to master contributory expertise – there is no distinction. This gives us a new question to ask about other abilities. Might it be possible to partition skills into those in which there is distinction between interactional expertise and contributory expertise and those in which there is none and would that distinction have an interesting significance? For example, does such a distinction apply to, say, literary criticism or, say, moral judgement?[52]

Language is important to most theories of knowledge because although language is not the only form know-how might take, it is the only form which something like Collins's interactional expertise, or other second-order activities, such as what Brandom calls "explicitation," can take.[53] Explicitation is usefully and subtly distinct from the explicit, because, as we have heard several times now, there is nothing implicit – in the sense of "hidden" – in knowledgeable acts or performances. If knowledgeable acts are always out in the open, and therefore explicit, explicitation is the act of laying bare what is going on in such acts: it is, if you like, second-order explication (the explication of the already explicit), as is Collins's paradigmatic case of interactional expertise – sociology of science. Where knowledge does not need to take written or spoken form in order to be explicit, explicitation cannot *not* be written or spoken. But the fact that we need writing and-or speech for all our second-order talking about and pointing at (other) forms of knowledge should not trick us into thinking that natural language is essential to *all* forms of knowledge. Being an historian of music or a musicologist is not the same game as being a musical instrumentalist. It's possible that a person may be all of these. But the instrumentalist's primary expressive form of their know-how is not natural language, or some parasitic version of it; it *is*, of course, for the historian and musicologist.

Conclusion

The tacit element of knowledge isn't a special mode or type of personal knowledge. It *is* personal knowledge. It is no more, but also no less, than a way of framing conversations we want to have about knowledge in terms of individual skill and capacity. The lecturer's sustained and more or less consistent ability to give a lecture on the problems of tacit knowledge is no more nor less practical than the weightlifter's ability to a pull a three-times-bodyweight deadlift. There can be no knowledge-of without knowers. And without knowers, the very idea of the codifiably true proposition would be meaningless: no utterances without utterers, no propositions without proposers. So-called propositional, context-independent, or codifiable knowledge doesn't rattle around "in" one's head like marbles in a bowl; nor is it simply, somehow, "out there." All knowledge exists in some socially constituted context or frame of reference, though some frames are more easily or commonly felt than others; some knowledge is thickly, some thinly, contextualized.[54] That there is thinly contextualized knowledge is a function of there being propositions to which most "reasonable" people, explicitly or implicitly, assent. Crudely put, there's a lot of stuff that a lot of us take for granted. "Reasonable" is being used in a deliberately weak sense here: it's nothing more than the presumption that our languages are close enough that we can have a discussion about *x*, and that (in the spirit of Brandom) when we do have such discussions, we are occupying shared spaces of reasons. Occupying a shared space of reasons does not require consensus (agreement on what, say, philosophical liberalism entails); it does require having enough in common – occupying a shared symbolic world, inhabiting a common milieu – to allow for coherent agreement and-or disagreement. On this model of "reasonable," Chaplin's character is an unreasonable boxer. To speak of propositional knowledge is to speak not of the conditions of possibility of *having* knowledge, but, again in keeping with Brandom, to presuppose discursive communities in which propositions are shared or have some purchase and can get a grip only against norms of use. Those norms of use are what presuppose some sort of symbolic or discursive frame, some "background" in Wittgenstein's rather than Heidegger's sense. But, to repeat, shared or common knowledge – the focus of the following chapter – requires knowers; received wisdom must be received (and given) *by someone*.

Natural language, spoken or written, is one privileged way of explicating knowledge or drawing attention to it and the discursive or symbolic systems which frame it. If, as Polanyi claimed, we do know more than we can tell, that's because explication, like giving grounds for Wittgenstein, could in principle go on forever. As Brandom puts it, "one cannot have *any* concepts unless one has *many* concepts," for "[c]onceptual content is in the first instance *inferentially* articulated" (as it was in T$_2$, the philosophy lecturer's assimilation and summary of several compatible accounts).[55]

To summarize, then.

Apparently context-independent knowledge refers to thinly contextualized symbolic worlds, the frames of which most of us needn't, don't, or can't notice for reasons of culture, expedience, and/or expertise. If all knowledge is context-dependent – in the dual sense of being dependent upon a knower and symbolically framed – then there is no knowledge that is not practical, because knowledge, as is often said, is a matter of knowing how to go on. Language may help us "point" to knowledgeable persons and their acts, but it does not sit nor get us "behind" them, for there is no behind to get to.[56] Natural language and its parasitic derivations (specialist discourse, jargon) are a privileged mode in which knowledge may be performed. They are not the only ones. But language is necessarily the form of second-order knowledge or punditry – those histories, philosophies, sociologies *of...* – because second-order knowledge is discursive knowledge. And – to be continued in Part III – language is, of course, the basic stuff of both schooled English and Creative Writing.

At least part of the problem underlying the widespread opposition of knowledge and skills, theoretical and practical knowledge, consists in how we think of certain activities and performances, or, rather, with our failure to recognize certain *practices* as such (think of Collins's attempt to separate language and practice). We fail to recognize the corporeal and therefore personal dimension of all knowledgeable acts when we think, for example, that kicking stones or turning back-flips is experiential and practical in ways that sitting at a desk and theorizing is not. Once we realize that both gymnastics and theorizing are *doings*, and that both require as their ground of possibility the corporeal person-knower-doer, the once sharp difference between context-independent and context-dependent knowledge, along with knowledge and skill, begins to dull. To echo an introductory remark, one aim of this chapter is to dissolve both the opposition of knowledge and skills and the subordination of the latter to the former, by showing that we fail to understand knowledge when we fail to understand it in terms of skilled, embodied performance or practical ability.

The viewpoint from which we see propositionality as a necessary condition of "real" knowledge is one from which we fail to see the ability to "put things into words" as itself a matter of practical ability and expertise. No doubt this is due in large part to the fact that a relatively high level of linguistic competence in persons is, in normal circumstances, taken as unremarkable. But it is a mistake not to see such quotidian expertise as part of our worldly, fluid copings, which are, according to Dreyfus, at once our most basic and most rarefied ways of being. Though most persons will, all things being equal, develop linguistic expertise, there are those among us whom we pick out as great wits, poets, orators, and so on: those who raise linguistic skill to "new heights" in certain relatively specialized contexts; there are, however, few if any persons whose exceptional linguistic expertise will be recognized as running the entire spectrum of specialisms – could that spectrum be exhaustively defined – in equal measure. Moreover, the ability itself of the person said to be "good with words" cannot itself, upon pain of regress, be put into words: we can theorize and generalize over it, put it under partial second-order linguistic descriptions. We can punditize it, but we cannot "drill down" to the propositional bedrock of the ability, because there is no such bedrock.

By acknowledging the importance of language to discussions of knowledge while decoupling it from the constitution of knowledge *per se*, I'm foreclosing any attempt to defend either schooled English and-or Creative Writing on the grounds that, because they deal in language and the construction of meaning, they have some privileged access to or relationship with knowledge. The point, which will be drawn out over the remainder of the book, is that schooled English and Creative Writing are no more nor less knowledge-based than any other subject or discipline.

Schooled English is in a peculiar situation: as a subject-area, it's hardly under threat; its cultural and academic importance seem to be taken for granted (perhaps because of the conflation of literacy with English; perhaps, too, because of the unassailability of certain authors and texts, and their invocation in certain narratives of national-cultural identity[57]). But despite the subject-area being secure – its disciplinary identity is, as we'll see, another matter – English hardly fits the mould of the so-called knowledge-rich curriculum, despite its high curricular status, any more than does Creative Writing.

In the view presented in this chapter, talk of replacing curricula overly concerned with skills at the expense of knowledge is little more than a bid for this curriculum rather than that; and in such talk "knowledge" is simply a term of prestige for the favoured curriculum and forms through which knowledge should be performed (and assessed). There may be convincing arguments why one curriculum is better than another – and such arguments *should* be had. But those arguments can't be played out on the battleground of knowledge. Knowledge is "there" regardless; whether it's the "right" knowledge is a different conversation.

Notes

1. To write this chapter, I have drawn heavily from an article I wrote some years ago ("On Tacit Knowledge for Philosophy of Education," *Studies in Philosophy and Education* 37 (2018), pp.347–365), which was, in part, an extended response to Neil Gascoigne and Tim Thornton's book *Tacit Knowledge* (Durham: Acumen, 2013; hereafter cited as *TK*). Although that article and this paper are broadly aligned, this chapter substantially revises and should be read as replacing the earlier piece, which, among other faults, overstated what I then read as Gascoigne and Thornton's residual Cartesianism. I tried, in the essay, to make it clear that my points of disagreement with Gascoigne and Thornton were relatively fine-grained, that I agree with them on a great deal. But I was not emphatic enough, and that didn't come across plainly enough. There are differences between us, of course; were that not the case, this chapter would hardly be necessary. And those fine-grained differences lead me, ultimately, to question the clarity and utility of the very idea of tacit knowledge, which Gascoigne and Thornton are keen to defend. Regardless, their book has a clear line of argument and is a superb synthesis of the field; and their answers to many of the problems of tacit knowledge are clearly stated. Were *that* not case, they wouldn't be this chapter's tacit knowledge touchstone.

   And what I failed entirely to say in that first piece was that, our differences notwithstanding, both Gascoigne and Thornton's book and mine are written in similar spirits of unease with, as they put it, a culture "of explicit rules and guidelines, of aims and objectives, of benchmarks and performance indicators, standardized tests and league tables" (*TK*, 1); a "culture that assumes that knowledge and expertise can be fully accounted for in a manual or a guideline" (*TK*, 192).

2. Department for Education, *The National Curriculum in England: Framework Document*, Department for Education (2014), <https://www.gov.uk/government/publications/national-curriculum-in-england-framework-for-key-stages-1-to-4> (accessed 01 March 2021).

3. Nick Gibb, "What is a Good Education in the 21st Century?," Department for Education (5 February 2016), <https://www.gov.uk/government/speeches/what-is-a-good-education-in-the-21st-century> (accessed 16 November 2020). See also Jonathan Simons and Natasha Porter (eds), *Knowledge and the Curriculum: A Collection of Essays to Accompany E.D. Hirsch's Lecture at Policy Exchange*, and Gibb's contribution therein, <https://policyexchange.org.uk/publication/knowledge-and-the-curriculum-a-collection-of-essays-to-accompany-e-d-hirschs-lecture-at-policy-exchange/> (accessed 21 February 2021). On the politicization of knowledge and education, see my pieces "Practically Speaking: Doing English in a Knowledge Economy," *The Use of English* 68(1) (2016), pp.56–63; "Creative Writing: Mapping the Subject," *The Use of English* 69(9) (2017), pp.45–53; and "Education, Knowledge, and Symbolic Form."

4. The National Curriculum framework document mentions "core knowledge" early on (p.6). See n.3 above for sources on the politicization of propositional knowledge, and also Chapter 4 of the present work for this in relation to Young and powerful knowledge.

5. Gilbert Ryle, *The Concept of Mind* (1949; London: Penguin, 1970), pp.30, 31 (subsequent references in text); Hilary Putnam, *Meaning and the Moral Sciences* (Boston, MA: Routledge & Kegan Paul), 99. The problems of regress identified by Ryle is close to Wittgenstein's insight that there are no rules for rule-following: *Philosophical Investigations* (hereafter *PI*), ed. by P.M.S. Hacker and Joachim Schulte, trans. By G.E.M. Anscombe, Hacker, and Schulte (1953; Oxford: Wiley-Blackwell, 2009), §§185–244.

6. See Ch. IV in the present work.

7 Belas, "Practically Speaking," "Creative Writing: Mapping the Subject," "Education, Knowledge, and Symbolic Form"; see the introduction and conclusion of Gascoigne and Thornton, *TK* (1–12, 191–92) for the terms in which they frame their analysis.
8 Michael Polanyi, *The Tacit Dimension* (Chicago: University of Chicago Press, 2009), p.4.
9 Paul K. Moser, "Epistemology (from Greek episteme, 'knowledge', and logos, 'explanation')," *Cambridge Dictionary of Philosophy*, 3rd Ed., Robert Audi (ed.) (Cambridge: Cambridge University Press 2015), via *Credo Reference*, <http://0-search.credoreference.com.brum.beds.ac.uk/content/entry/cupdphil/epistemology_from_greek_episteme_knowledge_and_logos_explanation/0?institutionId=210> (accessed 09 March 2021).
10 Wittgenstein, *PI*, §§179–181.
11 This seems to be the implication of Gascoigne and Thornton's philosophy of tacit knowledge (*TK*, *passim*, but see especially Chs 2–3).
12 Ryle, *Concept of Mind* (27).
13 Hubert Dreyfus, *Skillful Coping: Essays on the Phenomenology of Everyday Perception and Action*, Mark A. Wrathall (ed.) (Oxford: Oxford University Press, 2014).
14 See Dreyfus, "Overcoming the Myth of the Mental: How Philosophers Can Profit from the Phenomenology of Everyday Expertise [2005]," in *Skillful Coping*, pp.104–125, and "The Myth of the Pervasiveness of the Mental," in Joseph K. Schear (ed.) *Mind, Reason, and Being-In-The-World: The McDowell-Dreyfus Debate* (London: Routledge, 2013), pp.15–40. Dreyfus's defensiveness of non-conceptuality is, in part, a response to an ongoing debate with McDowell, who argues for the pervasiveness of conceptuality. See Schear, *Mind, Reason, and Being-In-The-World*.
15 See McDowell, "The Myth of the Mind as Detached" (hereafter "Myth") in Schear (ed.), *Mind, Reason, and Being-In-The-World* (41–58).
16 Immanuel Kant, *Critique of Pure Reason*, trans. Paul Guyer and Allen W. Wood (Cambridge: Cambridge University Press, 1998) [e-book], loc. 5979–94. Bolded text in original; italics added.
17 McDowell, "Myth" (41).
18 Call this everyday-being-lostness the Bugs Bunny Scenario, after the recurring joke in which Bugs, having lost his way while long-distance burrowing, consults a map and mutters "I knew I should have taken that left turn at Albuquerque." Bugs is in the wrong place – he's lost – but not radically disoriented.
19 On colour recognition, see McDowell, *Mind and World*, Lecture III, §5.
20 McDowell, *Mind and World* (57), qtd in "Myth" (44).
21 See Wilfrid Sellars, *Empiricism and the Philosophy of Mind* (Cambridge, MA: Harvard University Press, 1997); McDowell, "Avoiding the Myth of the Given," in Jakob Lindgaard (ed.), *John McDowell: Experience, Norm, and Nature* (Oxford: Wiley-Blackwell, 2008), pp.1–14.
22 McDowell, "Myth" (42), *Mind and World* (61, 46, 62).
23 See Wrathall's introduction to Dreyfus's *Skillful Coping* (1–22), as well as Dreyfus in that volume, "Overcoming the Myth of the Mental" and *passim*.
24 Dreyfus, "Heidegger's Critique of the Husserl/Searle Account of Intentionality," in *Skillful Coping*, pp.76–91 (88–90).
25 See Rorty's reading, via Derrida, of Heidegger's residual Kantianism in part I of "Philosophy as a Kind of Writing: An Essay on Derrida," *New Literary History* 10(1), pp.141–60.
26 McDowell, "Myth" (47).
27 See Martin Heidegger *Being and Time*, trans. John Macquarrie and Edward Robinson (Oxford: Blackwell, 1962), p.107.
28 Wittgenstein, *On Certainty* (hereafter *OC*), eds G.E.M. Anscombe and G.H. von Wright, trans. Denis Paul and Anscombe (Oxford: Blackwell, 1969), §141.

29 Thomas Nagel, *The View from Nowhere* (Oxford: Oxford University Press, 1986).
30 Wittgenstein, *OC*, §§97, 99. On language games, see *PI*, §§48, 64–71.
31 Jacques Derrida, *Of Grammatology*, trans. Gayatri Chakravorty Spivak (Baltimore: Johns Hopkins University Press).
32 David Lewin, "'The Sky is Not a Cow': Interpreting Religion Beyond the Propositional Frame," paper presented at PESGB Annual Conference, New College, Oxford (1–3 April 2016).
33 McDowell, "Non-Cognitivism and Rule-Following," in Alice Crary and Rupert Read (eds), *The New Wittgenstein* (London: Routledge, 2000), pp.38–52 (44).
34 What I'm exploring as system-relativity is compatible with Hilary Putnam's notion of internal realism. Internal realists, says Putnam, believe that linguistic meaning or reference cannot be explained so much as presupposed (that meaningful communication can take place in any language presupposes not a common psychology (all interlocutors having the same thoughts "in their heads"), but acculturation to shared language-use). Realism is important to Putnam, because it is a view that allows for objectivity, for knowledge proper. But what he calls metaphysical realism is exactly the impossible dream of a view from nowhere. Internal realism allows for innumerable, but nevertheless, true stories of the world. Putnam, "Realism and Reason," in *Meaning and the Moral Sciences* (123–140).
35 Stanley Cavell, *Must We Mean What We Say*, updated ed. (1976; Cambridge: Cambridge University Press, 2002), pp.47–48.
36 For an example of this "in action," see Alex Abramovich's article "Even When It's a Big Fat Lie," *London Review of Books* (08 October 2020), <https://www.lrb.co.uk/the-paper/v42/n19/alex-abramovich/even-when-it-s-a-big-fat-lie> (accessed 23 October 2020), and the accompanying podcast discussion, "The Categories are Stupid," *LRB Conversations*, 21 October 2020, <https://www.lrb.co.uk/podcasts-and-videos/podcasts/lrb-conversations/the-categories-are-stupid> (accessed 23 October 2020).
37 On the logical structure of exemplification (as related to and distinct from denotation) and on the logical functioning of samples and labels, see Nelson Goodman, *Languages of Art: An Approach to a Theory of Symbols* (Indianapolis: Hackett, 1976), pp.57–67.
38 Kant, *Critique of Pure Reasons* (loc. 4735; A51/B75). Peter Strawson has called this an ultimately "disastrous model," *The Bounds of Sense* (1966; Oxon: Routledge, 2019) [e-book], loc.678.
39 See Gascoigne and Thornton, *TK*, Ch. 6.
40 Robert Brandom, *Articulating Reasons: An Introduction to Inferentialism* (hereafter *AR*) (Cambridge, MA: Harvard University Press, 2000).
41 Jerry Fodor defends intellectualism in such a way that it neither falls into Ryle's regress, nor can it be reduced (quite) to mere neurology. The basic idea is that the sentences we might use to describe the "contents" of knowledge-that are *not* to be thought of as natural-language sentences rattling around "in" one's head, which then get expressed or performed in some way. They *are* to be thought of as the only form available to us by which we might refer to our mental "programming," by means of which we are able to perform such acts as shoelace-tying. For Fodor, tacit knowledge is this computational capacity or the psychological programming. Fodor, "The Appeal to Tacit Knowledge in Psychological Explanation," *The Journal of Philosophy* 65(20) (1968), pp.627–640.
42 Nelson Goodman, *Ways of Worldmaking* (Indianapolis: Hackett, 1978); Charlie Chaplin (dir.), *City Lights* (1931). The sequence is easy enough to find online – for example (for, respectively, the locker-room and boxing scenes): <https://www.youtube.com/watch?v=FxqfBRRVpz8> and <https://www.youtube.com/watch?v=NZt7bn-WYXs> (accessed 10 March 2021).

43 The idea of symbolic world or discursive frame is also drawn from the works of Ernst Cassirer, in particular his multi-volume work *The Philosophy of Symbolic Forms*. Goodman's *Ways of Worldmaking* begins with Cassirer, Goodman commenting that, among his and Cassirer's shared concerns, are "the multiplicity of worlds, the speciousness of 'the given,' the creative power of the understanding, the variety and formative function of symbols." Goodman notes that Cassirer's "emphasis on myth, his concern with the comparative study of cultures, and his talk of human spirit have been mistakenly associated with current trends toward mystical obscurantism, anti-intellectual intuitionism, or anti-scientific humanism." Yet, he concludes, "these attitudes are as alien to Cassirer as to my own skeptical, analytic, constructionalist orientation" (1). For an introduction to Cassirer's philosophy of symbolic forms, written by Cassirer in English for a then budding anglophone readership, see his *An Essay on Man: An Introduction to a Philosophy of Human Culture* (1945; New Haven: Yale University Press, 1972).

44 Maurice Merleau-Ponty, *The Structure of Behaviour*, 2nd Ed., trans. A.L. Fisher, (Boston: Beacon Press, 1966), p.169. See also Charles Taylor, "Retrieving Realism," in Schear, *Mind, Reason, and Being-In-The-World*, pp.61–90, and "Merleau-Ponty and the Epistemological Picture," in Taylor Carman and Mark B.N. Hansen, *The Cambridge Companion to Merleau-Ponty* (Cambridge: Cambridge University Press, 2005), pp.26–49; Wrathall, "Introduction," *Skillful Coping* (8); Dreyfus, "Merleau-Ponty and Recent Cognitive Science," in Carman and Hansen, *Cambridge Companion to Merleau-Ponty*, pp.129–150 (132); Robert Pippin, "What is 'Conceptual Activity'?", in Schear, *Mind, Reason, and Being-In-The-World* (91–109).

45 Taylor "Merleau-Ponty and the Epistemological Picture" (38).

46 On affordances see Dreyfus, *Skillful Coping* (*passim*) and Wrathall's introduction.

47 This dynamic may seem to be inverted in the case of a novice learning some new X for the first time. The novice's practical knowledge seems to be dependent – and thus parasitic upon – the teacher's theoretical knowledge. Dreyfus, though, would not allow that the novice is living in the same world as the expert, and thus of the practice. To stick with a familiar example: Dreyfus might say that the novice boxer is not really a boxer. Imagine that the novice develops into an expert: now, the "gap" between theory and practice disappears, because the expert doesn't attempt to execute abstract rules; rather practice produces "moves" in the game which become exemplary, or are subsumed to the language almost as general rules.

48 Gascoigne and Thornton, *TK* (179–183); Harry Collins, "Interactional Expertise as a Third Kind of Knowledge," *Phenomenology and the Cognitive Sciences* 3 (2004), pp.125–143, and "Are Experts Right or Are They Members of Expert Groups?," *Social Epistemology* 32(6) (2018), pp.351–57; Collins and Robert Evans, "Expertise Revisited, Part I: Interactional Expertise," *Studies in History and Philosophy of Science* 54 (2015), pp.113–123; Collins, Evan, and Martin Weinel, "Expertise Revisited, Part II: Contributory Expertise, *Studies in History and Philosophy of Science* 56 (2016), pp.103–110.

49 Collins, "Interactional Expertise as a Third Kind of Knowledge" (127).

50 Collins and Evans, "Expertise Revisited, Part I," and "Expertise Revisited, Part II."

51 The issue is complicated in our imaginary example because we've said that the coach once was a boxer, though by all likely measures and reckoning a less expert boxer than her current star pupil. What, then, would we say about this – that the coach once had contributory but now only interactional expertise? Would we prefer to say that her interactional know-how is dependent, in part, upon her once having possessed contributory expertise? To what extent was her contributory expertise ever truly contributory, if she were only ever a journeyman?

52 Collins, "Interactional Expertise as a Third Kind of Knowledge."

53 Brandom, *AR* (*passim*).
54 Brandom, *AR*; McDowell, "Non-Cognitivism and Rule-Following"; Putnam, "Realism and Reason."
55 Brandom, *AR* (15, 162). For engagements with Brandom in philosophy of education, see Jan Derry, "Can Inferentialism Contribute to Social Epistemology?" *Journal of Philosophy of Education* 47(2) (2013), pp.222–235, and "Inferentialism and Education," Paper presented at PESGB Annual Conference, New College, Oxford (1–3 April 2016); David Bakhurst, *The Formation of Reason* (Oxford: Wiley-Blackwell, 2011).
56 This is a lesson we may take both from Cassirer and Goodman (see n.40 above).
57 Some authors being in, of course, means others are out. Here's Michael Gove, former Education Secretary, "What does it Mean to be an Educated Person?," Gov. UK, <https://www.gov.uk/government/speeches/what-does-it-mean-to-be-an-educated-person> (accessed 03 June 2018): "There is a Great Tradition of English Literature – a canon of transcendent works – and [Stephenie Meyer's] *Breaking Dawn* is not part of it."

Chapter 4

Problems of Curricular and Disciplinary Knowledge
The Curious Case of School English

Introduction

This chapter is concerned with the epistemic rather than the epistemological; with, that is, the framing of subject-specific or disciplinary knowledge and with disciplinary identity, rather than the conditions of possibility, or structure, of personal knowledge.[1] Over the course of the chapter, we'll move from general epistemic matters to issues bearing on English and its disciplinary identity.

The previous chapter's epistemological concerns (about the structure or grounds of possibility of personal knowledge) *isn't non-epistemic*; the question *what is knowledge?* doesn't transcend the bounds of disciplinarity. It's a clearly philosophical question – or, at least, I've taken and attempted to address it as such. If the epistemological *seems* to aim for a higher level of generality than the epistemic, it certainly isn't prior to it. General epistemological questions are only possible in relation to – can only take place within – some epistemic frame.

Given the choice between a curriculum which did and one which didn't teach knowledge, who would opt for the latter? To say you favour some curricular programme because it's "knowledge-rich" or "knowledge-based" is like saying you favour the good over the bad because the good is good; or that you prefer a better over a worse curriculum because the better curriculum is better. The reasoning is circular and the "right" choice presupposed, though nothing is said about how the determinations *good* or *better* are made. Likewise, in talk which uses *knowledge* as a term of prestige over and above skills, nothing is said about how *knowledge-richness* is determined, nor how knowledge is distinct from and preferable to skill; certainly, nothing is said about what "knowledge-rich" is supposed to mean. Different curricula might be said to be more or less demanding or challenging (though *those* claims would need explanation); but a curriculum cannot itself be knowledge-rich. Curricula neither "contain" knowledge nor teach anything to anyone. Curricula can make demands, set out "standards," criteria, programmes of study. But they are neither rich nor poor in knowledge: persons are. Claiming that a curriculum is knowledge-based or -rich is no justification for that curriculum.

DOI: 10.4324/9781003042617-6

That opening gambit draws on the previous chapter's argument that there is no categorial difference between personal knowledge and skill; no hard line between what a person knows and what they can do, between their knowledge-of, -that, and -how. If that argument holds, then the idea that this or that curriculum can be knowledge-based while others are "merely" skills-oriented should begin to smell fishy (if it didn't already). Chapter 3's negative critique involved rejection of the idea that tacit knowledge is anything other than a name for personal knowledge (it *isn't* a special type or mode of personal knowledge); and also the categorial distinctions between practical and theoretical knowledge, contributory and interactional expertise. That last distinction is an epistemic, rather than epistemological, difference; a difference of perspective, context, frame, practice, but not necessarily of subject-matter: a boxing coach might have interactional expertise in relation to boxing itself, contributory expertise in relation to boxing coaching; to think that, when she is coaching, she has only or "merely" interactional expertise in boxing is to get wrong exactly what she *knows how to do* and, therefore, what's she doing when she's ringside.

When *knowledge* isn't being used merely as a term of prestige in a circular chain of reasoning, it might be used as a shorthand for *subject-knowledge*, in which case it's likely bound up in a way of thinking that takes knowledge as the "contents" of a given subject-area. If that *is* how *knowledge* is used, then it's a short step to thinking of subject-knowledge on the propositional model rejected in Chapter 3: as the canonical propositions, which may contain subject-specific technical terms, that are constitutive of a subject-area. Such thinking is broadly in line with Michael Young's notion of powerful knowledge, a focal point of this chapter. Some critics of powerful knowledge argue that while it may offer a plausible model for disciplinary knowledge in mathematics and the natural sciences, the same cannot be said for the arts and the humanities, because those latter subject-areas aren't characterized by specialist language, technical jargon, and-or canonical propositions, hierarchically or logically dependent upon one another. Those who set about defending English along these lines tend to accept, often implicitly, something close to the knowledge/skills or knowledge-that/knowledge-how distinction. From there, they aim to show that those subject-areas which are indeed primarily skills- or know-how-oriented are worthy of the same respect, are equally as valuable, as those built upon propositional or contentful knowledge.[2] While Ryle's analysis of knowledge-that and know-how was designed to show that, structurally, all personal knowledge is in some fundamental way practical knowledge (know-how first), in instances like these, we find Rylean language deployed in a most un-Rylean fashion – to bolster, rather than breach, the know-how/know-that distinction.

While I'm aligned with those who aim to defend the arts and humanities in education, and who wish to challenge the hierarchization of subjects, I depart from most for what are, by now, predictable reasons. The argument here is not that skills-based subjects and curricula need to be respected and defended because all subjects are equally valuable and some are knowledge-based, others skilled-oriented. Attaching greater or lesser value to subjects on the basis of their being more or less knowledge-rich is nonsensical for at least three reasons: (i) definitions of *any* subject or discipline that are criterion- and-or knowledge-based are bound to fail, because (ii) all subjects are skills-based, inasmuch as, in the spirit of Chapter 3, personal knowledge *is* skill; therefore, (iii) if knowledge-richness and-or propositional-knowledge theories are bad definitional frameworks for some subjects, they are bad for all. If one of the purposes of schooling – secondary schooling especially – is to introduce students to subject specialisms and disciplinary expertise, then a clear sense of what disciplinarity is and how it's constituted *should* have implications for curriculum design, not only at secondary- or high-school level but beyond.

The claim of Chapter 3 – that there can be no knowledge without knowers – rested on the idea that all knowledge is context-dependent in a dual sense: the individual is a context of possibility of knowledge; knowledge is symbolically organized, and is thus constrained by, relative to, a system or frame. That insistence, which drew on Wittgenstein and McDowell especially, pointed towards, but did not follow, further questions of shared or common knowledge. Our starting point in this chapter, then, is this: what is often framed as the difference between explicit and tacit knowledge is not the difference between different modes or types of individual knowledge, but, rather, the difference between shared, common, or received knowledge, on the one hand, and, on the other, individual know-how or capability. But while it may be useful to distinguish between these two levels, we should still resist the temptation to speak of different knowledge types. "Received knowledge" is a convenient shorthand, not a category. Matters of so-called "subject-knowledge," it will turn out, are in fact matters of disciplinary identity.

The model of disciplinary knowledge endorsed in this chapter is, broadly, social-realist and constructivist; it is *not* a form of frictionless relativism or textualism; it *does* care to preserve some notion of or standards for objectivity. But just as subject-areas cannot be defended on the grounds that different subjects involve different types of knowledge, neither can they be on the assumption that some are subjective, others objective. Not that there are no such things as the subjective and the objective (we'll come to *that* shortly); rather, they and their relationship to one another are often mistaken and misrepresented.

The Contents of Knowledge

I suspect that the idea of a "knowledge-rich curriculum" may be a convenient nickname for the demand that curricula be information- or fact-filled, and that the silliness of knowledge-richness is bound up with less silly concerns about "shared," "common," "standard," or "received" knowledge and its so-called transmission (the idea, roughly, that students are entitled to and should leave school, college, or university with some subject-specific knowledge-*of* that they didn't have before they entered).[3] Knowledge might appear to be something other than personal ability when it comes to curriculum design, because at issue here are questions of a common curriculum and, therefore, the received knowledge to which students should be exposed or have access; or even the knowledge they should "gain." If you've got to come up with a common curriculum, it's sensible to ask questions like "what do we think all students following this curriculum need to know by course's end?"; and for many, a sensible answer is that the knowledge all students need to know is the subject-specific knowledge that's true for all students of that subject, regardless of those personal differences that are accidents of birth, culture, and identity. This is not the only way to approach curriculum design.[4] But if this, or something like it, is indeed the line of thinking involved in "knowledge-richness," then it's easy to see how Creative Writing can be cast as a knowledge-poor, because apparently process-based, subject. From a knowledge-rich perspective, knowledge is the determinate contents of subject-specific curricula. Creative Writing likely seems, to many, to have little, if any, such contents. But English Literature is just as poor a fit for knowledge-richness as is Creative Writing. Its core practice is interpretative process. The difference isn't English Literature is, while Creative Writing is not, knowledge-based; the difference is simply that English Literature has become, over time, part of the very fabric of schooling, and isn't, therefore, as vulnerable a subject as Creative Writing: who in the Anglophone worlds can imagine mass schooling without literacy and literature lessons?

The doctrine of knowledge-richness is not a carefully worked out theory of education or knowledge; it's more a (relatively broad) political position, which aims to restore so-called knowledge proper to what is cast as an excessively – and so-called – skills-focussed education system.[5] There's nothing much wrong with the concerns that lead to and motivate the doctrine; on a presumption of good faith, this is nothing more than the belief that disciplinary knowledge matters and that it should inform curriculum design. What's wrong is to think that the doctrine of knowledge-richness is the only possible form that belief can take.

Knowledge-richness has been influenced in particular by E.D. Hirsch's notion of cultural literacy, which is indeed motivated by concerns with – as a matter of social justice – a common, minimal curriculum, rich in the general knowledge necessary to get along in life (Hirsch's benchmark for cultural literacy is "what the 'common reader' of a newspaper in a literate culture could be expected to know").[6]

Hirsch's curriculum theory is rooted in his early work in literature and hermeneutics. Against the presumption of essential semantic openness that he attributes to, among others, Gadamer, Hirsch argued that authorial meaning was determinate and determinable. The way to get "back" to original intended meaning is to historicize: the more thickly we can contextualize language-use, the better we can determine original intended meaning. Strangely, Hirsch's early hermeneutics simultaneously invokes and disavows historical contingency. The practice of history is, apparently, history-less, and Hirsch seems to believe that one can adopt a "frameless" perspective when one historicizes: history as a view from no- and everywhere. By historicizing meaning, the argument seems to go, we can ultimately bracket out historical change, because historicizing gets back to "original" and thus "ultimate meaning." History as a way out of history; or, if you like, a certain practice of History as a way around historicity.

Hirsch's epistemology and hermeneutics lead, eventually, to a curriculum theory that ends up looking and sounding, as Johann Muller and Michael Young put it, like a "laundry list" of facts and propositions.[7] Left out is how the propositions are to be integrated into something like understanding – and this gap is particularly odd, given that Hirsch's hermeneutics everywhere points to the sorts of "background" capabilities taken for granted both by the existential phenomenology he rejects, as well as by followers of Wittgenstein. Cultural literacy ends up espousing a crude model of propositional knowledge – one which sees knowledge as so many building blocks but is content to leave them in disorganized heaps and not to think about the structures of which those blocks are, could, or should be part. This is a view of knowledge which thinks the detail comes before the whole painting. But, just as knowledge-richness is not the only place a concern with knowledge can lead, things needn't have gone this way with cultural literacy.

Like McDowell, Robert Brandom takes it as read that knowledge must be conceptual. Unlike McDowell, the "fundamental form of the conceptual is," for Brandom, "the *propositional*, and the core of concept use is applying concepts in propositionally contentful *assertions, beliefs,* and *thoughts*."[8] While I don't agree that language is the only form of the conceptual, of interest here is Brandom's theory of how "content" is produced. Language-use isn't derived from prior already given and meaningful content – there isn't a single vertical line from isolated signifier down to isolated signified; nor is content inside a word as a kernel inside its shell. For Brandom, rather, a sentence or proposition means what it is used to say: saying is always a kind of doing. There *is* such a thing as propositional content, but this is *derived from*, not *given to*, use. The reverse sometimes *seems* to be the case, but only because certain forms of words (clichés and so-called "dead" or "frozen" metaphors, stock phrases, standard technical jargon) are stabilized by shared norms or habits of use.

"Starting with an account of what one is *doing* in making a claim," Brandom's brand of linguistic pragmatism "seeks to elaborate from [such an account another account] of what is *said*, the content or proposition […] to which one commits oneself," when making a claim of any sort (*AR*, 12). In

Brandom's inferentialism, propositional content can only be derived from use (what sentences are used to say or do); the content of a claim or statement can only be determined in relation to series of other claims or statements, because "to be propositionally contentful is to be able to play the basic inferential roles of both premise and conclusion in inferences" (*ibid*.). In other words, sentences have whatever meanings they do because they lead both to and from, are implicated in, a whole host of others. This is one reason why we're always, in discussions and theories of knowledge, bound to begin *in medias res*, and why formal discourses (subject-areas) are always parasitic upon presupposed natural-language competence: as Brandom says, "one cannot have *any* concepts unless one has *many* concepts" (*AR*, 15). Colour recognition, which we considered in the previous chapter, offers a simple case in point: my recognizing that my laptop casing is black is not only a matter of "correctly" ascribing a colour label to an object; it's also a matter of my having a larger palette of colour language, and of my being able to navigate that and make inferentially related judgements: my assertion that *this* is black is also a commitment to its not being green, blue, yellow…

For all its talk of "propositional contents," Brandom's inferentialism is not a propositional theory of knowledge on the model outlined and rejected above and in Chapter 3. Though Brandom's conception of knowledge is in some respects more language-fundamentalist than mine, the distance between us may seem greater than it really is, not least because while I, under the influence of Ernst Cassirer and Nelson Goodman especially, am interested first in the various forms knowledge might take and second in specifically linguistic forms of knowledge, Brandom is interested solely in the workings of knowledge *in* and *as* language.[9] But despite the difference between us on the place of language in knowledge, or the ways in which it's implicated, Brandom and I agree that knowledge is always socially constituted, because it often presupposes the possibility of persons speaking a shared language, which is to say the inhabiting of shared symbolic worlds or discursive frameworks.[10]

Just how and why Brandom's linguistic philosophy takes for granted the social constitution of knowledge takes a little explanation. Brandom takes up Wittgenstein's familiar notion of the language game, which, in Chapter 3, we used as a model for the discursive – and therefore symbolically organized – nature of knowledge. Brandom claims that there are circumstances in which we might have speech sounds *without* having discursivity. "Practices that do not involve reasoning are not," he writes, "linguistic or (therefore) discursive practices." Non-reasoning speech would amount to "a *vocal* but not yet a *verbal* practice":

> Inferential practices of producing and consuming *reasons* are *downtown* in the region of linguistic practice. Suburban linguistic practices utilize and depend on the conceptual contents forged in the game of giving and asking for reasons, are parasitic on it. Claiming, being able to justify one's

claims, and using one's claims to justify other claims and actions are not just one among other sets of things one can do with language. They are not on a par with other "games" one can play. They are what in the first place make possible talking, and therefore thinking: sapience in general. Of course we do *many* other things as concept users besides applying concepts in judgment and action and justifying those applications. But [...] according to [inferentialism], those sophisticated, latecoming linguistic and more generally discursive activities are intelligible in principle only against the background of the core practices of inference-and-assertion.[11]

"Content" is, then, a practical matter because the content of any sentence or set of sentences is determined in relation to those others by which they are implied and which they, in their turn, imply (or point to). And if Brandom's game of reason-giving- and -taking is, as he says, central to language (what it is and how we use it), then language by its very nature throws its users into the space of reasons: the possibility of rationalizing-discursive exchange *is* what it means to have a language *game*. Brandom ascribes to linguistic practices an essentially dialogic element: minus some social context, some situations in which interlocutors are engaged with one another, we might have verbal grunts, but we would not, according to Brandom, have vocality, linguistic practice. Antiphony, then, is the minimum requirement of discursivity. (And though Wittgenstein himself resists shooting as straight a definitional arrow as Brandom's, it's striking that those sections in the *Investigations* which deal with the problems of defining the concept *game* are conducted through the imagined antiphony of the philosopher answering his interlocutors.[12])

Working now in the light cast by Brandom, we need to make explicit what was only presupposed by and implicit in the previous chapter: the idea that someone can be a knower relative to some discursive or symbolic world takes sociality for granted. The very idea of a symbolic world or discursive framework presupposes worlds of shared meanings or common grounds (which is *not* the same as presuming agreement and consensus – not all philosophers, literary critics, musicians, and athletes see eye-to-eye on all matters bearing on their symbolic worlds). Without such a presupposition, the notion of knowledge as so many symbolic forms would have no purchase: the very idea of knowledge presupposes communities of knowers, and that entails insiders and outsiders – those who do and those don't know-how-to-x.[13]

Being a knower in some symbolic world is, then, a matter of identity, on roughly the bipartite model articulated by Kwame Anthony Appiah: one must identify as a knower (one might do this simply by participating in the language game or through "third-person" self-reflection and -identification); and one must be recognized as such, too.[14] Knowledge is socially constructed and – a critically important word for Brandom – *articulated* because for someone to have knowledge, the knowledge they have must answer to some norms of use. Those norms can only be norms by virtue of a community of knowers who subscribe to them:

> In calling what someone has "knowledge," one is doing three things: *attributing* a *commitment* that is capable of serving both as premise and as conclusion of inferences relating it to other commitments, *attributing entitlement* to that commitment, and *undertaking* that same commitment oneself. Doing this is adopting a complex, essentially socially articulated stance or position in the game of giving and asking for reasons. (*AR*, 119)

Truth is a necessary condition of knowledge. But it is not, for Brandom, some curious or mystical property. What is at issue, in fact, is less the metaphysical truth of any proposition, and more that "[t]aking a claim or belief to be true [...] is *endorsing* the claim oneself" (119). Scientific, mathematical – any discursively framed or disciplinary – truths are true by virtue of mass endorsement from expert communities, or, in Brandom's terms, those entitled to attribution and subscription.

The relationship between personal and disciplinary knowledge is, then, not the difference between skill, proper, and knowledge proper. It is the difference between being "inside" and "outside" a community of language users. And it is the difference between contextualized and decontextualized knowledge. Failure or, perhaps, refusal, to adequately contextualize knowledge allows for the illusion that knowledge can be absolutely depersonalized, as if its necessarily social conditions of emergence were somehow a threat to its objectivity, when, in fact, it's only through reference to some standard (framework, context) that objectivity can get a grip: as in McDowell's example of arithmetic, it's only with reference to the arithmetical system that arithmetical propositions are true or false. It's historical context that makes it misleading to say that, for example, phlogiston theory is no longer taught because it's wrong or untrue. Phlogistics worked perfectly well until it didn't, until its anomalous failures became more and more the norm. And it's discursive or disciplinary context that makes what Steven Rose calls "epistemological pluralism" – the fact that multiple interpretations (biomechanical, biochemical, and neurocognitive, say) of the same phenomenon can be equally "objective" or "true" – unmysterious.[15] Specialist knowledge is discursive or disciplinary. It is both objective *and* a human, social invention.

What's Wrong with Powerful Knowledge?

Though curricular questions such as *what should be taught?* and *what should be on the curriculum?* are important, the aim of this chapter is not to stipulate what should be on English Literature and Creative Writing curricula. Problems of canonicity were addressed in Chapter 1. Our interest in this chapter is with the general framing of subject-knowledge, and, indeed, with whether a general framework that holds good for any and all subjects and-or disciplines is even possible. I think it is, and usefully so. *Descriptions* of any given subject or discipline will need to be *sui generis*; but no description could ever be exhaustive, and no particular description is a *general theory* of disciplinary identity. If we want to avoid the banal sorting of subjects into different types of knowing – those that are supposedly knowledge-based and objective, those that are supposedly skills-oriented and subjective – then it's worth having a unifying framework which recasts the objective/subjective difference, and which recognizes disciplinary identity as a practical matter in ways that flow from Chapter 3's account of personal knowledge. My claim isn't that there are no differences between disciplines, but that trying to cash those differences out in the currency of different types of knowledge is unsound, unnecessary, and is to play into politicized debates over the relative value of different subject-areas.

The account of shared or common knowledge I've outlined with help from Brandom is broadly in keeping with social realism. Michael Young's idea of powerful knowledge offers a social-realist framework for curriculum design and for stipulating what should count as disciplinary knowledge proper. Young and his colleagues have been at pains to explain that powerful knowledge is not "knowledge of the powerful."[16] In contrast to forms of dominative power – which, among other things, might be behind the suppression of some forms of knowledge – the power in powerful knowledge lies in its ability to transform and to liberate, to broaden the horizons of those who have it;[17] and it is a power warranted by disciplinary expertise.

Powerful knowledge is specialized disciplinary knowledge and is decoupled from everyday experience and thinking. It is those forms of knowledge (epistemes) that need to be taught, that aren't common-sense or intuitive. Informal modes of knowing (tying one's shoelaces, knowing one's way around the neighbourhood) are *not* intrinsically less valuable than powerful knowledge, they're just more easily learned through social osmosis.[18] All powerful knowledge is specialized knowledge, but the same is not true *vice versa*. Young and Muller offer Scientology as an example of specialized, but not powerful, knowledge (PK, 231). According to powerful knowledge and its advocates, the purpose of formal education is to teach those forms of knowledge that can be neither taught nor caught outside of some such formal educational context.

Powerful knowledge has undergone numerous revisions, but on what we might call the "standard" formulation[19] it must: (i) be systematically organized around sets of logically related, tightly defined concepts,[20] as well as criterion-based norms of practice and validity; (ii) be subject to revision by the relevant expert community (that is, it's socio-historically produced); and (iii) have explanatory or predictive force – that is, it must tell us something about how the world works (accepting, of course, that what it tells us may be subject to change, as per condition (ii) (PK, 236-38)). The "disciplinary community" governs its episteme, because the disciplinary community controls the criterial norms bounding subject-areas and disciplines (conditions (ii) and (iii)). This applies as much to the social as natural sciences. The weaker or stronger the disciplinary community, the weaker or stronger the domain of knowledge as specialized – and thus powerful – knowledge (PK, 244). Once the opposition of "natural" to "social" or "cultural" kinds morphs into the received opposition of the rational and non-rational, however, the arts and humanities – which are not "vertically" arranged around logical conceptual hierarchies[21] – are easily misunderstood as domains of non-specialized, non-powerful, "soft" or "folk" knowledge.[22]

Among the various criticisms of powerful knowledge is the concern that most of the subjects Young and his collaborators would want to bring into powerful knowledge's ambit do not in fact meet its basic conditions. John White points out that what we'll call the "conceptual criterion" – the demand that forms of powerful knowledge are built around networks of logically related, strictly defined concepts – is met only by mathematics and the natural sciences.[23] In a similar spirit, Robert Eaglestone, focusing specifically on English Literature, argues that powerful knowledge can provide us with an adequate model of scientific but not literary knowledge, because it privileges knowledge over the knower, *sofia* over *phronesis*; and because it cannot account for the interpersonal and dialogical character of literature study: English Literature is, Eaglestone writes, "a living conversation," a creative, improvisational dialogue between persons and texts, in which "*how* we say something is as important as *what* we say."[24] What I want to suggest is not that powerful knowledge is fine for the "hard" sciences but not the humanities; but, rather, that if a *general* theory of disciplinary identity – quite distinct from *sui generis* descriptions of particular subject-areas – is good for the sciences, then it ought, if it *is* a good general theory, to be good for the arts and humanities. If it isn't, then it may not be especially good for the sciences, inasmuch as it isn't a good general theory at all, but only a partial subject description. That formulation is deliberately circular. More simply, the idea here, concerning the idea of a general theory of disciplinarity, is: yes, such a general theory should be possible, and might be useful, but only, of course, if what's good for one subject or discipline is good for all.

Young and his colleague Johann Muller admit that early statements of powerful knowledge did indeed take scientific knowledge as paradigmatic of disciplinary knowledge *per se*, and that, because of this, the arts and humanities appeared to be excluded.[25] In order to correct this, they relax the conceptual criterion by referring it to Bernstein's notion of vertical and horizontal epistemic arrangements – the idea that concept-bound subjects like Physics are vertically, or hierarchically, arranged, their permissible conclusions foregone;[26] whereas subjects like History are horizontally, or narratively, arranged, their conclusions arrived at through processes of inferential and speculative reasoning. One difficulty here, at least as far as the coherence of powerful knowledge is concerned, is that, for Bernstein, horizontal discourses are not systematically organized around sets of logically interrelated, semantically specified concepts; so although we can take Bernstein as offering a systematizing label for the non or loosely systematized, this surely amounts to saying that a revised definition of powerful knowledge will simply have to give up on the conceptual criterion altogether – which is, it seems, Young and Muller's next step: "The power of both History and Physics as subjects lies in the *augmentation of possibilities* afforded by the progressive deepening of *their distinctive disciplinary form of reasoning and argumentation* that constitutes the discipline."[27] Notice that by substituting *forms of reasoning and argumentation* for *conceptual schemes*, Young and Muller move closer to the expansive view of language – as discursive game – and symbolic world developed in the previous chapter.

Replacing the conceptual criterion with the broader claim that all subjects have their own discursive practices is a change in powerful knowledge's conceptual machinery, another moving part of which is replaced when the arts are brought into the fold of powerful knowledge:

> What distinguishes arts from the sciences and social sciences is that although they are specialised and subject to the constraints and the boundaries associated with other types of specialised knowledge, they are not exclusive to specialist practitioners. You do not need to play the violin to appreciate Mozart, to write a novel to have read Jane Austen, or to be able to dance to enjoy the Bolshoi Ballet. In each case though it is possible to gain a kind of freedom from everyday melodies, texts and movements, and to imagine an enhanced set of possibilities in each of those domains. (PK, 246)

Here, the condition that powerful knowledge have explanatory or predictive power – on the model of reliable mechanical theories – has been superseded by an enhanced-set-of-possibilities clause. Muller and Young recognize that not all disciplines have prediction (material-mechanical exposition) as their aim,[28] and this seems to have led them to a humanistic recalibration: the question now is not how, or the extent to which, all knowledge domains carve nature at the joints, but how they might change our perspectives on the world. This goes some way to addressing Eaglestone's complaint that powerful knowledge is concerned with knowledge rather than knowers; now, attention is on how knowledge might *affect* its knowers, how it might transform their worldviews. The way Young and Muller position arts-knowers, however, is not without problems.

While it's true that one doesn't have to be a musician to be moved by a piece of music, it's also obviously though not unimportantly true that the expert violinist and non-musician will, in very real ways, experience the "same" performance of the "same" symphony differently. There are no good grounds for gainsaying individual responses to artworks, but the proficient musician will have access to a way of knowing – a mode or style of being – that is not part of the non-musician's habitus. And just as Young has stressed that powerful knowledge is, though specialist, not intrinsically more valuable than "common-sense" knowledge, so too can we say that although the musician has no greater entitlement to their opinion of a concert than does any other audience-member, nevertheless theirs is the perspective of a specialist: right or wrong, *that* is exactly what powerful knowledge is supposed to be interested in, and it's a perspective which *will* carry weight when we are transplanted from the space of the auditorium and context of an audience-member to, say, a performance workshop in an elite music school (once again, *pace* Chapter 3, the dual rings of context: epistemic frame; knower as context). The verbally articulate musician, moreover, may be able to explicate their experience and assessment of a musical performance to both non-musicians and music students alike, in terms to which the latter groups may not (otherwise) have had access (intersection of participatory and interactive expertise; or, better, cross-domain expertise (in teaching and musical performance)).

In the passage from Young and Muller quoted above, music, literature, and dance are treated as domains of knowledge, when in fact they are subject-matter or, more broadly still, objects of interest. Several disciplinary positions, and therefore practices, are implied, but little is made either of the parallels between the player-musician and the dancer, the composer and the author, the work itself (whether musical or literary), the reader and audience; nor of the differences between them. Disciplinary knowledge, the central concern of powerful knowledge, is entirely left out: yes, one can appreciate a musical performance without being a musician, but the fact that one can sit through a concert or read a book doesn't mean one can write a symphony or write a novel. Nor does it mean that one can produce articulate music or literary criticism, which, presumably, is what's at stake in positioning the arts student as an audience member (as a critic-in-waiting). The capacity to enjoy a *performance* of a musical work is not exclusive to musicians, true; but the form of literacy required to read the score of that work is. Musical performers and actors, composers and writers, music and literary critics may have common subject-matter or objects of interest, but they practice different disciplines and thus occupy different disciplinary positions.

Failure to distinguish subject-matter from discipline leads, then, to ambiguity as to how arts students should be positioned in relation to arts subjects. The assumption seems to be that arts students are being trained to be spectator-consumers rather than producer-participants, though the issue is not quite as cut-and-dried as that: Young and Muller do imply that students *might be* meaning-makers in the particular case of History, when they state that "conclusions in History are arrived at" (this in distinction, they claim, from the foregone conclusions of physics).[29] And there is perhaps the suggestion of an interplay between receptivity and productivity when they suggest that

Problems of Curricular and Disciplinary Knowledge 71

"the teacher's understanding of Romeo and Juliet [sic.] might enable a pupil to imagine love relationships in a new way"[30] – though notice, here, yet another shift in the framing and focus of powerful knowledge, from disciplinary norms to pedagogical skill: are we now to take pedagogy as a form of powerful knowledge? This is no insignificant question; and on this point, Young and Muller's failure to distinguish between the musical work and its performance is instructive.

One problem Young and Muller have created for themselves is whether or not the raw fact of aesthetic experience can be counted as powerful knowledge, or whether it needs to or can be "translated," as it were, into knowledge.[31] This phenomenological question – which is not a problem, *per se*, but *is* a problem for powerful knowledge, and yet is a question which doesn't get answered – *appears* not to matter to the sciences, as if the knowledge of those domains simply "speaks for itself." In fact, the phenomenological awareness that's missing from Young and Muller's account of the arts is also missing from their account of the sciences. Teachers *are* skilled performers, no less in the science lab than in the drama studio; and in this respect, they stand in the classroom, in relation to their students, similarly as do performers in an auditorium in relation to their audience. Science teachers are not mere conduits for forms of knowledge that speak for themselves. Being able to say what disciplinarity is in general is one thing; being able to say what's learned and how in some given educational context is another. What's learned, whether in the classroom or the concert hall, cannot be modelled on the transmission of propositional content (sentences supposedly characteristic of a discipline or subject), because learning itself is always an existentially charged occurrence.[32] We'll pull on this thread a little more in the final section.

Problems of Subjectivity and Objectivity

Let's bring our attention back to powerful knowledge's positioning arts students as spectators. Part of the problem, I suspect, has to do with received notions of objectivity and subjectivity – or, rather, objective and subjective knowledge domains – and the passing comment Young and Muller make about foregone and speculative conclusions (in the sciences and humanities respectively). Remember that early articulations of powerful knowledge took scientific knowledge as paradigmatic of disciplinary knowledge in general, and that an important aspect of the idea was that powerful knowledge forms tell us something objective about the world. Young and his colleagues have, as we've seen, revised some of the conditions of powerful knowledge, in order for it to accommodate arts and humanities subjects. But the more the definition is revised and expanded, and the more inclusive it becomes, the more powerful knowledge's commitments to so-called "objective" knowledge is put under strain. What was a matter of concepts giving us improved purchase upon the world becomes, in the case of Music, an expanded capacity for melodic, harmonic, and rhythmic appreciation.

It's common to hear talk of the objectivity of the sciences and the subjectivity of the arts. Anyone wishing to preserve the idea that truth is a real property in the world and of things will want to resist the idea that there can be both subjective *and* objective knowledge. If knowledge proper presupposes truth, then the idea that there can be subjective or objective knowledge seems to smuggle in two kinds of truth (the subjectively true and the objectively true). But if truth is an absolute – things either are or aren't true – then the subjectively true must either be rejected as nonsense (truth is or isn't; you can't have varieties), or accepted as a charitable way of saying that in certain domains – such as discussions of literary works or the production of creative texts – there can be a variety of tastes and opinions but no final appeal, as there can be in mathematics and the natural sciences, to the high court of truth.

Because, on the model of powerful knowledge, the conclusions of physics are foregone, students can be positioned unproblematically as scientists-in-training; their performances can be assessed based on whether (and perhaps how) they arrive at the right answers. When there appear to be no right answers but only the chaos of subjective evaluation, however, things are a little harder. Muller and Young avoid the difficulties of objectivity and-or subjectivity in relation to arts knowledge, first by positioning the model student as an audience member (a recipient of knowledge), second by imagining what, presumably, are meant to be uncontroversially (perhaps objectively?) "great" works (Mozart, Austen; elsewhere, Shakespeare).[33] What's in play here is the presumption that the imagined scenario can still be made to answer to standards of objectivity in cases where students are faced with objectively great works. Accepting these presumptions, the question becomes whether students' sensibilities can be opened to the qualities of great works and aligned with standards of appreciation and taste. If the work of art just is a great work, then the question is whether students can be taught to genuinely appreciate – rather than merely accept – that.

In the previous chapter, we dispensed with any substantivist notion of truth by saying that truths were system-relative (true or false according to the discursive frame or symbolic world in which truth claims circulate). In principle, powerful knowledge advocates can have no disagreement with this position, because, as Young and Muller have stressed repeatedly, powerful knowledge is not epistemologically focussed (on the what and the how of knowledge, its conditions of possibility); instead, powerful knowledge's concerns are socio-epistemic (it cares about how disciplinary knowledge is framed). But although this is the case in principle, and although powerful knowledge does not attempt to cash out its value in the currency of truth, what gets left out both by banal objectivity/subjectivity talk, and by powerful knowledge's default positioning of arts students as audience-members, are the normal aims and activities of different disciplinary areas. Instead of asking *what do we need to know?*, we might try asking *what should we be trying to do?*.

Typically, English Literature is modelled as a mode of reader appreciation. The discipline asks that we report on our encounters with literary texts, to respond to texts and explain or justify those responses. Take the sentence "The language in Shakespeare's *Othello* is beautiful, but its plot is full of holes" as a starting point in just such a report. What *should* – in the normative disciplinary sense – come next is an explanation of *why* one stands by this claim. Working on a presumption of good faith – that students' responses to literary texts are their own and are sincere – English Literature knowledge is subjective not because it can't be set on firm epistemic footings, but in the sense that it consists in objective reports on subjective experience. The objectivity of such reports *can be*, and often *is*, subject to testing: it's relatively easy, in many instances, to explain linguistic or textual misunderstanding – to explain why someone might not, in fact, want to stand by their original claims. We could even test, in principle, whether someone really did stand by their statements (is this judgement consistent with others they've made, here or elsewhere; are they committed to the statement and others it entails, or merely to getting a rise out of their interlocutors? And so on.).

For now, take for granted that subjective experience of a special sort – one's experiences with and of literary texts – is English Literature's subject-matter. In schooled English contexts, it's common to be asked how you respond to a text, how you feel about it, and why. In the contexts of schooled mathematics and the natural sciences, such questions are less common. Students are not, typically, asked how they feel about algebra, or what their favourite subatomic particle is. But a serious case might be made for asking *why* such questions don't get asked; why we don't invite students to consider the possible elegance or beauty of this theorem or that equation – exactly as scientists do.[34] Perhaps we do not ask how one feels about algebra because our feelings don't affect the truth of the equation. But neither do my feelings about the play *Othello* or the writer Attica Locke affect the truth of the one being a play, the other a writer of crime fiction and thrillers. Such simple statements of easily verifiable fact occur all the time in English Literature and Creative Writing classes. Often, they pass unremarked; sometimes, though, uncertainty as to what kind of a text we are dealing with is, from the point of view of the critic and-or author, a matter of significance – just as not knowing quite what one is looking at may be a point of fascination for the physicist. All too often, mangled presumptions regarding objectivity and subjectivity, and their apparent binary opposition, are mapped respectively to presumptions of the anaesthetic nature of the sciences, the aesthetic nature of the arts. This, I think, is true of powerful knowledge. But, it should be stressed, it is an unfortunate side-effect; it is not part of Young and Muller's, or their associates', ostensible projects.

What's Right with Powerful Knowledge?

Up to this point, my reading of powerful knowledge probably seems to be converging with its critics. If disciplines are now understood to have distinctive modes of reasoning and argumentation – rather than definitive networks of "key concepts" – and if they are now understood to have the capacity to enlarge possibilities – rather than as having strictly predictive force – then, implicitly, powerful knowledge has moved away from any propositional model of knowledge and any criterion-based disciplinary definition it might, in the early days, have seemed to imply, and towards a practice-based or dynamic model – one which, as touched upon earlier, points towards but doesn't engage with experiential or phenomenological accounts of learning. Minus conceptual canons and predictive force, what's left of powerful knowledge's original conditions is the expert community as arbiter of what counts as knowledge. Implicitly, we're left with the following model of disciplinarity: disciplines are whatever their practitioners do. In fact, no more than this is needed for a disciplinary definition: it amounts to a simple statement of the Wittgensteinian and Brandom-esque ideas on which I've been drawing. Such a definition allows for the interaction of what goes on in schools, colleges, and universities (disciplines do not only trickle "down" into their school-subject equivalents); of these with cognate activities outside of the academy (the impact of independent writers and scholarship on academic activity), and within other relevant institutional settings (education policy, funding, and so on have the potential to affect disciplinary practice); and it allows for those limit cases that seem simultaneously to test and reaffirm received ideas of disciplinary norms.

(Two examples here: whether Richard Rorty remained an academic philosopher after *Philosophy and the Mirror of Nature*, or was more a philosopher turned literary and cultural critic, is a moot point. But the answer doesn't matter much. The point is that the very question (*is Rorty (still) a philosopher?*) points toward the possible limits, the contested and possibly shared borders of disciplinarity. A second case: Martha Nussbaum, after appearing in the documentary film *Examined Life*, published a journalistic piece disavowing the film, for two related reasons: first, she believed that the film misrepresented what philosophy as a discipline is; second, she objected that the film drew its insights on philosophy largely from non-philosophers (the exceptions are Nussbaum, Appiah, and Peter Singer). Her rejection of the film turns on her belief that a film supposedly about philosophy operates almost entirely outside of philosophy's borders, and her argument takes for granted her right as an expert to map (and possibly police) those borders.[35])

Young and his collaborators have been generous and receptive to their critics; but this has led to a situation in which powerful knowledge's terminological framework has undergone so many additions and revisions that we're left with a definitional theory which is itself lacking definition. If subjects' language games can be *either* vertically *or* horizontally organized, and if they can reveal to us *either* the way world just is *or* the way it might be, then virtually anything can be powerful knowledge once it has institutionalized identity and recognition: powerful knowledge is in danger of becoming defined not by epistemic coherence, but by whether or not you can sign up for a course in it – and this is exactly the sort of thing Young is seeking to avoid. The revisions needed to bring the arts and humanities in from the cold make scientology – for Young and Muller, remember, an example of specialist but not powerful knowledge – a candidate for powerful knowledge: it has its own conceptual scheme, the meanings of which are closely guarded by its expert community; it shapes the worldview of its larger community. But whether or not scientology should be taught in schools is not an argument that can be or needs to be settled on the basis of epistemic criteria (whether it is or isn't epistemically coherent, specialist, powerful, whatever). Were such a question to be asked (in good faith), it could be settled easily enough, *pace* John White and others, on the basis of moral and political questions about educational aims.[36]

The only cultural domain I can think of for which participation likely meets the criteria of verticality *and* horizontality, real-world predictability *and* aesthetic transformation, as well as epistemic governance by a community of experts, is that of elite sport – in particular, sports fandom and punditry. Hans Ulricht Gumbrecht has written about the structure of aesthetic experience in general and of sports fandom in particular.[37] He argues that aesthetic experience consists in the oscillation between presence and meaning. Presence is Gumbrecht's shorthand for worldly, thickly contextualized, here-and-now encounters; experience in the raw, or as close to that as is possible (Gumbrecht is a Kantian of sorts). Gumbrecht's notion of presence has a whiff of Heidegger's existentialism about it; the precise experiential feeling or "meaning" of presence is, in the moment, always just beyond language's grasp. As soon as we do articulate something of presence in and as language, we have moved to the (retrospective, or past-oriented) domain of meaning. Gumbrecht doesn't want to dispense with meaning; rather, in light of the claim that the academic humanities "have lost not just a tone of writing but an affective disposition," he wants to promote a "relation" to experience "that could oscillate between presence effects and meaning effects," so that academic work in the arts and humanities might regain an aesthetic disposition that Gumbrecht calls "praise" – the unembarrassed investment of non-instrumental value in aesthetic objects and our encounters with them. For Gumbrecht, sport, rather than canonical "great" art, best encapsulates the truly transformative aesthetic encounter.[38]

Accepting Gumbrecht's account of the aesthetics of sports fandom, we must recognize that to be able to praise a sports event on its own terms, one must understand the sport's grammar. Sports and games are, like the classic formulation of powerful knowledge, organized around logically interrelated concepts (the rules or, in the case of Rugby Union, the Laws). Sports are regulated by their expert governing bodies, which are responsible for managing any epistemic shifts – they are epistemically closed, while nevertheless being subject to change.[39] If one speaks the language of a particular sport and is immersed in its discursive culture, then one may make predictions that are about as evidence-based and reliable, perhaps, as weather forecasting. And, of course, the experience of participating – either in the sport itself or in spectatorship – is, potentially, an aesthetic one (the aesthetics of spectatorship is Gumbrecht's point of entry).

While I think the discursive worlds of sports a pretty neat exemplar of powerful knowledge on virtually all fronts, I doubt that a stadium full of cheering fans is what powerful knowledge advocates have in mind. Criterion-based definitions of subjects and disciplines, rather like criterion- or content-based genre definitions, are destined to fail, either because they admit much that doesn't belong and-or exclude much that does.[40] If disciplines are what their practitioners do, then to learn a subject is to practice it by taking part in its language game(s). Eaglestone's definition of English as a conversation is good – but it is good as a general definition of all disciplines, not as a definition that marks out English Literature's uniqueness. Indeed, Writing Across the Curriculum advocates have used conversation as a figure for inducting students into any discipline-specific set of academic conventions. To learn the conventions of this or that discipline, says Susan McLeod, is to join a conversation already underway.[41]

While powerful knowledge doesn't work as a theory, its broad political project should be preserved. It is explicitly *not* an approach to curriculum in the laundry-list tradition of E.D. Hirsch's cultural literacy and core knowledge programmes.[42] It *is* committed to preserving conceptual and cultural space for disciplinary identities and to handing responsibility for those identities to practitioners. There is a scene in David Fincher's neo-noir film *Seven*, in which Detective Mills (played by Brad Pitt) says of the serial killer he and his partner Somerset (Morgan Freeman) are tracking: "just because the fucker's got a library card, doesn't make him Yoda!"[43] When it comes to educational politics, however, it often feels as if that's exactly what having a library card makes you. To be Education Secretary in England is to be Yoda by appointment; and it's against such political structures, which give governments a direct hand in epistemic construction and legitimation, that Young imagines powerful knowledge to be pushing. The interventions of White, Eaglestone, and others are, in a nice twist of irony, precisely the sorts of powerful displays of disciplinary knowledge that Young and his friends wish to support: they are statements from the expert community about what their disciplines are (and what they are not). Often, such statements push back against overweening governmental intervention, the norm, in England, since the Education Reform Act of 1988;[44] and this, again, is in keeping with Young and Co.

Disciplines as Practice

The concern that literature students aren't imagined as meaning-makers and practitioners is not only a concern with powerful knowledge – one of the more thoughtful and carefully articulated accounts in which disciplinary knowledge is *the* going concern. It's also a problem of policy and curriculum design.

Not all students will become mathematicians or scientists in the powerful knowledge sense of the term; but we *do* ask that they aim or play at or take on such a *being* while they are in maths or sciences classes. Such is not the case with English, however. We've seen that powerful knowledge imagines the literature student as a recipient of others' artworks, whereas the science student is imagined as a doer – though perhaps a replicator of others' science, rather than an originator. We find the same positioning of the imagined literature student in the curricular framing of English. The following passage is from the Department for Education's statement of the "purpose of study" of English:

> English has a pre-eminent place in education and in society. A high-quality education in English will teach pupils to speak and write fluently so that they can communicate their ideas and emotions to others and through their reading and listening, others can communicate with them. Through reading in particular, pupils have a chance to develop culturally, emotionally, intellectually, socially and spiritually. Literature, especially, plays a key role in such development. Reading also enables pupils both to acquire knowledge and to build on what they already know. All the skills of language are essential to participating fully as a member of society; pupils, therefore, who do not learn to speak, read and write fluently and confidently are effectively disenfranchised.[45]

Here's the equivalent passage in the Key Stage 3 Science document:

> A high-quality science education provides the foundations for understanding the world through the specific disciplines of biology, chemistry and physics. Science has changed our lives and is vital to the world's future prosperity, and all pupils should be taught essential aspects of the knowledge, methods, processes and uses of science. Through building up a body of key foundational knowledge and concepts, pupils should be encouraged to recognise the power of rational explanation and develop a sense of excitement and curiosity about natural phenomena. They should be encouraged to understand how science can be used to explain what is occurring, predict how things will behave, and analyse causes.

The above paragraph is *not* reproduced in the programme of study for Science at Key Stage 4. Instead, the introduction to that document tells us that

> [t]eaching in the sciences in key stage 4 continues with the process of building upon and deepening scientific knowledge and the understanding of ideas developed in earlier key stages in the subject disciplines of biology, chemistry and physics.
>
> For some students, studying the sciences in key stage 4 provides the platform for more advanced studies, establishing the basis for a wide range of careers. For others, it will be their last formal study of subjects that provide the foundations for understanding the natural world and will enhance their lives in an increasingly technological society.[46]

Notice how closely the science statements can be mapped to powerful knowledge — its early articulations, at least; or, perhaps, powerful knowledge on the "orthodox" reading. Science is presented explicitly as a cluster of "specific" or "subject" "disciplines." With English, things are more muddled. English is both culturally valuable ("pre-eminent") and sociopolitically (functionally) necessary. There is relatively little of the disciplinary or the specialized; none of the verticality presupposed of the sciences; neither linguistic nor literary knowledge or expertise feature much here, as they do in the science statements, nor anywhere else in the documents. Mention of spiritual, emotional, and cultural development might be read as consistent with later articulations of powerful knowledge, in which disciplines are characterized by their *trans*formative rather than *in*formative power; and literature is singled out, briefly, as being particularly important on that score. But the government document doesn't frame English in terms consistent with powerful knowledge, precisely because English is presented as a means to other forms of non-domain specific and non-powerful knowledge. Indeed, the fact that reading is said to "enabl[e] pupils both to acquire knowledge and to build on what they already know" shifts the purpose of study from English as a subject or discipline to functional literacy, to language as a cross-disciplinary bearer of information and trans-domain capacity: language as, implicitly, a condition of the very possibility of knowledge acquisition and transmission (whereas, according to Chapter 3, it is only a strictly necessary condition of language-based and second-order knowledges). Here, when one reads, one is not inhabiting any particular way or mode of being; reading is not part of any disciplinary language game; it's simply a central mechanism of the transmission-reception model of learning presupposed by knowledge-richness and cultural literacy.

Positioning students as consumers, receivers, spectators of the arts, rather than as makers, invites the conclusion that the arts are less specialist or knowledge-based than the sciences, because, as per Muller and Young, one doesn't need to be an artist to appreciate art. Such a conclusion, however, fails to distinguish between the different specialist practices of the artist and the critic, and the non-specialist (which is *not* to say invalid or uninteresting, or unwarranted) judgements of the casual observer (reader, watcher, listener …).

Disciplinary identity has been a persistent problem for English. Eaglestone puts it this way:

> Teaching and learning a subject involves more than knowing about a list of texts, equations or processes: it teaches ways of thinking and approaching material, it teaches *habits of mind*. Because of this, a discipline also teaches an identity, a way to be. [...] But what do we teach our students in English to be when we teach them literature? Possibly not "Englishers"[.][47]

The essay that is the typical form of English Literature assessment is derived from the tradition of literary criticism. And the Literary Critic is the disciplinary identity into which, says Eaglestone, English Literature inducts its students. But perhaps *the* principal problem with the framing of schooled English (as in, for example, the Department for Education's programmes of study) is a failure to understand what literary criticism *is* – why anyone would undertake it in the first place, and what we're doing when we're doing it. The forms of active and specialist reading that constitute literary criticism – which we'll consider in the next chapter – are not adequately distinguished from the *seemingly* more passive modes of reading associated with functional literacy (reading comprehension, knowledge "transmission").

All too often, the essay is taken to be the "natural" byproduct of assessment in English, the means by which students can demonstrate comprehension and appreciation of texts, and teachers can adjudicate those demonstrations.[48] Less often is it framed as a *writerly* mode with its own histories and traditions (of, for example, articulating either shared cultural identities or personal aesthetic experience).[49] The idea that you do not need to be a specialist practitioner to appreciate the arts is redundant because trivially true. Being transformed through aesthetic experience – *and* crucially, in a Brandom-like spirit, being able to recognize and explicate one's transformation[50] – relies on an openness to those experiences that is more than mere pleasure-or-appreciation-in-the-moment; it is a comportment of oneself in relation to the experience that is itself part of the way-of-being-of the artist and, indeed, of the critic.[51] But this is no different from the comportment of the would-be scientist. Attending a scientific lecture and reporting what you thought of it doesn't make you a scientist. Attending a reading and reporting what you thought of it doesn't make you a writer or a literary critic.

Conclusion

The general *epistemic* question of disciplinary identity, as it's being pursued in this chapter, needs to be answered in two parts: firstly, there's a question of canonicity – from what sources do we draw the language and its rules of use that constitute the game; in relation to what and to whom are our disciplinary practices contextualized? A thoroughgoing acceptance of the historicizing-decolonizing gesture would mean that every subject should be taught through both first- and second-order practices: one would study not only mathematics, but the history of mathematics; not only English literature, but also the history of English literature. What we're imagining here isn't history as a simple timeline of incontrovertible facts, but as the stories of social, political, philosophical change; literary history not as a chronological list of great works, but as the stories we can tell of *how* English literature emerged as a schooled subject, which political and philosophical fields of force shaped it ... In short, precisely the sorts of stories reviewed and recited, briefly, in Chapter 2.

Secondly, there's the issue of practice — what do *x*-ers do when they *x*?

The knowledge gained from English may seem at once less specialist, less like knowledge proper than that learned, say, in a physics class (there are no left-wing electrons or jealous neutrons). But this is only *seemingly* the case, both because of confusions over objectivity and subjectivity, and the tendency to position students of Mathematics and the Sciences — and, indeed, of the various Performing and Expressive Arts — as disciplinary participants, whereas English Literature students tend to be positioned as recipients or spectators. Because we *do* tend to position English students as spectator-recipients, stipulative accounts of English (who and what should and should not be taught) can quickly descend into arguments over literary taste that are based precisely on non-disciplinary "common" knowledge of the sort Young and Muller attempt to guard against, but on which they nevertheless rely when they presume that the works of Mozart, Austen, and Shakespeare are unproblematically "great" art.[52] (Notice that when such names are mentioned, the works themselves need not be — the name underwrites or countersigns the quality of the work; it's enough that the imagined work is a Shakespeare, an Austen, a Mozart. Such names undergo antonomasic transformation and become bywords for their associated form, mode, genre: a promising student, a "natural," is said to be a budding Shakespeare-Austen-Mozart ...)

Although Young and Muller are far from the reformist politics of knowledge which underpins current policy in England and which motivates Hirsch-inspired curriculum design and talk of knowledge-richness, they seem to take for granted the self-evidentiality of aesthetic value. On powerful knowledge's own principles, however, if one is to study a curriculum of "great works" of literature, then one needs also to study the values and processes by which those works are established as great (philosophy and history, say, of aesthetics). Likewise, if historical importance is the guiding rationale of a literature curriculum (apart from our valuations of their literary merit, the argument might go, the writers worth studying are those who've shaped the course of English literature), one must study not only the literary texts but also the history of their reception — not as mere "bolt-on" context, but as central to the texts' meaning(s) (the social histories of how they've come to mean at all). One might argue, for example, that it's now impossible to understand Conrad's *Heart of Darkness* without understanding something of the historical and biographical circumstances that made the novella possible, nor without knowing something of the history of its critical reception.[53] One needs, that is, to be inducted into the interdisciplinarities of literary scholarship, and to be able to participate, *pace* Brandom, in the spaces of literary reasoning.

The difficulties that Young and Muller have in finding common disciplinary ground between the arts and the sciences disappear once the imagined student of any subject or discipline is positioned as a practitioner (no matter their relative level of expertise). On the basis of powerful knowledge, English Literature's core "knowledge" domain – its core practice or language game – *should be* the production of literary texts, because to undertake this is surely, *pace* Eaglestone, to inhabit the way-of-being of the writer and their work, the primary subject-*matter*, surely, of both English Literature and Creative Writing;[54] and doing that is, in fact, exactly what's at stake in powerful knowledge. To ask students of literature to act as if reader-writers is to position them in ways analogous to that of science and mathematics students when we ask them to "do" science and mathematics.

This perspectival change – from viewing students as spectators to viewing them as makers – *doesn't* entail the removal of critical-analytical writing from English Studies. It *does* entail a shift in our understanding of what critical writing is and what it's for, a shift that reframes critical writing as a poetics. We misunderstand what literary criticism is and what it does if we think its purpose is to demonstrate "understanding" of a text on the model, say, of solving a puzzle (the purpose of literary criticism is *not* to figure out what the text "really means"). Literary criticism's interpretative acts are constructive and reconstructive, creative; they are, if you like, (re-)mappings which indicate the routes we've taken through texts, and which reduce the apparent gap between reading and writing: writing always entails and implies reading, as reading does writing (inasmuch as to retell, interpretate, evaluate a text is to formulate in language our thoughts about and our relationship to it; to tell stories about the text; to have conversations about it).[55]

To suggest that schooled English might need to be rethought so that its students are asked to inhabit the way-of-being of a writer (to produce readerly-writings) is to bring the argument back to the constitutive account of knowledge-as-embodied practice developed in Chapter 3. The suggestion here is that literary criticism needs to be approached and explicitly framed as a mode of creative writing, one which offers objectively reliable accounts of readers' subjective experiences of texts. The claim that literary criticism is in part the objective rendering of subjective experience is the claim that literary criticism attempts to make personal experience – non-linguistic experiences of, or encounters with, language – communicable in more general terms; and it is *that* which makes literary criticism an exercise in poetics.

Notes

1 This chapter draws on but significantly develops and revises some ideas first explored in my article "Knowledge, the Curriculum, and Democratic Education: The Curious Case of School English," *Research in Education* 103(1) (2019), pp.49–67. During the period in which this chapter was drafted, the UK government made the several aggressive interventions into English education outlined in Chapter 2.

2 Such arguments are being made both in academic publishing and more generalist, widely accessible contexts. See, for a few examples, Barbara Bleiman's recent volume (which collects numerous blog posts and other occasional pieces), *What Matters in English Teaching: Collected Blogs and Other Writing* (London: EMC, 2020), as well as her conference paper of the same title (*EMC Blog*, 23 March 2020), <https://www.englishandmedia.co.uk/blog/what-matters-in-english> (accessed 21 February 2021), and this related comment on Twitter (<https://twitter.com/barbarableiman/status/1227598366319706112>) (accessed 01 February 2021). Robert Eaglestone addresses issues of subject knowledge and knowledge types, or forms *Powerful Knowledge, "Cultural Literacy" and the Study of Literature in Schools*, *IMPACT* 26 (PESGB/Wiley Online Library: <https://onlinelibrary.wiley.com/doi/epdf/10.1111/2048-416X.2020.12006.x>) (accessed 01 October 2021)); with Steve Connolly, he discusses English and Media subject-knowledge in relation to powerful knowledge and cultural literacy in an episode of the *Ed. Space* podcast, Episode 5, 13 September 2020, <https://anchor.fm/oliver-belas/episodes/Ed-Space-Episode-5-Steve-Connolly-and-Robert-Eaglestone-on-Disciplinary-Knowledge-and-Subject-Identities-ejihb1> (accessed 13 September 2020); Eaglestone has also addressed disciplinary identity and subject knowledge in "What do We Teach when We Teach Literature?" *The Use of English* 67(3) (2016), pp.4–12, *Literature: Why it Matters* (Cambridge: Polity, 2019), and *Doing English: A Guide for Literature Students*, 4th Ed. (Oxon: Routledge, 2017). Some writers have sought to defend literature study on an implicitly knowledge-that basis, on the grounds that literature "contains" moral lessons: see David Carr and Tom Harrison's *Educating Character Through Stories* (Exeter: Imprint Academic, 2015), and, though the approach is rather different, Marth Nussbaum, *Not For Profit: Why Democracy Needs the Humanities* (Princeton: Princeton University Press, 2010). Such approaches are, arguably, species of the reductive hermeneutics (which imagines literature to be distillable to determinable and determinate meaning) that Rita Felski discusses early in *The Limits of Critique* (Chicago: University of Chicago Press, ch.1), and at which the likes of Susan Sontag, in *Against Interpretation and Other Essays* (1961; London: Penguin, 2009), and Hans Ulrich Gumbrecht, in *Production of Presence: What Meaning Can't Convey* (Stanford: Stanford University Press, 2004), aimed their critiques of interpretation.

3 See Section II Introduction, n.2; Winch and Gingell, "Knowledge," in *Philosophy of Education: The Key Concepts* (109). Even the seemingly uncontroversial idea of educational being "for" knowledge gain is not quite as simple as it may sound. How to measure exactly what has been learned is difficult, and cannot be captured by tests. This difficulty is exacerbated when what schools, colleges, and universities offer is presented in terms promised economic prosperity, and when they're expected to capture and represent learning as data – attainment, value-added, progression (to higher education, "graduate" jobs). Entitlement is an important component of Michael Young's powerful knowledge, explored in this and the next chapter. See Young, "The Curriculum and the Entitlement to Knowledge [2014]," Assessment Network and Research, Cambridge University Press and Assessment, available online<https://www.cambridgeassessment.org.uk/insights/the-attack-on-knowledge/> (accessed 06 December 2021).

4 See, for example, Michael J. Reiss and John White, *An Aims-Based Curriculum: The Significance of Human Flourishing for Schools* (London: Institute of Education Press, 2013); White, "The Weakness of 'Powerful Knowledge'," *London Review of Education*, 16(2), pp.325–335 (DOI: 10.18546/LRE.16.2.11).
5 See the previous chapter; see also my "Education, Knowledge, and Symbolic Form," *Oxford Review of Education* 44(3) (2018), pp.291–306 (DOI: 10.1080/03054985.2017.1389711); Jim Clack, "Distinguishing Between 'Macro' and 'Micro' Possibility Thinking: Seen and Unseen Creativity," *Thinking Skills and Creativity* 26 (2017), pp.60–70 (DOI: 10.1016/j.tsc.2017.06.003); John Yandell, "Classrooms as Sites of Curriculum Delivery or Meaning-Making: Whose Knowledge Counts?" *Forum* 56(1), pp.147–155 (DOI: 10.2304/forum).
6 E.D. Hirsch, "Cultural Literacy," *American Scholar* 52(2) (1983), pp.159–69 (166). On Hirsch's influence on education policy in England, see my "Education, Knowledge, and Symbolic Form," and John Yandell, "Culture, Knowledge, and Power: What the Conservatives have Learnt from E.D. Hirsch," *Changing English: Studies in Culture and Communication* 24(3) (2017), pp.246–52 (DOI: 10.1080/1358684X.2017.1351231).
7 Muller and Young, "Knowledge, Power and Powerful knowledge Re-Visited," *The Curriculum Journal*, 30(2) (2019), pp.196–214 (205) (DOI: 10.1080/09585176. 2019.1570292) (hereafter cited in the text as RV).
8 Robert Brandom, *Articulating Reasons: And Introduction to Inferentialism* (Cambridge, MA: Harvard University Press, 2000, p.12). Hereafter cited as *AR*.
9 The opening sentences of Goodman's *Ways of Worldmaking* (Indianapolis: Hackett, 1978, p.1) led me to Cassirer. How could they not? "Countless worlds made from nothing by [*sic*.] use of symbols – so might a satirist summarize some major themes in the work of Ernst Cassirer. These themes – the multiplicity of worlds, the speciousness of 'the given,' the creative power of the understanding, the variety and formative function of symbols – are also integral to my own thinking. Sometimes, though, I forget how eloquently they have been set forth by Cassirer, partly perhaps because his emphasis on myth, his concern with the comparative study of cultures, and his talk of human spirit have been mistakenly associated with current trends toward mystical obscurantism, anti-intellectual intuitionism, or anti-scientific humanism. Actually these attitudes are as alien to Cassirer as to my own skeptical, analytic, constructionalist orientation." For a flavour of Cassirer's work, see *Language and Myth* [first German ed. 1925], trans. Susan K. Langer (1946; New York: Dover, 1953), *An Essay on Man: An Introduction to a Philosophy of Human Culture* (1945; New Haven: Yale University Press, 1972). Cassirer's *An Essay on Man*, written in English by Cassirer, offers Anglophone readers a single-volume introduction to his multivolume philosophy of symbolic forms, untranslated in the '40s.
10 For an account that may or may not agree with my talk of symbolic worlds and discursive frames, but which certainly complicates it in interesting ways, see Donald Davidson's account of prior and passing theories (his substitutes for what is often called linguistic competence), "A Nice Derangement of Epitaphs [1986]," in *The Essential Davidson*, eds Ernie Lepore and Kirk Ludwig (Oxford: Clarendon, 2006), pp.251–65.
11 Brandom, *AR*, pp.14–15. Without wishing to disturb a theme we put to bed in the last chapter, it's worth noting that where Wittgenstein's background is one of conceptual inheritance, Brandom's is one of inherited linguistic competence. It's unclear whether this is exactly the sort of tacit competence that Gascoigne and Thornton are likely to admit exists, but which can count not as knowledge but mere neurology; or whether it might count as tacit knowledge because our linguistic competences are something we can work on and develop, but could not get "behind" or "inside" (in the sense that meanings are often said to be "behind" or "inside" speech-acts).

12 See, for example, Wittgenstein, *Philosophical Investigations*, §§64–77; the difficulty of giving *game* sharp definitional edges leads, of course, to Wittgenstein's notion, almost as famous as language games, of "family resemblance." It's also worth noting that the developmental aspects of language acquisition isn't part of Brandom's general philosophy. He's concerned with the logical structure of linguistic – which is to say dialogic and discursive – practice; his starting point, therefore, is the already-fluent language-user.

13 A person who speaks natural language but does not speak this or that disciplinary language game will, usually, still be considered a person. But because language is not the only, but rather the paradigm, form of knowledge and is often taken as a condition of sentience, those who do not speak language at all, or who do not speak certain varieties of a natural-language game, may be marginalized or radically depersonalized. In *Learning from My Daughter: The Value and Care of Disabled Minds* (Oxford: Oxford University Press, 2019), Eva Kitay has written about how her profoundly/multiply disabled daughter, who is nonverbal, isn't "seen" by standard academic philosophy. In the 1970s, sociolinguist William Labov drew attention to the linguistic intersection of racial and class politics and challenged the deficit view of Black American English (he demonstrated the linguistic ingenuity and efficacy of Black American English over and above so-called middle-class speech and Bernstein's elaborated code). Labov, *Language in the Inner City: Studies in the Black English Vernacular* (Oxford: Blackwell, 1972). More recently, April Baker-Bell has studied anti-Black linguistic racism and education: *Linguistic Justice: Black Language, Literacy, Identity, and Pedagogy* (New York: Routledge, 2020).

14 Kwame Anthony Appiah, *The Ethics of Identity* (Princeton: Princeton University Press, 2005), pp.65–71. On the taking a third-person perspective of one's self, see Chapter 3 of this book. A person's know-how doesn't suddenly evaporate in the absence or refusal of recognition from others; but without recognition the status of knowledge as such may be affected, and so too its availability as knowledge to others.

15 Steven Rose, *Lifelines: Biology, Freedom, Determinism* (London: Allen Lane-Penguin, 1997).

16 Michael Young and Johan Muller, "On the Powers of Powerful Knowledge," *Review of Education* 1(3) (2013), pp.229–250 (DOI:10.1002/rev3.3017) (hereafter cited as PK).

17 See Young & Muller, PK; Muller & Young, RV.

18 Young & Muller, PK. This is not to say, however, that disciplinary and "everyday" knowledge do not exert pressures on, or interanimate, one another. See Lew Zipin's Vygotsky-influenced account, "Pursuing a Problematic-Based Curriculum Approach for the Sake of Social Justice," *Journal of Education* 69 (2017), pp.67–92.

19 The "standard formulation" of powerful knowledge is the one which, for example, White ("Weakness of 'Powerful Knowledge'") and Eaglestone (*Ed. Space* podcast; forthcoming IMPACT pamphlet) critique; it's also the one to which Young and his colleagues look and which they attempt to revise in light of their critics (in, for example, RV).

20 Basil Bernstein, "Vertical and Horizontal Discourse: An Essay," *British Journal of Sociology of Education* 20(2) (1999), pp.157–173.

21 Ibid.

22 Young & Muller, PK, Muller & Young, RV, *passim*.

23 White, "Weakness of 'Powerful Knowledge'," *London Review of Education*, 16(2) (2018) pp.326–327.

24 Eaglestone, *Literature: Why it Matters* (6, 9). See n.2 for Eaglestone's other related work.

25 See Young & Muller, PK, and Muller & Young, RV, in the latter of which the authors directly address some of the criticism White makes in "Weakness of 'Powerful Knowledge'."

26 Muller & Young, RV (207); Bernstein, "Vertical and Horizontal."
27 RV (207, emphases added).
28 RV (203).
29 RV (207).
30 RV (203)
31 Young and Muller, for all their attempts to carve out a privileged space in powerful knowledge for the arts, elide expressive arts practices with aesthetic appreciation. Maxine Greene distinguishes carefully between the two domains. Though she doesn't limit aesthetic appreciation strictly to the arts, she does tend to assume the arts are its first home. Greene, *Variations on a Blue Guitar: The Lincoln Center Institute Lectures on Aesthetic Education* (New York: Teachers College Press, 2001).
32 David Aldridge, "Reading, Engagement and Higher Education," *Higher Education Research and Development* 38(1), pp.38–50.
33 Young & Muller, PK.
34 See, for example, Graham Farmelo (ed.), *It Must Be Beautiful: Great Equations of Modern Science* (London: Granta, 2002). Scientists' aesthetic attachments to their fields are neatly dramatized in the documentary film *Particle Fever* (dir. by Mark Levinson, 2013), which is about CERN's Large Hadron Collider project.
35 On Rorty's standing after *Philosophy and the Mirror of Nature*, see Richard. J. Bernstein, *The Pragmatic Turn* (Cambridge: Polity Press), ch.9. Martha Nussbaum, "Inheriting Socrates," *The Point* 2 (2010), <https://thepointmag.com/criticism/inheriting-socrates/> (accessed 01 March 2021); reprinted in *Philosophical Interventions: Reviews 1986-2011* (Oxford: Oxford University Press, 2012). Astra Taylor (dir.) *Examined Life* (2008); Nussbaum's contribution to the film can be viewed online (<https://www.youtube.com/watch?v=cbcGbflpFzI>), and the transcript read in the accompanying book, edited by Taylor, *Examined Life: Excursions with Contemporary Thinkers* (New York: New Press, 2009).
36 Reiss and White, *Aims-Based Curriculum*; White, "Weakness of 'Powerful Knowledge'."
37 Gumbrecht, *Production of Presence* and *In Praise of Athletic Beauty* (Cambridge, MA: Harvard University Press, 2006).
38 Gumbrecht, *Athletic Beauty* (21), *Presence* (xv), *Athletic Beauty* (24).
39 Consider, for example, the current debates around concussion in football and rugby, or the decision ahead of the 2016 Olympics that male boxers would not wear protective headgear. BBC Sport, "Concussion in sport: Group Including Josh Navidi Call for Radical Reforms for Player Safety" (18 February 2021), <https://www.bbc.co.uk/sport/rugby-union/56098989>; Ken Belson, Making Olympic Boxing Safer by Eliminating Head Guards," *The New York Times* (06 August 2016), <https://www.nytimes.com/2016/08/07/sports/olympics/making-olympic-boxing-safer-by-eliminating-head-guards.html>; Sean Ingle, "Issa Diop Incident Shows Concussion Rules 'Deeply Flawed,' Brain Charity Says," *The Guardian* (10 February 2021), <https://www.theguardian.com/football/2021/feb/10/diop-incident-shows-new-concussion-rules-deeply-flawed-brain-charity-says-headway> (all electronic sources accessed 04 March 2021).
40 See Oliver Belas, "Genre," *The Encyclopedia of Literary and Cultural Theory*, Michael Ryan (ed.) (Oxford: Wiley).
41 Susan H. McLeod, "Introduction," in McLeod and Margot Soven (eds), *Writing Across the Curriculum: A Guide to Developing Programs* (1992; e-book; WAC Clearing House, Colorado State University, 2000), available online, <https://wac.colostate.edu/books/landmarks/mcleod-soven/> (accessed 23 July 2021), p.3.
42 Muller & Young, RV (205).
43 David Fincher (dir.), *Seven* [stylized as *Se7en*] (1995).

86 Problems of Knowledge

44 See, for example, Stephen J. Ball, *The Education Debate*, 3rd Ed. (Bristol: Policy Press, 2017).
45 Department for Education, *English Programmes of Study: Key Stage 3 National Curriculum in England* (2013), p.2, <https://assets.publishing.service.gov.uk/government/uploads/system/uploads/attachment_data/file/244215/SECONDARY_national_curriculum_-_English2.pdf> (accessed 03 June 2018); *English Programmes of Study: Key Stage 4 National Curriculum in England* (2014), p.3, <https://assets.publishing.service.gov.uk/government/uploads/system/uploads/attachment_data/file/331877/KS4_English_PoS_FINAL_170714.pdf> (accessed 03 June 2018). "All the skills of language are essential to participating fully as a member of society": true, possibly; but what are "all the skills of language"? "[P]upils, therefore, who do not learn to speak, read and write fluently and confidently are effectively disenfranchised": are we to read this as thinly veiled prescriptivism (*you need to get the language right if you're going to get along*), or as resigned pragmatism (it may not be right that you've got to speak the Queen's English if you want to get along, but that's just the way it goes)?
46 Department for Education, *Science Programmes of Study: Key Stage 3 National Curriculum in England* (2013), p.2, <https://assets.publishing.service.gov.uk/government/uploads/system/uploads/attachment_data/file/335174/SECONDARY_national_curriculum_-_Science_220714.pdf> (accessed 26 November 2018); *Science Programmes of Study: Key Stage 4 National Curriculum in England* (2014), p.3, <https://assets.publishing.service.gov.uk/government/uploads/system/uploads/attachment_data/file/381380/Science_KS4_PoS_7_November_2014.pdf> (accessed 25 November 2018). The Programmes of Study apply to schools in England; governmental oversight of education in the UK is devolved. The statement quoted appears in the documents for English at Key Stages 3 and 4, the equivalent of ISCED 2-3. England's A Level system bridges the transition from ISCED 3-4, 4 being equivalent to the first year of a university degree.
47 Eaglestone, "What do We Teach" (4).
48 Belas, "The Perfectionist Call of Intelligibility: Secondary English, Creative Writing, and Moral Education," *Philosophical Inquiry in Education* 24(1) (2016), pp.37–52 (44–46) (DOI: <https://doi.org/10.7202/1070553ar>).
49 The Harlem Renaissance was, at least in Alain Locke's view, an attempt at carving out a shared, yet plural, Black American, literary and cultural identity. I.A. Richards's emphasis on aesthetic experience suggests a link to the educational and aesthetic philosophies of John Dewey. See Alain Locke (ed.), *The New Negro: Voices of the Harlem Renaissance* (1925; New York: Touchstone, 1997); and also George Huthcinson, *The Harlem Renaissance in Black and White* (Massachusetts: Belknap Press-Harvard University Press, 1995). See I.A. Richards, *Principles of Literary Criticism* (1924; London: Routledge, 1989); and also Dewey, *Democracy and Education: An Introduction to the Philosophy of Education* (1916; New York: The Free Press, 1997), *Art as Experience* (1934; New York: Perigee, 1980), *Experience and Education* (1938; New York: Touchstone-Simon and Schuster, 1997). In passing, it's worth saying: see Hutchinson's book for Dewey's connections to the intellectual currents of the Harlem Renaissance.
50 This moves us from the Aristotelian cathartic model to something closer to Maxine Greene's notion of aesthetic education.
51 Despite n.29, it is this ontological aspect that is sometimes missing from Greene, who, ironically, writes in precisely this mode of being-as-artist on the subject of aesthetic experience.
52 Take, for example, the presumptions underlying this from Michael Gove "What does it Mean to be an Educated Person?" Gov.UK, <https://www.gov.uk/government/speeches/what-does-it-mean-to-be-an-educated-person> (accessed 03 June 2018): "You come home to find your 17-year-old daughter engrossed in a book. Which would delight you more – if it were *Twilight* or *Middlemarch*?"

53 Joseph Conrad, *Heart of Darkness*, Norton Critical Edition, 4th Ed. (1899; New York: Norton, 2006).
54 What "subject-matter" isn't transparent, however, as we'll find in the final section.
55 See, for example, Roland Barthes, *S/Z: An Essay*, trans. Richard Miller (New York: Farrar, Straus, and Giroux, 1991); Jacques Derrida, *Acts of Literature*, ed. Derek Attridge (London: Routledge, 1991); Jacques Rancière, *The Emancipated Spectator*, trans. Gregory Elliott (London: Verso, 2009); Felski, *The Limits of Critique*.

Chapter 5

Reading/Writing and a (Very) Rough Sketch of Revised English Studies (Coda to Part II)

Introduction

With this chapter, our narrow focus on English Literature and Creative Writing ends. In Part III, I consider the importance of writing practices to university-level education generally, beyond the subject-specific interests of English Literature and Creative Writing. As a coda to the subject-centred portion of the book, we'll review a debate over English Literature's disciplinary and methodological identity. Simply put, the debate is concerned with whether English Literature is a practice rooted in close reading or other contextualist methods (historicism, theory, and so on). This is sometimes framed as the difference between literary criticism and literary scholarship.[1] In recent years, there's been a groundswell of work advocating for close reading, though it's not always clear whether "close reading" should be read as a narrowly prescribed method or a broad approach virtually synonymous with "literary criticism."[2] This debate needn't be decided one way or the other, so long as there are specialists producing both criticism and scholarship. Instead, we'd do better to reframe – and, indeed, to rename – English Literature: "Textual Criticism," "Ways of Reading," "Literary Criticisms"? The name itself is less important than the gesture of foregrounding critical reading as multiple overlapping practices, multiple possible methods. To capture that gesture, towards the end of this chapter I'll use the last alternative, Literary Criticisms, in place of English Literature. What's commendable about the pro-criticism lobby is its resistance to assessment frameworks and curriculum designs that reduce literature study to feature-spotting and programmatic comprehension, and which encourage students to treat texts as puzzles to be solved or barriers to be crossed: "this is what the text *really* means, beneath its literary surface …" What's confusing about the pro-criticism group is its assumption that aesthetic appreciation is only on the side of close textual analysis (and not, say, on the side of historicist interpretation). The criticism/scholarship debate will lead us into a brief consideration of aesthetics and aesthetic experience. From there, we move to what I think is an obvious though often overlooked matter: reading – of the special kind associated

DOI: 10.4324/9781003042617-7

with English Literature – is a writer's game. This brings us full circle, back to one of the points with which this book began: it's seldom asked why literary criticism should be *the* central practice or default mode of literature studies. The chapter ends with a brief and rough plan for a revised English Studies, one centred around creative writing practices.

The Criticism/Scholarship Debate

There's a debate in English Literature studies – less new than resurgent – over disciplinary identity. Participants tend to rely on a broad-level distinction between textual and contextual methods – between literary criticisms rooted in close reading on one side; literary history, historicism, and theory on the other. Both text- and context-centred approaches involve reading closely, but reading closely is not necessarily close reading. The former "describes many different practices of reading from antiquity to the modern era."[3] The latter identifies a distinct, but not static, methodological tradition. Typically, this tradition has its "inaugural moment" in the work of I.A. Richards, from whom we move to the Leavises and then onto the New Criticism in America.[4] Though it was the New Criticism that offered positive strategies for close reading, it was Richards who "laid the foundation" for close reading by developing "a set of tactics for removing the sources of misreading."[5]

Among those who find in favour of literary criticism and-or close reading is a tendency to assume that this is the side on which aesthetic appreciation lives: the argument, roughly, is that close reading attends to the text as an aesthetic end in itself; close reading is attentive both to the literary character of literary texts and to readers' personal responses. Contextualist approaches treat texts as means to other, more broadly "cultural," ends; in doing so, they tend to ignore or rationalize away the literariness of literature (literary language is something to be overcome so that we can get to the picture of history, the moral message, the "real" meaning "behind" the language).[6]

J.W. Phelan claims that attending to literary fiction's fictionality but not its literariness makes it all too easy to treat texts as standing for or "containing" some other "content" or significance (the text as container for some moral lesson, or some set of facts about the world). Such readings tend to be reductive: they assume that one can say, with certainty, what the "real" "value" or "meaning" of the text is, and they do this by stripping out the literariness of literary language, proceeding as if language were simply a transparent window on the world, and as if literary texts were simply attractive theatres for the staging of philosophical dramas. It's important to Phelan that we can identify a definite "cognitive gain" from literature study, *and* that the cognitive gain offered by the study of literature involves the aesthetic: cognitive gain is the general mark of educational value, while the aesthetic is the mark of the literariness of literature. The cognitive gain promised by close reading is not new propositional content, but rather the ability to think critically, creatively, sensitively: this is cognitive gain as know-how rather than knowledge-that.[7]

Where Phelan's currency is *individual* cognitive gain, Joseph North cashes out the value of close reading in terms of an aesthetic education aimed at a broadening of our collective horizons. Literary criticism, he writes, was once a project that aimed at "cultivating new ranges of sensibility, new modes of subjectivity, new capacities for experience"; and though the literary-critical project of the early twentieth century was not without its problems, North wishes to recuperate much of that project. Like Phelan, North believes it's the aesthetic dimension – the literariness of literature – that's lost if literature is "reduced" to historical evidence or theoretical exemplar; but for the latter, the importance of aesthetic education is political rather than cognitive: close reading is critical reading and is "part of a longer history of resistance to the economic, political, and cultural systems that prevent us from cultivating deeper modes of life."[8]

Robert Eaglestone reads both cultural literacy and powerful knowledge as crudely scientific discourses which, interested only in forms of knowledge reducible to propositional "content," mistake particular forms of knowledge for knowledge *per se*. This – a fairer assessment of cultural literacy than of powerful knowledge (as discussed in the previous chapter) – leads to the claim that framing literature study in terms of cultural literacy and-or powerful knowledge leads to literary works and readers' responses to them being displaced by overweening contextualism. Literary knowledge can be more easily rationalized *as* knowledge (on the scientific model) if literary texts are treated as either mirrors of or ciphers for history, and if history is conceived as nothing more than lists of time-, place-, and date-stamped facts. As an example, Eaglestone cites the English Literature curriculum map of one large chain of schools, "which seems not to be interested in literature but in simplified versions of history as context." He continues:

> The key knowledge in the curriculum map for *Oliver Twist* is, first, "life in Victorian London; Victorian crime," and only then, "the form of the novel" [...]. Worse, nowhere in the map [...] is there a discussion of character, plot, narrative voice, how a novel works or even what a novel is. This is not teaching the student how to read novels but offering an ersatz Victorian social history.

In such cases, Eaglestone argues, "historical context is prioritised over how [the text] works," or how the genres of which they're a part function. Prioritizing context over text "implies I have to know the history before a [text] moves me or before I can understand it. Versions of second-hand history make easy-to-assess subunits of 'valid' knowledge, but they do not lead to a deeper understanding."[9] Crucially, Eaglestone doesn't present his defence of close-reading-as-personal-response as a new or radical perspective. Quite the opposite: he aligns himself with the *ideals* of England's National Curriculum, but not the instrumentalist realities of its national examinations system and assessment frameworks.[10]

Eaglestone is less concerned to preserve close reading as a tightly defined method than he is to resurrect a relatively broad tradition of literary criticism (of which Richardsonian close reading is an essential part). Where Phelan's interest is in the cognitive gain afforded by aesthetic and literary education, and North's is in a left-wing emancipatory project, Eagestone's focus is the importance of allowing space for personal responses to literature.[11] He believes scientistic conceptions of disciplinarity and curricula an ill fit for English Literature, because, "while there may be wrong answers in science, this is rarely so in the study of literature […]. An interpretation might be more or less skilful or interesting or persuasive, but a sophisticated appreciation of […] a literary work […] cannot be *invalid*, especially if there is evidence to support it."[12]

This is right so far as it goes (recall our earlier discussion of subjectivity and objectivity in Chapter 4). But it needs to be said that there's plenty in literature study one *can* get wrong.[13] Here's a textbook example of how we might get something right or wrong, or at least righter or wronger. This is David Crystal glossing a passage from Jane Austen's *Emma*, in which Miss Bates recounts Mr. Churchill's response to some baked apples:

> "Oh!", said he, directly, "there is nothing in the way of fruit half so good, and these are the finest-looking home-baked apples I ever saw in my life." That, you know, was so very – And I am sure, by his manner, it was no compliment…"
>
> It is easy to let the speaker carry us on past this point, so that we do not notice the existence of the problem: if the first comment means anything at all, it is surely a compliment, yet Miss Bates seems to be denying it. The apparent contradiction is resolved when we know that *compliment* had an additional sense in Austen's time, which it has since lost: it could mean simply "polite or conventional praise." What Miss Bates means is "It wasn't just flattery."[14]

Eaglestone himself offers an example of a limiting right/wrong kind of response in literature study: "Without understanding that Satan is evil – a value judgement – *Paradise Lost* makes no sense."[15] Eaglestone's point is that mathematical and scientific knowledge can be presented as value-free, inasmuch as many of our answers to mathematical and scientific questions can be marked either right or wrong (molecular bonds are as they are regardless of how we feel about them), and right answers are the products of following right methods. By contrast, he argues, the very idea of value-free English Literature knowledge is incoherent. Notice, however, that in the example of *Paradise Lost*, one can make either the right or wrong moral call: you *must* judge Satan as evil, otherwise you just won't get *Paradise Lost*. The idea, then, is that irrespective of your own moral values (your "personal" response), you must understand that Satan is evil in the *Paradise Lost* world. But if this is right, understanding that is less about primary moral judgement and value (what do *I* believe; who and what do *I* think is right or wrong, good or evil?), and more about second-order chains of moral reasoning (how and why is So-and-So positioned, presented, constructed as good or evil or somewhere in between, within the moral logic of this literary world?).

It turns out, then, that in the *Paradise Lost* example, the gap between so-called scientific and literary knowledge is not so wide: chemical bonds are what they are, regardless of how I feel about them; Satan is *positioned* as evil, regardless of how I feel about him (and, indeed, if I fail to see this, I may struggle to articulate why I, reading *Paradise Lost* in the early twenty-first century, feel the way I do about him). The issue isn't, in the end, the distinction between value-full or value-free knowledge, but whether we're required simply to make claims (of belief, say), or to make claims *and* give reasons for them. I may remember the answers to simple arithmetical problems without ever understanding the arithmetical processes by which those answers should be reached. Similarly, I can be told that in *Paradise Lost* Satan is evil; I can accept that and remember and recite it whenever *Paradise Lost* comes up in conversation. Without ever conceptualizing how or why he's evil, without ever exploring the contingencies on which such a judgement hangs, I can still know that Satan is evil. In either example, we'll never know how or why I've reached the answer I have unless I'm asked to give my reasons (to "show my working").

The point, then, isn't that you don't get *Paradise Lost* if you don't know that Satan's evil; it's that one way of demonstrating understanding of *Paradise Lost* is to be able to discuss *why* we do or should assent to the claim that he's evil (or, indeed, why we might recognize but reject that characterization). And articulating this *why* is impossible without drawing on some sort of contextual or paratextual resources – political, religious, (auto)biographical ...

A final, anecdotal example. At a recent symposium on schooled English and England's National Curriculum, a writer, critic, and educator claimed that government policy meant not only that literature students had access to a narrow range of writers and literary traditions, but also that the scope for students to respond in genuinely personal terms was severely limited. One of the examples of the kind of writer students are missing out on was Toni Morrison. Leave to one side the fact that Morrison *is* regularly studied at upper secondary level and has been for more than twenty years in England: the speaker's broad point about curriculum diversity was – and at the time of writing remains – absolutely right. The interesting thing here is the choice of Morrison as example in a presentation that pressed the personal over the contextual (very much in the spirit of Eaglestone). Morrison's *Beloved* is historical fiction not only in the familiar sense – the novel stages the history and legacy of slavery in the United States – but also in the metahistorical and metafictional senses that it excavates and interrogates the writing of history itself, the ways in which national memory is selectively narrativized, the ways in which we are haunted by our collective and individual pasts. In Morrison, poetics is always a politics and vice versa; her writing always challenges what Rancière calls the "distribution of the sensible," the political-historical forces that determine which cultural forms are permissible and perceivable.[16]

What does it mean to respond "personally" to *Beloved*? If one's response isn't shaped by the lived histories Morrison attempts to recover and the national history she attempts to revise, then one's personal response counts for nothing.

One cannot, at last, prise text and context apart, though we might centre one or the other at various times. The difference that some commentators draw between historicist and personal responses is the difference between responses that articulate the text with general or with personal histories: the issue is one of scale (or level) and perspective – not of historicism versus ahistoricism, contextualism versus subjectivism – and of *how* we articulate the general with the personal.[17] This *how* is a matter, mostly, of writing more or less well; and that is the subject of the book's final part.

There are plenty of situations in which *contextual* – that word is as useful as it is catch-all and vague – understanding cannot be separated from the range of likely "personal" responses, because framing the text in particular ways makes certain interpretative options more or less likely. Understanding the changing use of a particular word can open new possibilities in meaning; explicating and articulating these requires a bit of etymological work (as in the Crystal example). One cannot begin to address Morrison's *Beloved* without appreciating the national- and world-historical and the poetic-political questions to which she addresses her novel. And, as with the example of Milton's Satan, to question, frame, and reframe the construction of goodguys and badguys is to reframe one's entire moral reading of a text, and, perhaps, to adjust one's understanding of the social construction of morality. Explicating *that* demands some sense of how moral norms may or may not have changed over time, of how and why they have the grip on us that they do. It's only an appreciation of moral contingency that allows William Blake, to give a famous example, to ironize evil as nonconformism – creative desire unrestrained – to equate nonconformism with true poetry, and to celebrate Milton for being "a true Poet and of the Devil's party without knowing it."[18]

Location of the Aesthetic

While the writers mentioned above all wish to recuperate some version of literary criticism, Eaglestone's position differs from Phelan's and North's in at least one important respect. Phelan's and, especially, North's work focusses on intra-disciplinary practice – on what practitioners do, how they do it, and what's valuable (or not), appropriate (or not) in those practices. By contrast, Eaglestone's defence of disciplinary identity is made in opposition to government interventions in education policy which, he rightly argues, have impoverished schooled English.[19] I don't reject the arguments nor dismiss the concerns of close-reading advocates: we agree on far more than we disagree, and there can be no literary criticism without some kind of close textual attention. It's easy, however, to *appear* to overstate the case for text-centred criticism: the exploratory and ludic elements of textual interpretation characteristic of literature study should be defended from *reductive* contextualist approaches that treat literary texts as merely decorative containers for some other "content" or "meaning." But defending close reading methods and the importance of aesthetic education doesn't mean committing oneself to a- or de-contextualist methods. Indeed, a radically decontextualized literary criticism is unthinkable: as soon as we get down to the *why* of our responses to this or that text – as soon as we start explicating and articulating – we're setting about the business of contextualizing. To rationalize is always, in some way and on some level, to contextualize.

Eaglestone, it must be said, chooses his words carefully, and while he is concerned with the political narrowing of schooled English's scope, he is not methodologically prescriptive. He's worried about literature study being reduced to an "ersatz" or "simplified version of" history, and he plays this notion of an ersatz history off against a vision of what literature study could or should be. So, to repeat, the argument isn't against contextualizing, per se, but against *reductive* contextualism. The danger, however, in comparing a best-case version of one discipline to a worst-case version of another is that an appeal against an impoverished model of a *subject-area* (in this case History) can be misread as an argument against certain approaches or *methods* (in this case, historicism). If *this* happens, then what is in essence a political argument – which wishes to open educational space for literature to be experienced with a sense of wonder – is likely to be muted by and mistaken for an apparently methodological argument.[20] And if *that* happens, the tragedy is that the argument against current education policy and, more broadly, the political construction and policing of knowledge may be misread as its opposite: professional infighting over this or that method, this or that way of thinking.

Apart from Eagelstone's methodological generosity, there is a tradition of assuming a close tie between aesthetic appreciation and close reading, and this assumption invites confusion over the location and structure of the aesthetic.[21] *Aesthetic* is a vague term, as Richards points out.[22] Just as it doesn't single out any particular textual property (or "content"), neither does it denote a special category of experience,[23] for once we've picked out *an Experience* from the general experiential flow, the idea of aesthetic (as opposed to anaesthetic) experience is meaningless: an experience has the significance it does because we have been *affected* by it (and what marks it out as coherent is often its narratability: retrospectively, an experience has the quality of a story and of an event).[24]

We may speak of someone "having an aesthetic." When we do so casually, we mean something like, "they have a consistent, predictable, yet distinctive style." More formally, saying that someone has an aesthetic is a way of saying they have and practice a philosophy of style, beauty, or, perhaps, art – and it's solely in reference to philosophy of art that R.G. Collingwood believes "aesthetic" should be used. Aesthetics, he claims in *The Principles of Art*, cannot be the philosophy of beauty, because beauty has nothing essential to do with art proper. Philosophically, he says (drawing on Plato), the beautiful is a means of yoking desire, morality, and knowledge: in Plato, what is good is true, and what is true is good, and it is these that we should desire and pursue. To regard something as beautiful, then, is simply to acknowledge its formal or technical excellence: just as a painting may be beautiful, so too may a mathematical proof; but to judge either as beautiful is to say nothing about whether or not they're art.[25] Equally, amusement or entertainment art and propaganda art may be technically sound and pleasing, and therefore beautiful, but they aren't, for Collingwood, art proper.[26]

Because it's concerned in large measure with negative critique – with clearing aesthetic philosophy's cluttered decks – *The Principles of Art* is a relatively long book. Its positive thesis, however, is relatively simple, a variety of the Mirror of Nature species of argument:

> Writers are to-day beginning to realize that important literature cannot be written without an important subject-matter. In that realization lies the hope of a thriving literature yet to be written; for the subject-matter is the point at which the audience's collaboration can fertilize the writer's work.
>
> [...]
>
> [There is a] characteristic which art must have, if it is to forgo both entertainment and magical value, and draw a subject-matter from its audience themselves. *It must be prophetic.* The artist must prophesy not in the sense that he foretells things to come, but in the sense that he tells his audience, *at risk of their displeasure,* the secrets of their own hearts. [...] As spokesman of his community, the secrets he must utter are theirs. The reason why they need him is that no community altogether knows its own heart; and by failing in this knowledge a community deceives itself on the one subject concerning which ignorance means death. For the evils which come from that ignorance the poet as prophet suggests no remedy, because he has already given one. The remedy is the poem itself. Art is the community's medicine for the worst disease of the mind, the corruption of consciousness.[27]

Art, for Collingwood, provides a diagnostic voice we didn't know we needed; it resonates with the tradition from which it has grown and with the history of the now.[28] Just *why* this view necessitates a separation of the aesthetic from the beautiful, though, is unclear. Perhaps it's because pleasure and approval, to which Collingwood attaches beauty, suggest ease, familiarity, comfort; while art proper is initially uncomfortable (and only therapeutic *because* of this).

Dave Hickey, writing in the 1990s about contemporary visual art, was convinced that if "beauty is the agency that causes visual pleasure in the beholder," then "any theory of images that is not grounded in the pleasure of the beholder begs the question of art's efficacy and dooms itself to inconsequence."[29] Unlike Collingwood, then, beauty *is*, for Hickey, essential to any aesthetic philosophy; yet neither "beauty" and "pleasure" nor the art that asks us to confront them entails ease, familiarity, comfort. "[T]he beautiful," writes Hickey, citing Baudelaire, "is always strange."[30] Aesthetic theory worthy, in Hickey's view, of the name will be willing and able to reckon with art written in what he calls "the vernacular of beauty," a vernacular that "engage[s] individuals [...] in arguments about what is good and what is beautiful."[31] Comfort and ease, Hickey writes, accompany beauty only when the political questions to which the artwork gives form are no longer going concerns. On this matter, Collingwood and Hickey are surprisingly close. Both Collingwood and Hickey have something to say about the aesthetic illiteracy of those who look only to yesterday's canonical art; they both identify a tendency to mistake historical importance for art's strange, disruptive beauty. Collingwood:

> The philosopher-aesthetician who sticks to classical artists is pretty sure to locate the essence of art not in what makes them artists but in what makes them classical, that is, acceptable to the academic mind.

Here's Hickey:

> It is, perhaps, "good" for us to look at [Caravaggio's] *The Madonna of the Rosary* without blanching at its Counter-Reformation politics, because those politics are dead.[32]

In question for both Collingwood and Hickey is our ability, perhaps our willingness, to dwell in discomfort. Both writers turn to contemporary art: Collingwood to Eliot and *The Waste Land*, Hickey to the pornographic photography of Robert Mapplethorpe, whom, Hickey laments, is only defended – where he is at all – on the sacrosanct grounds of "freedom of expression," not for the political poignancy of his art, his ability to speak "the vernacular of beauty, in its democratic appeal."[33] Collingwood and Hickey share a belief in the local rootedness and disruptive potential of art, and, in this concern, they are hardly alone nor original: identity-centred art and artists have long known this. From Collingwood, we get the idea that art might furnish us with ways of articulating the world anew; from Hickey, the idea that only by attending to particular instances of terrible, even terrifying, beauty can we understand the work of the work of art. For both, close attention to art is morally and politically important. So too is the ability to give verbal form to one's encounters with them; but, to return to an earlier claim, this can't be done effectively without articulating the personal with the contextual: if art rattles us, it must be because it speaks somehow to present concerns.

Collingwood's philosophy is not without its problems: in particular, his claim that art proper offers a social palliative without political commitment is hard to defend.[34] Like Hickey, however, he's sceptical of academia's ability to account for and confront head-on the cultural work that art does; and his positive thesis regarding art is attractive because it assumes that art proper emerges between the art-object and the spectator, and that it does so because it gives form to things faintly sensed but, until now, unexpressed.[35] Hickey's general claim, with Mapplethorpe a then-recent case in point, is that it's in the interests of certain culture brokers – not the markets, but, rather, academic, and educational institutions – that the masses *not* know how to experience nor articulate the experiencing of art. As this chapter – and with it this book's narrower subject-specific focus – starts drawing to a close, let's focus on aesthetic experience as emerging, in the case of literature, between readers and texts.

Aesthetic experience happens in the interaction *between* two or often more agents.[36] Aesthetic experience is nonrational attachment, but *non*rational doesn't connote faulty reasoning, poor or mistaken judgement, unreasonableness. The nonrational is simply that which has or needs no prior reason or cause other than the affective experience itself. The necessarily retrospective articulation or explication of aesthetic experience takes place dialogically; absent other persons to speak to, we find ourselves (in the essays we choose or are required to write) writing out and writing through our experiences; to the extent that we do think of ourselves as interacting with artworks, we treat them *as if* agential.[37]

Literature has the power to move us in the same way that alcohol has the power to intoxicate us: only if imbibed. Like booze, literature's power to affect us is parasitic: it relies on a suitable – that is, a susceptible, responsive – host. Aesthetic experience occurs on the cusp of the autonomic (the involuntary response) and the reflective. We can, to some extent, train our aesthetic sensibilities, just as we can, to some extent, train ourselves to tolerate alcohol or develop a taste for certain foods and-or flavours; we won't, however, always have the feeling of being able to control or manipulate our aesthetic experiences. I won't push the comparison too far: my suggestion isn't that there's an exact symmetry between biochemical functions and aesthetic experiences; rather, it's that we shouldn't mistake a text's moving us emotionally with its somehow "containing" or "having" that emotion (and certainly not with its "containing a 'deeper' meaning"): a story can make us sad, it can tell a story *of* sadness; it doesn't (despite our common ways of talking) make sense to say it itself *is* sad. Sad stories are (potentially) saddening, in the same way that bourbon is (potentially) intoxicating.[38]

If the aesthetic is not a set of qualities "in" the text, but is rather something that happens in the encounter between reader and text, then to be able to say how and why a literary text interests us is, in part, to choose a way of reading and attempt a special type of description. Just as we've no business saying that some persons' aesthetic lives count for more than others, we've no business saying which ways of reading are more or less valid than others, which are more or less plugged into the aesthetic than others. It's absolutely right that educators and critics should (as do Eaglestone and Bleiman) argue for greater space for the personal and the exploratory in schooled literary criticism. But commitment to what is, in essence, a form of structured play shouldn't shade into methodological prescriptivism. As soon as we shift gear from raw feeling to its attempted explication, as soon as we start trying to say *why* we think-or-feel as we do, we are bringing context to bear on text, text on context. It may be that the linguistic character of the text is of interest; that the text speaks to our lived experiences (we feel seen by a text; we relate to it); that it hooks us into history in new and exciting ways; that it *does* stage a philosophical drama in a way that matters to us ... These and other angles of approach are all within the compass of the aesthetic. One of the most important messages from powerful knowledge, as we've already heard, is that the expert community should be the final arbiter of disciplinary and epistemic issues. On that view, it's pointless trying to decide between, say, literary historicism and criticism, at least for as long as there are specialists participating in and producing works of both.

Close reading began as an attempt to help us better articulate the ways we're affected by literature. Richards's starting point: "Criticism [...] is the endeavour to discriminate between experiences and to evaluate them."[39] Arguments over the disciplinary identity of literature study are arguments over preferred methods (how you read) and method*ologies* (the rationalization of your preferred method: *why* you'd read this way and not another). Rather than trying to decide on *the* model for doing literature, we'd do better foregrounding differences of approach, and teaching these as equally valid, available ways of reading closely, critically, even creatively.

Reading Is a Writer's Game

"A book is a machine to think with," begins *Principles of Literary Criticism*, "but it need not, therefore, usurp the function either of the bellows or the locomotive. This book might better be compared to a loom on which it is supposed to re-weave some ravelled parts of our civilization."[40] Richards's images do interesting work here: *machine* is an abstract idea; the specific machine makes all the difference: different mechanism, different result. Methods, then, are production machines. When it comes to literature study, differences of approach will force and forge differences of style, just as stylistic choice, the genres and traditions upon which we draw, will affect and determine what we write: what we say and how we say it are mutually determining. Close reading, then, is not only a method, it's a genre: a way of reading that manifests itself as a largely conventionalized way of writing.[41]

Differences of method produce stylistic differences (those more or less conventional differences between the literary theorist, historian, journalist, and so on). That much is true, but to leave things there could suggest that writing is secondary to method, style somehow secondary to (some "basic" or "pre-stylistic" act of?) writing – something somehow added to language. That can't be right – certainly not when it comes to literature study, creative writing, or arts criticism and scholarship in general. There's no such thing as style-free writing, though (as I'll discuss in greater detail in the final chapter) there is writing that adheres so strictly to certain conventions that it seems almost to dissolve or, perhaps, to aspire to a sort of transparency; writing which wishes, as Richard Rorty puts it, that it weren't writing.[42]

Certainly, there are disciplines in which the norm is to "write up" research in prose that doesn't call attention to itself. Research reports are still telling stories, of course; but the aim may be for us not to notice the language, but rather whatever the language points to. Where this is the case, the work, the subject-matter, appears to lay "behind" the writing. We imagine a linear process from research design, to research itself, to the write-up (though this image is likely a product of the formal ("literary") conventions of research reports, and not necessarily a good reflection of the realities of empirical research). In literature study and creative writing alike, however, writing is itself a method; or, if you like, it occupies the same functional space as does method in other disciplines. Research reports are substitutes for other modes of inquiry, for other work carried out; they stand for the fieldwork: they are writing which, perhaps, sometimes, would like not to be writing, while literary criticism and creative writing are always turning inwards – not in the sense that they must always be overtly self-reflexive, but in the sense that they are substitutes for nothing else, they *are* the work. The work, or the subject-matter, is "in" the writing, not "reflected" by it, not "behind" it.

The idea that close reading is not only a method but also a genre is easily missed or forgotten; and this likely has a lot to do with the close reading assignment's longstanding centrality to schooled English. What Heather Murray writes of university-level English could also be said of schooled English from secondary level on:

> So pervasive and persistent is the "close reading" as an assignment at the university level that it is tempting to consider it as a synecdoche for the English essay. Certainly, there are many types of literature assignments [...] in even the most conservative or restricted programs. But there is something integral about this one. The close reading is basic to the pedagogic practice we tend to value most highly, the detailed discussion that takes place in the seminar session. It occurs as an assignment in a number

of guises and a variety of contexts, most particularly in the essay and in the examination sight passage.[43]

The writerliness of literary criticism in all its traditional, generic, methodological varieties is easily lost when it becomes a vehicle for conveying understanding, a means of assessing comprehension and appreciation.[44] Critical reading is a writer's game, in the dual sense that writers and their works are the stuff of English Literature, the *matter* of the subject-matter, *and* that literary criticism has its own generic writerly conventions (just as all traditions, forms, and genres of writing must). The methods we adopt for critical reading will be, in part, a product of our trying to say certain things in certain ways, just as what we're able to say about a text will be shaped by our methods. No way of reading that isn't also a way of writing – and vice versa.[45]

If ways of reading critically are necessarily also ways of (usually expository) writing, then the recalibration that's needed in schooled English is not only the centring of the personal and the text (over and above impersonal context), but the centring of writing practices. In the English classroom, the essay should be framed not as the byproduct of having to assess students' comprehension of texts, but as a genre and tradition of creative critical writing. What Elizabeth Hardwick wrote of book reviewing we might extend to criticism more generally: "Book reviewing is a form of writing. [...] It *does* matter what an unusual mind, capable of presenting fresh ideas in a vivid and original and interesting manner, thinks of books as they appear."[46] To produce criticism of this sort, we'd do well to put creative writing practices (not necessarily a highly schooled subject-area), and not the critical practices associated with English Literature, at the beginning of schooled literature study. If, as Eaglestone suggests, we want students of literature to understand the mechanics of character, narrative voice, plot, setting, and so on, why wouldn't we want students to write them, rather than write *about* them?[47] To repeat a point made several times in this book, it's an oddity of schooled English Literature that doing the thing you're studying is a marginal and not a central practice.

A (Very) Rough Sketch of a Revised English Studies

It isn't the aim of this book to give pedagogical advice, nor to offer a detailed alternative curriculum.[48] However, given all that I've written up until this point, I'll conclude with a very brief and rough outline of a model for a recalibrated English Studies. What follows is only a sketch, not a curriculum plan; and nor is it a total reinvention of the subjects and disciplines we call English. It is, if anything, an attempt to shift where the emphasis falls.

English Studies, at secondary- or high-school level, would begin by centring writing practices and writer's craft: students' first project in secondary English Studies would be their own literary work. But this couldn't be done without reading and discussing texts, and those discussions would generate a sort of analytical archive (annotations, critical and-or journalistic fragments, and so on). That archive would range from personal responses to exemplar or source texts, to stylistic analyses, to accounts of what the students were aiming for in their own work and how they hoped to achieve that.

In a relatively non-technical way, lower-secondary English Studies would cover textual analysis and criticism, and language study, mostly through creative writing projects. By the end of upper-secondary, the different disciplinary practices of Creative Writing, Literary Criticisms, and Language Study would be parcelled out a little more. Creative Writing would remain. Literary Criticisms – formerly English Literature – would explicitly teach different critical approaches to literary analysis. Language Study – formerly English Language – would be primarily sociolinguistics and stylistics, not because these are the only areas of language study, but because sociolinguistics foregrounds those political and cultural dimensions of language that shape all of us; it invites us to grapple with the intersection of language with race, class, region, gender, sexuality, age, and so on. Stylistics would keep a close contact between literature and language studies.

This is, as I say, only a very rough and brief sketch, designed to indicate a desirable reorientation or recalibration of English Studies. Turning this sketch into a curriculum plan would be a significant undertaking – one, perhaps, for the future. From even so brief a sketch as this, though, it's clear that there would be implications for university-level English courses: there would need to be some compulsory Creative Writing elements to undergraduate English degrees, given that most secondary-level English teachers are English Literature (rather than Creative Writing or Linguistics) graduates. No doubt some will baulk at that idea. For what I hope are, by now, obvious reasons, I see no problem with (though nor do I hold out much hope for) it. As I claimed at the very beginning of this book, English has never existed outside of a certain kind of educational logic. What I'm proposing, then, is less a change to English *per se* – there will always be literary critics, historians, journalists; novelists, poets, playwrights; linguisticians – and more a shift in educational culture, a shift in widespread attitudes about how English should be studied, and especially about what is worthwhile or most valuable in English and literature studies.

Notes

1 As in Joseph North, *Literary Criticism: A Concise Political History* (Cambridge, MA: Harvard University Press, 2017).
2 Examples include Barbara Bleiman, *What Matters in English Teaching: Collected Blogs and Other Writing* (London: English and Media Centre, 2020); Robert Eaglestone, "Powerful Knowledge," "Cultural Literacy," and the Study of Literature in Schools, *IMPACT* 26 (PESGB/Wiley Online Library: <https://onlinelibrary.wiley.com/doi/epdf/10.1111/2048-416X.2020.12006.x> (accessed 01 October 2021)),

Literature: Why It Matters (Cambridge: Polity, 2019), "What Do We Teach When We Teach Literature," *The Use of English* 67(3) (2016), pp.4–12; John Guillory, "Close Reading: Prologue and Epilogue," *ADE Bulletin* 149 (2010), pp.8–14; North, *Literary Criticism*; J.W. Phelan, *Literature and Understanding: The Value of a Close Reading of Literary Texts* (Oxon: Routledge, 2021). What they have in common is a commitment to the importance of paying close attention to the text: each is committed to reading closely, but this doesn't mean they advocate or share the same conception of close reading.

3 Guillory, "Close Reading: Prologue and Epilogue" (8).
4 "Inaugural moment" is Guillory's phrase (*ibid.*). See also Eaglestone, "What Do We Teach...?"; Heather Murray, "Close Reading, Closed Writing," *College English* 53(2) (1991), pp.195–208; North, *Literary Criticism*. Jesse Cordes Selbin, in "'Read with Attention': John Cassell, John Ruskin, and the History of Close Reading," *Victorian Studies* 58(3) (2016), pp.493–521, pushes close reading's origins further back than do most scholars, to the mid nineteenth century and the works of John Cassell and John Ruskin.
5 Guillory, "Close Reading" (13).
6 Surface/depth approaches to interpretation, while convenient, are more often than not misleading, and relatively poor ways of modelling how literary language, so-called, works. Donald Davidson explores this brilliantly in his essay "What Metaphors Mean," *Critical Inquiry* 5(1) (1978), pp.31–47. His thesis is that metaphor denotes a special category of use, or affect, not of meaning. What we commonly call the "meaning" (or "real meaning") of a metaphor is, in fact, an explication of our encounter with metaphorical language and its affect. This, he suggests, might be written off as a pettifogging difference, but it isn't: metaphors do not contain special, yet determinable, meanings; they trigger affective responses.
7 Phelan, *Literature and Understanding*. At times, Phelan seems to suggest that literary language is simply devices or features (metaphors, similes, and so on). While obviously metaphor-rich texts are in many ways easier, more convenient, in the classroom (because they seem to cry out for a little "decoding"), this can't serve as a definition of what makes literature literary, not least because Phelan is interested in something like a "high-art" concept of literature, and the mere presence of "literary" features is surely no marker of high art. Douglas Cowie offers a cleverly circular definition of literary language as original combinations of words that couldn't be otherwise, that no one else could have written (Nicole Acquah, "Epiphanies Are the Result of Process": Interview with Author Douglas Cowie," *The Artist's Toolkit* [podcast] (3 August 2021), accessed via <https://douglascowie.com/?p=1958> (05 October 2021)).
8 North, *Literary Criticism* (6, x).
9 Eaglestone, *"Powerful Knowledge," "Cultural Literacy," and the Study of Literature in Schools* (27). and NC.
10 Eaglestone, *"Powerful Knowledge"* (34).
11 Eaglestone and Bleiman are closely aligned here (see n.2).
12 Eaglestone, *"Powerful Knowledge"* (26–27).
13 Equally, there *is* scope in mathematics and science classes for personal reactions, depending on the types of question being asked. Yes, one can misunderstand or misapply an equation; but there are no grounds for telling science and mathematics writers that their aesthetic attachments to their favourite equations are wrong. In literature study, a point of debate might be the type of text we're dealing with: do we count the text as a poem, a short story, an essay...? Some composite of each of these? Often, text-type is *not* the centre of discussion; we take that for granted and get on discussing the text's significance. Similarly, there may be cases in the sciences where the raw data are not a point of contention, but their significance is.

14 David Crystal, *The Cambridge Encyclopedia of the English Language* (London: BCA/Cambridge University Press, 1995), p.76.
15 Eaglestone, *"Powerful Knowledge"* (17).
16 Jacques Rancière, *The Politics of Aesthetics*, Gabriel Rockhill (ed. and trans.); London: Bloomsbury, 2004), pp.1–14. Two refrains from *Beloved* (London: Vintage, 1987/1997) exemplify what Rancière has in mind, and the ways in which Morrison addresses the distribution of the sensible: "Unspeakable thoughts unspoken," "This is not a story to pass on." In the first, Morrison raises ethical questions of a world-historical magnitude: how to give linguistic form to slavery, and in particular the middle passage, the sea voyage from west Africa to Europe and the United States which killed many thousands of enslaved Africans, and of which there are no known first-hand accounts.* The second refrain occurs in the book's closing lines and occurs in two forms, the past and present: "This was not a story to pass on," and "This is not a story to pass on." Morrison juxtaposes the wilful burying of a politically inconvenient past with the need to remember, in the dual sense of not forgetting and reconstituting, literally re-membering. This brief reading of Morrison, clumsy, imperfect as it is, cannot take shape without recourse to context. It is personal, inasmuch as it comes "from" me and I stand by it, but it isn't original (it is not "mine," nor am I the first or only person to think of it).
*For some time, Olaudah Equiano's was thought to be the only extant first-hand narrative of the middle passage, but Vincent Carretta's biography of Equiano casts doubt on that. Equiano, *The Interesting Narrative and Other Writings*, Vincent Carretta (ed.) (London: Penguin, 1995); Carretta, *Equiano the African: Biography of a Self-Made Man* (Athens, GA: University of Georgia Press, 2005).
17 On the place of personal experience in the classroom, see Diana Fuss, *Essentially Speaking: Feminism, Nature and Difference* (London: Routledge, 1990), ch.7.
18 William Blake, *The Marriage of Heaven and Hell* [1870] in *Blake's Poetry and Designs*, 2nd Ed. (Mary Lynn Johnson and John E. Grant, eds.; London: Norton, 2008), p.71.
19 Bleiman has a similar political focus to Eaglestone.
20 Not that the political and the methodological are entirely separate: political aims will lead us to certain methods, just as methods serve political projects. Methods produce, they delimit what can be sensed or perceived. This much is made obvious by the idea of methodology, distinct from method. Methodology is the *why* of method, its epistemic framing or justification. Just as the aesthetic cannot be hived off from the ethical and the political, nor can the methodological be separated from the aesthetic, the political, the ethical. Rancière theorizes this, at a general level, as the distribution of the sensible (see n.16 above). The intersection of method, politics, ethics, and poetics is often raised by work that questions how research is done to – as opposed to alongside, in relation to, or partnership with – marginalized, oppressed, or endangered groups. See, for example, Linda Tuhiwai Smith, *Decolonizing Methodologies: Research and Indigenous Peoples* (London: Zed Books, 2012).
21 This confusion, claims I.A. Richards, is at least as old as Kant's attempt at an aesthetic philosophy, and "has made the term [aesthetic] nearly useless." *Principles of Literary Criticism* (1924; London: Routledge, 1989), p.10.
22 Richards, *Principles* (ch.2).
23 Aesthetic philosophy from the eighteenth century on is, in various ways, primarily concerned with the complexities and varieties of aesthetic experience (for a brief overview, see Peter Gilgen's entry, "Aesthetics," in *The Encyclopedia of Literary and Cultural Theory*, Michael Ryan (ed.) (Oxford: Wiley, 2011)). On aesthetic properties, see Frank Sibley's "Aesthetic Concepts," *The Philosophical Review* 68(4) (1959), pp.421–450. The question for Sibley is what our aesthetic discourse is *doing*; he's interested in asking what the language of the critic does

when it's used to persuade others of the aesthetic qualities of this or that work. So even when we appear to be pointing linguistically to properties "in" the artwork, what we're really doing is giving voice to our own aesthetic experiences, beliefs, and values.

24 See the next chapter and my engagement therein with Aldridge. Among the many philosophers interested in narrative and narratability are Kwame Anthony Appiah, *The Ethics of Identity* (Princeton, NJ: Princeton University Press, 2005), *The Lies that Bind: Rethinking Identity* (London: Profile, 2018); Eddie S. Glaude, Jr., "Pragmatism and Black Identity: An Alternative Approach," *Neplanta: Views from South* 2(2) (2001), pp.295-316; Alasdair MacIntyre, After Virtue: A Study in Moral Theory, 2nd Ed. (London: Duckworth, 1985); Richard Rorty, *Contingency, Irony, and Solidarity* (Cambridge: Cambridge University Press, 1989), *Achieving Our Country: Leftist Thought in Twentieth-Century America* (Cambridge, MA: Harvard University Press, 1998); Charles Taylor, *The Ethics of Authenticity* (Cambridge, MA: Harvard University Press, 1991).

25 R.G. Collingwood, *The Principles of Art* (1938; Oxford: Oxford University Press, 1958), pp.36–41.

26 Collingwood, *Principles* (chs 4–5).

27 Collingwood, *Principles* (332, 335–336, emphases added). "Magical" art is, for Collingwood, not art proper; it is closer to propaganda and-or, perhaps, kitsch, as it aims at provoking predetermined responses or emotions in its audiences. Not everyone would draw this distinction between art and propaganda. There is, for example, the engaged/autonomous art debate, associated especially with Sartre and Adorno (see their contributions to *Aesthetics and Politics* (London: Version, 2007)). Famously, in his 1926 article for *The Crisis*, "Criteria of Negro Art," W.E.B. DuBois wrote: "Thus all Art is propaganda and ever must be, despite the wailing of the purists. I stand in utter shamelessness and say that whatever art I have for writing has been used always for propaganda for gaining the right of black folk to love and enjoy. I do not care a damn for any art that is not used for propaganda. But I do care when propaganda is confined to one side while the other is stripped and silent" (David Levering Lewis (ed.), *The Portable Harlem Renaissance Reader* (London: Penguin, 1995), pp.100–105, (103).

28 This is, perhaps, a pseudo-Romantic view of art and the artist, tinged with localism and even a little early twentieth-century managerialism: where Shelley's poet is the unacknowledged legislator of the world, Collingwood's is diagnostician, spokesperson, and teacher only of the nation ("I write chiefly for English readers and about conditions in England," p. 332). Modest by comparison to Shelley, perhaps, but still no meagre claim.

In his attempt to navigate between individuality and tradition, one can sense the influence not only of Eliot the poet, but also Eliot the critic on Collingwood. T.S. Eliot, "Tradition and the Individual Talent" [1919] in *20th Century Literary Criticism*, David Lodge (ed.) (London: Longman, 1972), pp.71–77.

29 Dave Hickey, *The Invisible Dragon: Essays on Beauty* (1993; Chicago: University of Chicago Press), p.1.

30 Hickey, *Invisible Dragon* (9).

31 Hickey, *Invisible Dragon* (16).

32 Collingwood, *Principles* (4); Hickey, *Invisible Dragon* (14).

33 Hickey, *Invisible Dragon* (16).

34 The standoff between so-called "engaged" and "autonomous" art is often exemplified, as noted above (n.27), by the standoff between Sartre (on the side of engagement) and Adorno (on that of autonomy). But Adorno's commitment to autonomous art was not, of course, apolitical; it was part of a left-wing

emancipatory project. He was concerned that politically didactic art, even when it espoused the right politics, deployed the same tactics and cultural logic that made fascism possible.

35 Collingwood does place limitations on the role of spectator experience: he assumes that authentic aesthetic experience consists in some sort of replication in the spectator of the artist's emotional experience, to which the artist gives form in the artwork. Though there can be no guarantee of identical experience, those closer the experiences of artist and spectator, the better the work is understood. One roughly gauges understanding of art through conversation and the convergence of viewpoints. Not only does Collingwood's theory raise predictable and largely unimportant questions about artist intentionality, it works from other strange presumptions: that critical consensus is a likely benchmark of "correct" or "reasonable" understanding; and that the particular work of the artwork is the expression of a single, particular emotion. The essence of the artwork proper, Collingwood claims, is the imaginative-emotional work, and that is there from the very beginning. So it's as if, quite apart from the medium and final form of any art-object, the artwork proper comes to the artist fully formed and perhaps even unbidden (*Principles, passim*).

36 The brief account I offer of aesthetics and aesthetic experience owes much to Maxine Greene, *Variations on a Blue Guitar: The Lincoln Center Institute Lectures on Aesthetic Education* (New York: Teachers College Press, 2001); Hans Ulrich Gumbrecht, *Production of Presence: What Meaning Cannot Convey* (Stanford: Stanford University Press, 2004), *In Praise of Athletic Beauty* (Cambridge, MA: Belknap/Harvard University Press, 2006); and Phil Ford's "Style as Analysis" (ch.2 in Ciro Scotto, Kenneth Smith, and John Brackett (eds), *The Routledge Companion to Popular Music Analysis: Expanding Approaches* (e-book; New York: Routledge)), as well as the journalistic work of William Youngren and Whitney Balliett with which Ford is in dialogue. Gumbrecht's deformed Kantianism is particularly interesting: for Gumbrecht, aesthetic disinterestedness is not dispassionateness, but simply non-instrumentalism. Aesthetic attachment has no prior reason, is not a means to some other end.

37 Think of some of the familiar figures of speech we use for both our artistic and social contacts: we interact-engage-dialogue with, interrogate-read-question-analyze artworks and persons alike.

38 Claire Colebrook makes this point with respect to Deleuze's philosophy of art, the work of which is to present us with (new) affects. She gives Pinter as an example of an artist able to dramatize and present "boredom" as affect, without inducing boredom in the audience. Colebrook, *Gilles Deleuze* (London: Routledge, 2002), pp.21–25.

39 Richards, *Principles* (vii).

40 Richards, *Principles* (vii).

41 Rita Felski makes a similar claim of critique, which she regards as the dominant genre of literary criticism in *The Limits of Critique* (Chicago: University of Chicago Press, 2015), p.3 and *passim*.

42 See the final chapter of this book; Richard Rorty, "Philosophy as a Kind of Writing: An Essay on Derrida," *New Literary History*, 10(1) (1978), pp.141–160.

43 Murray, "Close Reading, Closed Writing" (195).

44 I explore this in more detail in "The Perfectionist Call of Intelligibility: Secondary English, Creative Writing, and Moral Education," *Philosophical Inquiry in Education* 23(1) (2016), <https://journals.sfu.ca/pie/index.php/pie/article/view/934> (accessed 10 October 2021).

45 Not a new idea, this; it is Barthes's starting point in *S/Z: An Essay* (trans. Richard Miller; New York: Hill and Wang, 1974).

46 Elizabeth Hardwick, "The Decline of Book Reviews" in *The Collected Essays of Elizabeth Hardwick* (e-book; New York: New York Review of Books, 2017). Tymon Adamczewski's considers the literariness of criticism in European theory since the 1960s in "A New Territory? Literary Criticism as a Literary Genre," in Jacek Fabiszak, Ewa Urbaniak-Rybicka, and Bartosz Wolski (eds), *Crossroads in Literature and Culture* (London: Springer, 2013), pp.11–23.

47 On the critical-creative nexus, see Jesper Guldal and Alistair Rolls, "Detective Fiction and the Critical-Creative Nexus," *TEXT* 20 (Special Issue 37) (2016), available online <https://textjournal.scholasticahq.com/article/27044>, DOI: <https://doi.org/10.52086/001c.27044> (accessed 05 December 2021); on literature as enacted criticism, see Andrew Green, "Death in a Literary Context: Detective Novels of the Golden Age as Enacted Criticism," *Clues* 39(2) (2021), pp.41–50.

48 In England, an alternative English curriculum was proposed by John Richmond and colleagues. Their report is available online and is published as a book: *Curriculum and Assessment in English 3 to 19: A Better Plan*, UKLA, <https://ukla.org/ukla_resources/curriculum-and-assessment-in-english-3-to-19-a-better-plan/> (accessed 10 October 2021); Richmond, Andrew Burn, Peter Dougill, Angela Goddard, Mike Raleigh, Peter Traves, *Curriculum and Assessment in English 11 to 19: A Better Plan* (Oxon: Routledge, 2017).

Part III

Writing Beyond the English Studies Classroom

Chapter 6

Thinking as a Kind of Writing, Writing as a Kind of Philosophy; or, On Lightbulb Moments

> *I've never been in a lesson with so many lightbulbs going on!*
> (Alex, Year 10 Student, during an English lesson)

Introduction

This final chapter considers, beyond English and Creative Writing and with a focus on university education, writing's significance to learning in general. I'm particularly concerned with the ways in which we teachers and our students navigate between the creative potential and conformist demands of academic writing, in particular academic writing in the form of the assigned essay. While the essay is perhaps the most flexible and capacious of forms,[1] its career as a mechanism of academic assessment, especially in university education, means it's often perceived as the opposite: if you've never written an essay that wasn't an academic assignment, chances are your sense of the essay is that it's a rather narrow, limited, and limiting form.

In many ways, the concerns and recommendations of this chapter are nothing new; a return, really, to the ethos of the Writing Across the Curriculum (WAC) programmes that emerged in the United States in the mid '70s and which prompted a flurry of research in the '80s and '90s.[2] WAC is tailored to the North American university, where students start by taking courses in a range of subject-areas before specializing around the midpoint of their degrees.[3] The guiding rationale of WAC, as Susan McLeod puts it, is "that writing and thinking are closely allied, that learning to write well involves learning particular discourse conventions, and that, therefore, writing belongs in the entire curriculum, not just in a course offered by the English department."[4] WAC programmes "help introduce students to the conventions of academic discourse in general and to the discourse conventions of particular disciplines – much as we would try to introduce newcomers into an ongoing conversation."[5] This is the side of WAC often summarized, straightforwardly enough, as "learning to write."

DOI: 10.4324/9781003042617-9

WAC isn't just about learning or being inducted into academic discourses or genres, however; WAC advocates presume the reciprocity of learning to write *and* writing to learn. On the second, William Zinsser offers this:

> Writing organizes and clarifies our thoughts. Writing is how we think our way into a subject and *make it our own*. Writing enables us to find out what we know – and what we don't know – about whatever we're trying to learn.[6]

But if learning to write is about being inducted into disciplinary norms and conventions, and writing to learn is expressive – "a 'knowledge-transforming' rather than a 'knowledge-telling' task," as MacLeod puts it[7] – then WAC's basic mission may be founded on a tension: to what extent might learning to write stifle the personal-transformational potential of writing to learn? How are we, in Zinsser's spirit, to make a subject our own if we are also being asked to submit to conventions that limit our linguistic choices?

One answer to such concerns is to treat the two sides of the WAC coin as distinct approaches to or modes of writing. Expressive writing is on the side of writing to learn. It's personal, for no one but ourselves, a way of giving shape to thoughts we may or may not share with others down the line. On the side of learning to write, the purpose of transactional writing *is* to share ideas with others; and here writers have an obligation to their readers, imagined or actual, to make their work comprehensible; to pitch it appropriately, according to intended audience and purpose; in short, to work out which language game they're playing and to play by the rules.

The distinction between expressive and transactional writing is neat and useful in its way, so long as we don't mistake distinction for isolation. As we'll see, Peter Elbow uses free, uninhibited, careless writing as a starting point for careful writing: the former, he believes, is the material from which the latter is sculpted.[8] Nor should we assume that, on the side of learning to write, all the rules of the language game are already in place and immutable – another of this chapter's aims is to raise questions about the perceived or apparent "standards" of academic writing. WAC, then, is not *necessarily* conservative and conformist, but it *could* be practiced as such.

The link presumed in WAC literature between thinking and writing might seem to conflict with my insistence in Chapter 3 that language is one, but not the only, form knowledge might take. When it comes to writing to learn and the connection between writing and thinking, however, WAC advocates have in mind not the existential dynamics of know-how and skill, but the process of externalizing thought in-and-as language. Language isn't the only form knowledge might take. But we can hardly escape language and the need to verbalize if what we want or are required to do is communicate what we think to others: and if communication with others *is* the aim, then we can't gainsay the importance of learning how to write for an intended or imagined reader. There are surely those times, as Zinsser says, when we're not quite sure what we think until we attempt to write: writing *can* be a way of trying ideas on for size, of seeing whether or not they fit together coherently and complementarily. Sometimes, it's only once an idea is written that we can ask whether it looks and sounds right; whether we're prepared to stand by it; whether it coheres with or contradicts our other more or less corrigible beliefs (or, perhaps, will force us to revise them[9]). What the WAC principle of writing to learn gets absolutely right is that, often, thought takes form, becomes available to us, *in the act* of writing. Writing to learn articulates – in the dual sense of expresses and connects – the existential and the rational, because it gives communicable shape to thought dimly *felt*.

By chapter's end, we'll have moved beyond the scope of the WAC ethos, but not because I disagree with it: WAC has refocussed and, on many points, reaffirmed my recent thinking, which has been shaped by England's secondary and university education systems, about the educational importance of writing. But I want to turn, late in the chapter, to the question of how writing practice might bear on educational issues of identity and expression, and how these in turn might require educators to loosen our grip on so-called academic standards and conventions (which, more often than not, are poorly if at all formulated). I want to consider what scope there may be for the classroom to be a space in which what counts as (good?) academic writing and research might come under some much-needed pressure. Asking why we ask our students to write, who and what they're writing for, might encourage us teachers to rethink our deeply ingrained – our second-nature – commitments to so-called academic standards.

On the way to those thoughts concerning students' writing and academic standards, a modest defence of discipline – distinct from disciplinarity – will be made: often, educational philosophy of a humanistic stripe idealizes education proper as that which cannot be planned or demanded. I'm not unsympathetic to such views. But while teachers can neither demand nor strive to bring about the transformational, epiphanic, authentic moment (call it what you will) in students, they can strive to create spaces in which such moments might stand a chance. This is where discipline as routine, repetition, familiar movement patterns might be the friends, not the enemies, of education. And it's as preparation for this defence of discipline that we begin with a conflict, one well-known to education studies.

Going Over Old Ground: Education versus Schooling

It's a commonplace in education studies to distinguish between, perhaps to oppose, education and schooling. Sometimes, this distinction is the entry point into education studies. In his *Education: A Very Short Introduction*, for instance, Gary Thomas reminds us "emphatically […] that education isn't just about what happens in schools and colleges," "for the two phenomena, schools and education, are not, sadly, necessarily linked at all."[10] In some of the most enduring quotes and quips that pitch education and school against one another, school always comes off worse. Thomas cites Mark Twain, Winston Churchill, and Albert Einstein:

> I have never let my schooling interfere with my education. (Twain)
>
> The only time my education was interrupted was while I was at school. (Churchill)
>
> Education is what remains when we have forgotten everything that has been learned at school. (Einstein)[11]

It's hard to gainsay such testimony; if Twain, Churchill, and Einstein say they had crummy experiences at school, then presumably they had crummy experiences at school.

Philosophical writing on education commonly makes use of similar distinctions. Sometimes, *education* points to something like an ideal of subject-disciplinarity, shorn of the institutional and sociopolitical trappings which *school* connotes. One finds this in R.S. Peters, for example, and also in Richard Rorty.[12] In the latter, disappointingly, the suggestion is that schools should function as agents of socialization so that universities can receive citizens ready to be inducted into subject-specific education. Well before Rorty and Peters, William Blake had something to say, in both prose and verse, about the tensions between creativity and schooling. "As none by traveling over known lands can find out the unknown," he writes in the philosophical pamphlet, *All Religions Are One*, "So from already acquired knowledge Man could not acquire more"; and, as his School Boy wonders in *Songs of Innocence and Of Experience*, "How can the bird that is born for joy,/Sit in a cage and sing."[13] (In similar spirit to Blake, a student of mine once presented me with a poem that contrasted the oppressiveness of school with the truer education he'd received from grime music.[14]) In Maxine Greene's work, *school* is a pejorated term – "We are interested in education here, not in schooling," she begins one of her talks – while *education* points to the semi-effable, phenomenal rupture that occurs when our minds (or "body-minds" as Greene has it) get good and blown.[15]

It's often hard to resolve educational ideals – education *for* liberty, equality, conformity, tradition (its recuperation, continuity, revision) – with the complex of power-relations in which formal education (massified, state-sanctioned, systematized) is enmeshed. Some time ago, Michael Fielding worried that if Third Way educational ideology in England were left unopposed, teachers and educators would have to "surrender our capacity to think and act differently." The charge that creativity and criticality are quashed by schooling is the kernel of Ivan Illich's idea of a deschooled society.[16]

It may be that the tension between schooling and education is produced by the mechanisms built into the mass education machine. Gert Biesta suggests that mass formal education is powered by three gears – qualification, subjectification (roughly, self-formation), and socialization – all of which turn simultaneously. This idea counters and complicates Rorty's uncharacteristically clumsy formulation of schools' and universities' educational roles – not only because all three gears are, for Biesta, always already turning; but also because socialization can operate in both disciplinary and non-disciplinary domains: schools *and* universities might (try to) socialize us into certain standards or norms of "polite" interaction (behaviour policies in schools; "codes" of expectations and talk of "professionalism" in universities), and-or into certain disciplinary norms or ways of knowing (how to be a scientist, historian, and so on). While all three gears are necessary to formal education, Biesta argues, prioritizing qualification above all else takes what should be properly educative out of education.[17]

What the writers mentioned above, and many others, are concerned with is the extent to which formal education impedes learning, the latter imagined as unpredictable, unplannable *event*; or what I'll be calling the lightbulb moment – because "sometimes only a cliché will do."[18]

For David Aldridge, engagement proper (as opposed to its use as an educational buzzword) is more or less synonymous, because experientially symmetrical, with learning. Aldridge exploits the difference between education, on the one hand, and schooling or even merely inhabiting the school site: engagement, he writes, is "characteristic of a higher *education* rather than, say, going to university, or attending lectures. It is quite possible [...] to spend hours in the library without becoming engaged."[19] Engagement proper "constitute[s] an existential orientation towards the world." Crucially, it has an "'eventful' character," which emerges from "an intentional relation between student, teacher and object of study, [which] transcends the will or action of any individual participant." "It is not," Aldridge continues, "in the power of teacher or student to 'bring about' engagement; rather it 'befalls' them. Engagement is also a contingent relation, and maybe a fragile or fleeting one. There is no method or technique for ensuring that participants, once having fallen into it, will remain in this relation." Engagement, as Aldridge formulates it, is the process by which subject-matter, as distinct from the *object* of study, emerges as such or presents itself. The object of study can be planned and prescribed, while subject-matter, to which both teachers and students "'belong' [...] in the moment of engagement," is "a shared concern [and] is necessarily emergent." Aldridge substitutes *subject-matter* for what usually goes by the name *knowledge*, not least because while the former *doesn't* prioritise professional or expert (teacher) knowledge, it *does* offer an ontological (rather than epistemological) account of learning as a "stylistics of existence."[20]

For Aldridge (whom I'm treating as broadly representative of educational philosophy in the existential-phenomenological tradition[21]), subject-matter emerges in the moment of engagement. One of his aims is to trace the phenomenological symmetry, if not the identity, of his central concept with other similarly "eventful" terms: *reading, education, understanding*.[22] These terms are synonymous, in that they refer to different modes or styles of the same basic experiential structure: the phenomenal *event* of learning. Drawing on Gadamer, Aldridge claims that, "ultimately, all educational moments are self-educational."[23] There is little, phenomenally speaking, distinguishing *engagement, reading, understanding, education* from the general structure of revelation or (Heideggerian) "unconcealedness" – roughly, the idea that one experiences the revelation of truth as the world emerging or being brought forth anew. That which is unconcealed is made manifest for us in the midst of some aesthetic experience; it does not, according to Heidegger (another reference-point for Aldridge), have the character or feeling of our having constructed it. The truth of unconcealedness is not sudden attainment, recognition, or discovery of an ultimate Truth, but rather an altered orientation in and towards the world (the revelation of the untruth in which one previously dwelled).[24] Like unconcealment, engagement is "eventful," it "befalls" us, we are "thrown" into the situation and "projec[t] possibilities into" it.[25]

Aldridge's is a "weak" conception of engagement, for at least two reasons: (i) it can't be stipulated, demanded, narrowly defined, quantitatively represented (this would constitute a "strong" conception or definition);[26] (ii) its phenomenal structure makes it, as I've already suggested, virtually synonymous with other existential events (reading, understanding, education itself) that are educative inasmuch as they are self-affecting, authentic, transformative. To repeat, engagement – one's leaning into unconcealment – is always educative because transformative, but it can't be planned for or cooked up by following a recipe (the carefully planned lesson that flops is a common enough experience among teachers).

Education as Learning. Learning as a Lightbulb Moment?

When I gave a presentation based on an earlier version of this chapter,[27] there was some dissatisfaction with my use of the lightbulb-moment figure. I considered dropping it, but decided against that, not least because Alex, the student quoted at the top of the chapter, made her comment in the period when I'd been writing that early draft, and the story of what she'd said helped me pull together some of the looser strands of my thinking. (Some readers may be familiar with the improvisation game *Yes, and ...*, in which participants keep an idea going for as long as possible by accepting whatever another says ("yes") and developing it ("and...")). Alex made her comment during one of my wife's English Literature lessons, one of those in which the plan is jettisoned early on because the session is powered by spontaneous, generative discussion. The focus of the lesson was Lady Macbeth; what my wife remembers of the session is a profusion of interesting and creative responses, each subsequent comment urged on, yes-and..., by the last.)

One concern raised at my talk was that my use of the lightbulb figure seemed to stand for something like an ungrounded moment of epiphany. That being the case, two objections followed: firstly, that the very notion of educational epiphanies is fraught with problems (therefore, lightbulb-moment as epiphany needed careful theorizing); secondly, that my talk of what sounded like epiphanic moments seemed to sit uneasily with my defence of discipline, training, and routine (see third and fourth sections below) – lightbulb moments seem to "just happen," whereas discipline seems to presuppose sustained commitment and effort. A third objection was that the lightbulb figure, or at least my use of it, seemed to take for granted a confused temporal structure which I never addressed.

Apart from the fact that Alex's comment, and the short educational story for which it's a sign, spoke to some of the ideas I was trying to work through, I also chose the lightbulb figure in an attempt to deflate or demystify some existential-phenomenological accounts of learning. Sometimes, the complicating gesture is an ethical gesture, one that forces us to think twice and to go slow over what is often taken for familiar ground.[28] There may be good reasons for signalling to our interlocutors that some things are not as cut and dried as we might think, that some things, often ignored, are worth rethinking. However, I'm not convinced that rendering what are supposed to be everyday experiences in perfect Heideggerese, say, brings us any closer to the everydayness of those supposedly everyday experiences. The deflationary gesture, then, was simply an attempt, through the use of a cliché, to bring the *feel of the moment* of revelation closer. It was a gesture made in the full knowledge that clichés don't do the same work for everyone, but also a belief that such a cliché was no more obscure than much philosophical writing.[29] What has been interesting to me is that – among an admittedly small sample – the lightbulb figure has been received more positively by literature specialists than by philosophers.

In an article published some years before his piece on engagement, Aldridge critiques the very possibility of educational epiphany as an experiential moment: educational epiphanies, he argues, may not be experience-able in the present (the moment they are supposed to have occurred); nor can we make sense of them *as* moments.[30] Aldridge notes a tension in the philosophical literature between epiphany imagined as continuity and discontinuity – epiphany, on the one hand, as a "gradual process of becoming," and, on the other, epiphany as interruption (particularly of "habitual learning"). Aldridge associates the first model with Paul Smeyers, the second with Pádraic Hogan; and he makes a link between their work and Andrea English's analysis of "transformative" education as a process of "negativity and interruption."[31] Epiphanic time, Aldridge suggests, is a problem. The idea of epiphany seems to suggest a signal event, a moment in time that changed everything for us. But "[w]hat," he asks, "is the duration of this moment? When does it occur?"[32] Is epiphanic time indeterminately long (epiphany as becoming), or infinitesimal (the moment of interruption)? Aldridge's answer is to cast suspicion on epiphany as an experience we can have in the here and now, and to reframe it as a necessarily retrospective, perhaps distinctly literary narrative form. Epiphanies, he suggests, are born in the act of (re)telling. In Aldridge's piece, epiphanies appear to be doubly utopian: utopian in the sense that epiphanic narratives tend to isolate and idealize the importance of signal, transformative moments in our pasts; and utopian, too, in the sense that, if epiphanies are born only in the act of narration, then the epiphanic moment itself is simultaneously idealized yet nowhere – a good-place and no-place, an *ou-topos* and *eu-topos* – existing only in and as text.[33]

Andrea English's characterization of transformation as interruption, on which Aldridge draws, involves two existential movements – the inward and outward turns – constitutive of transformative learning:

> The inward turn happens when the individual begins to reflectively think about the pre-reflective interruption in his experience and thereby to make it into a conscious moment that he can examine. The outward turn involves the changed outlook on the world that arises out of coming to understand oneself […] and the world differently or otherwise than before the learning experience. This new understanding is not necessarily a gain or a loss, though it can feel like either or both to the experiencer, but primarily a different way of seeing and being in the world.[34]

Both the inward and outward turns are interpretive and narrative. The inward turn is close to Aldridge's narrativized epiphany; it involves coming to know the significance of an experience by putting it under some conceptual or narrative description. In both Aldridge and English, transformation or epiphany is not a matter of seeing how things "really" are in the metaphysical sense: transformation and epiphany do not bring us closer to the ultimate truth of things; they do not provide us with a view from nowhere. To this end, English's outward turn is a *reframing* of one's worldview. It is how things look as a result of the inward turn.

Aldridge is right that the possibility of *recognizing* the epiphanic moment as such means that it relies on narratability (more simply, tellability). There are economies of scale to be considered, and, to be sure, this *is* where momentariness may well be a function not of the "original" experience, but of narrative: we might look back and remember a period of weeks or months as "the moment" when It all changed; equally, the lightbulb moment might be the work of a few seconds, minutes, or hours. True, too, that lightbulb moments don't follow clock-time: as in Dewey's characterization of *an* Experience, they necessarily have a certain structural unity (regardless of the time-scale, we can nominate beginnings and ends); and, as in Aldridge, *identifying* the unity of an Experience is retrospective, narrative work.[35] Nevertheless, Alex said what she said, in terms of clock- rather than experiential-time, just moments after and also just ahead of several yes-and ... lightbulb flickers. The story (of the lesson and what Alex said) was not told to me as itself an epiphanic moment (a moment when everything changed for my wife (the teacher who told me this story)), but simply as a nice thing that happened in class today. The lightbulb moments I'm interested in are not necessarily epiphanic narratives in Aldridge's sense; the former don't require the sense of narrative or poetic profundity seemingly required of the latter. I'm interested in those commonly occurring moments when our orientation with respect to an object of interest or study simply shifts: we can feel the shift, but might, for now, be unable to articulate its portent.

Lightbulb moments may not have – because they do not need – the interpretive clarity of Aldridge's epiphanies or English's transformative experiences; rather, they are the material out of which epiphanic and-or transformation narratives are fashioned. The lightbulb moment occurs as an (as-yet) unarticulated response, as a turning towards; and it's situated on the cusp between the effable and the ineffable. Here are two examples.

In Chapter VI of Kate Chopin's novel *The Awakening*, the narrator interrupts the action with a brief meditation (the entire chapter is just 250 words) on the transformational moment that will set the course of protagonist Edna Pontellier's life:

> Edna Pontellier could not have told why, wishing to go to the beach with Robert, she should in the first place have declined, and in the second place have followed in obedience to one of the two contradictory impulses which impelled her.
>
> A certain light was beginning to dawn dimly within her, – the light which, showing the way, forbids it.
>
> At that early period it served but to bewilder her. It moved her to dreams, to thoughtfulness, to the shadowy anguish which had overcome her the midnight when she had abandoned herself to tears.
>
> In short, Mrs. Pontellier was beginning to realize her position in the universe as a human being, and to recognize her relations as an individual to the world within and about her. [...]
>
> But the beginning of things, of a world especially, is necessarily vague, tangled, chaotic, and exceedingly disturbing. How few of us ever emerge from such beginning! How many souls perish in the tumult!
>
> The voice of the sea is seductive; never ceasing, whispering, clamoring, murmuring, inviting the soul to wander for a spell in abysses of solitude; to lose itself in mazes of inward contemplation.[36]

The chapter, which is at once the existential kernel of the novel and yet has little ostensible bearing on the novel's action, is itself a narrative interruption.

Chopin – whose prose is anything but vague, tangled, chaotic – captures something of English's double turn: Chopin's protagonist feels the inward pull of a *dim* light which both beckons and forbids. This is hardly light as a vision-based metaphor for knowledge or clear understanding, however: nothing distinct is illuminated here. We have not emerged from Plato's cave; we are simply drawn towards a changed quality in the play of light and shadow. This inward stirring, which the protagonist doesn't yet comprehend, perhaps is prompted by and perhaps produces Edna's receptiveness to the voice of the sea, which, taking on a new and emerging significance, invites her not to know but simply to wander – to orient herself in relation to it and to feel. Though this chapter doesn't move the plot on, it ripples outwards to all that will come: Chopin gives us the image of the sea, the metaphor of its voice; the rest of the novel takes place in the wake and echo of this interruption. Note, however, that Edna – referred to by her first name, rather than "Mrs. Pontellier," for the novel's first time in this chapter – is not yet in a position to realize her own double turn. The omniscient narrator must tell us what Edna cannot yet fully express: that her connection to the sea is sensual, not rational, and that it has *begun* to change her. All that is available to Edna is the vague stirring, the sense simply that something has changed.

The second example comes from my philosophy seminar room. At the end of a session focussed on philosophies of identity, a student hung back. Among several topics she wanted to discuss were the tensions between gender-critical feminism and trans rights advocacy. She was not, at that point, able to verbalize exactly what her views were, nor was she able to chart a course between what *appeared* to be two radically opposed positions. She did not quite know what she wanted to say, other than she was trying to think through her parallel desires to be an ally to trans persons (this student was a cis-gender woman) and to stay true to her belief that women's sex- and body-based rights matter and need to be protected. The student had had, I want to suggest, a lightbulb moment of sorts: it's not that she had nothing to say about women's sex-based rights, or about trans rights. But something had stirred her to reconsider *what* she thought about these, to think about the pressures the different positions might exert on one another, and to think about where she now stood in relation to them. She left the session making the inward turn. But that turn had been preceded by something like the non-propositional, non-rational feeling identified by Chopin.

Let me briefly address the concern that there's a conflict between lightbulb moments and discipline. My comments below on discipline are offered as a rough sketch of what I think are conditions not of the very possibility of lightbulb moments happening at all, but of their *likelihood* in the classroom. Here, then, I need only say a few words about why I think there's no conflict to worry about. The objection was that while lightbulb moments seemed to require very little effort – they either happen or they don't; they're not the products of planning and practice – discipline requires quite the opposite: it requires sustained commitment or engagement. Fine. But though one is committed to the life, say, of a writer, philosopher, athlete, one cannot control the ups, downs, flows, and blockages encountered in such a life. Crudely put: regardless of commitment, sometimes things go well, sometimes they don't. Equally, one doesn't need to commit to, say, the life of a writer, or to becoming a writer, in order for writerly lightbulb moments to happen; one does not need to commit to being or becoming a philosopher to have philosophical lightbulb moments. One need only commit to the situation (the seminar, say, or the reading of an article), to be open, in the manner suggested by Maxine Greene, to the possibilities of that situation. (This is why I write, below, of lightbulb moments as being a little like momentary expertise.)

I've taken this detour, have allowed this interruption, because my use of "lightbulb moment" seemed to cause as many *philosophical* problems as I'd hoped it would avoid. The danger, though, in attempting to respond to critics and head off problems is that one makes a mountain of a molehill. It would be easy to overcook the significance and overcomplicate the structure of the lightbulb moment. All I want is a linguistic figure that is almost as familiar as the experience itself, and which helps me point to those *aha!* moments, the full significance of which can only be teased out and articulated retrospectively. There's no attempt here at a systematic philosophy of the lightbulb moment, simply an attempt to describe in general (and, I'd hoped, unmysterious) terms a common experience: the feeling that something is being learned, though just *what* may take some figuring out. The lightbulb moment is worth mentioning, because, when it comes to writing practices and their general educational value beyond English and Creative Writing, I'm interested in processes and practices that allow us to first shape and then to share what it is we think, or perhaps only tentatively think we think.

Expertise, Routine, and Educational Space

It's true that lightbulb moments must be allowed to happen; they can't be taught or demanded (to do the latter would surely be a form of pedagogical kitsch[37]). Educators can attempt to create background conditions in which lightbulb moments might be more likely; they can attempt to clear a little space in the place of the classroom. Heideggerian and post-Heideggerian phenomenology make a big deal about the so-called background – the always-already familiar, non-theorized or -thematized contexts in which we dwell.[38] Our backgrounds shape us; it's in dynamic relation to them that we develop our particular styles of being: barely awake in the morning, I move from bedroom to kitchen in a particular way – with a particular style – because I'm habituated to my environment, and such habituation allows for seamless, thoughtless (in the sense of automatic, habituated) interaction: thinking without Thought. Presumption of such background familiarity is, on the one hand, part of a normative or descriptive method common to phenomenology (**this** *is what usually happens in* **these** *quotidian circumstances*); on the other, it's part of the ethical project running through much work in or inflected by the existential-phenomenological tradition, the insistence that certain qualities of experience emerge from or between our ethical relations with others, from or between our bonds of care, duty, love, trust, and so on.[39] Both the normative and the ethical project begin strategically *in medias res*, because existential-phenomenology is typically interested in the warp and weft of everyday experience – whether simply to describe those structures that are so familiar they are often hidden in plain view, or, in so describing them, to disrupt and possibly change them. Background familiarity is presupposed, too, in a good deal of phenomenological educational philosophy, again because it takes aim at what is supposedly familiar, typical: "the teacher," "the student," "the classroom" are spoken of as (if) familiar parts of routine structures; against such and such a background the lightbulb is now more, now less, likely to flare.

Hubert Dreyfus, whom we encountered in Chapter 3, draws upon the phenomenological concept of background to develop a structure of expertise, or, as he calls it, fluid coping.[40] Novices (musicians, craftspersons, athletes …) have limited repertoires of moves to which they have recourse regardless of the circumstances. Novices always work in a sort of abstraction from the background; one might even say that there's a sense in which there is no background for novices, because they cannot interact fluidly – automatically, Thoughtlessly – with their environment, cannot bend their performance to the particular conditions. Experts, by contrast, are responsive to, because thickly embedded in, the moment. It's against a sense of the generically familiar (*I've been here – in this sort of situation – before*) that experts are able to cope as fluidly in the particular situation as they do. Reading is an excellent example of and general model for this: there are backgrounds of reading, against which we might sight-read this or that text with more or less "success" (some generally fluent readers ("functionally literate") will be more, some less, able than others to sight-read philosophy, poetry, and so on); similarly, expert skiers can read the snow, boxers and dancers the bodies of their opponents, jazz musicians their bandmates. One characteristic of expertise, according to both Dreyfus and John McDowell (despite other points of disagreement between them), is that expert activity is performed in a flow state.[41] Experts just do whatever it is they're experts in (there is nothing, as it were, "behind" the performance), whereas novices consciously recall the moves they wish to execute before executing them. Lightbulb moments are much like the flow-state associated with expertise, though they are, of course, only moments: situationally specific (thickly embedded; "backgrounded"), unreflective as "it" happens (though one might reflect on "it" retrospectively, and, doing so, epiphanize it in the way Aldridge suggests). The lightbulb moment is "momentary expertise."[42]

Think of how sporting, musical, artistic, crafting, and other expertises are developed, and it's obvious that training – routine cycles of repetition and variation – and discipline are crucial. Though the automaticity and repetitiousness that *training* connotes may seem to conflict with notions of education proper, etymologically *train* and *educate* are close (they share the Proto-Indo-European root *deuk-*, meaning "to lead"). *Training* involves shaping, drawing out, manipulating, handling, and the defining or delimiting of a field. Despite its authoritarian associations, *discipline*, derived from *disciple*, suggests not only punishment, but one who follows a path of learning and who grasps or takes hold of the object of learning. Training involves developing background familiarity, making increasingly natural otherwise unnatural movement patterns. The more expert one becomes, the more responsive to background conditions one is, the less one is separated from a "mere" inanimate backdrop, and the more one is imbricated dynamically in one's living environment. Background familiarity, achieved through discipline of one sort or another, establishes conditions in which lightbulb moments are more or less likely, because it's in relation to these that movement patterns are "drilled in" and habits formed. Background familiarity guarantees some sort of habituation; it doesn't guarantee desirable or healthy habituation. In any sustained formal educational context – and I'm thinking here not only of school but of other forms and domains of education: expressive arts and sports training, for example – habituation goes on, and so we'll want to ask ourselves to just what – what attitudes, what movement patterns – we and-or others are being habituated.[43]

Though phenomenological accounts of education are very often proffered against educational instrumentalism, we shouldn't take them as arguments against *any* sort of routine. The classroom as physical site is a place in which some sort of educative space is opened. If the presumption is that education only happens when the "right" lessons have been learned, then it's natural enough to think that sometimes learning does, while at other times it doesn't, happen in the classroom. But if, in keeping with phenomenological accounts of learning (as revelation, disclosure, engagement …), we recognize that new perspectives are always partial, that a turning-towards is also necessarily a turning-away – if *that's* recognized, then we have to accept that *something* is always learned in the classroom, some space is always opened; but neither teacher nor student is in total control of just *what* is learned, or of the kind of space that's opened. To the extent that it's often in the teacher's power to set the tone of the classroom, we might say there's a sense in which teachers carry their classroom spaces with them, almost as an aura. The classroom becomes a space wherein students' perceptions of self (positive, negative, anywhere in between) are trained into them, where their engagement (positive, negative, anywhere in between) and disengagement with a subject and its emergent subject-matter are established, over time, as routine.[44]

Aldridge is right, of course, that one could spend hours in a library without ever becoming engaged: this could be just the sort of routine movement pattern that prevents engagement, that prevents lightbulb moments, precisely because one thinks one *is* learning simply by putting in the time. But it doesn't follow that because one style or habit of existence doesn't guarantee the eruption of learning it necessarily prevents it. Teachers are, in part, diagnosticians; they (try to) intervene when certain habits of action, certain patterns of movement, appear to block learning, and they (try) to bring to students' attention those habits of action that they think will be more conducive to learning. This is as true of teachers who are sports coaches as it is of teachers who teach writing.

Writing Beyond the English Studies Classroom

At this point, I want turn, by way of lengthy conclusion, to the general importance of writing practice, beyond the subject-areas or disciplines associated with English.

Imagine that you have been struggling to set some thought down in writing: the right form of words won't come. You don't know – you can't say – what the right form of words is (if you could, you would have used it); but you *do* know you haven't found it yet. Suddenly, the turn of phrase is at hand – often, we'll say the words "presented themselves." Very likely, we'll not be able to give reasons why this happened as and when it did. There's no reason or rationale "behind" the phenomenon, though we may be able to say what we were doing (or had ceased to do) when the solution presented itself (I left the computer and went for a walk; I stopped writing and started reading (and a particular phrase jolted me); I poured myself a bourbon; I went for a run; I switched from keyboard to pen and paper; I talked to someone about it; I talked to someone about entirely unrelated stuff; I listened to Archie Shepp's most recent album, and *that* prompted a redrafting of a sub-section...).[45] The "right" form of words says or does something that other attempts haven't; it makes explicit some facet, some inflection, we feel is essential to the sentiment of (not the meaning "behind") the sentence. It emerges in the act of writing.

The example of writing offers a clear case of an aesthetic moment being given objective form; it exemplifies what Hans Ulrich Gumbrecht calls the "oscillation" between "presence" and "meaning"; it might also be taken as an example of what Robert Brandom calls explicitation – the making explicit of the inferential commitments and entailments of our beliefs, the (second-order) explication of the already-explicit.[46]

Though writing is not the only form that learning-as-affect might take, the written assignment is the most commonly used form of assignment in formal educational contexts. It's also the form most taken for granted (particularly if what's asked for is the explication of (the giving of reasons for) one's thoughts),[47] in that it's too often treated — in academic contexts especially — as if merely a set of conventions. What's all too often left out of academic writing guides is the role writing to learn can have on the road to learning to write. *How* we say affects *what* we say. Style is not a mere adornment; it runs all the way through writing.[48]

Understood as both a mode of thinking and a form of thought, *writing* can take its place alongside other eventful terms (*education, reading, engagement* ...). Just as teachers can offer instruction in or demonstration of pianoplaying and weightlifting but not in how to be pianists and weightlifters, so might writing teachers also show students the forms of words one *might* use to express an idea. We might be able to go some way to explicating our own linguistic and syntactic choices. But we cannot teach students how to be writers. Of course, there's no need for all students (in all subjects and disciplines) to become *writers* — in the literary or quasi-literary sense in which *writer* is often used — nor to *become* writers in the phenomenologically committed sense of being and becoming, either. But it might not be such a bad thing for them to think of themselves as, say, "essay-writers" rather than "assessment-completers-or-satisfiers." Better yet, it might be desirable for students to think of themselves as expert language users and, therefore, expert thinkers — expert on Dreyfus's model, that is, as persons able to wield language thoughtlessly and in flow. This is unlikely to happen if — and this is where routine and discipline, and, perhaps, a little school(ing) come in — little or no writing is done between assignments; if writing, as a process by which thought is made manifest as such, is not part of the academic background; and, too, if students are made to feel captive to a language that they feel isn't theirs.

In the Creative Writing classroom, there is, arguably, little need for supervised or group writing: Creative Writing courses are so structured that it would be hard to stay in the programme without getting with the programme. And of course, Creative Writing as a subject-area is neatly circular: its primary medium is also its primary subject-matter. But in subjects where writing appears to be a byproduct of having to do assessments, and appears, therefore, to be a means quite distinct from its end, clearing space for writing practice may be useful.

For Peter Elbow, "careless" speech is a springboard to "serious" writing. It is, he says, "useful [...] to invite *wrong* writing on the way to right writing."[49] Starting with the assumption that "*'correct writing' is no one's mother tongue*," his aim is not to dispense with context-dependent conventions of "correct" and "serious" writing (though notice the contingency of these, indicated by *his* quotation marks of ironic suspicion).[50] He hopes, rather, to bridge the gap between one's linguistic home and other more "alien" discursive worlds,[51] and his approach shares something implicit in the phenomenological story: the way to bring about "more" learning is not, necessarily, more schooling. To translate this into the quasi-phenomenological language used above, Elbow advocates an approach to writing that allows thinking to flow untrammelled, so that later – perhaps much later – thought might emerge. Language is the background against which something might be said, the ground in which, as Merleau-Ponty puts it, we might "shape [...] certain hollows, certain fissures [...] to bring into the world that which is strangest to it: a *meaning*."[52] Elbow's project, both through the use of freewriting – which is often "lively and even clear (though often not usable as it comes out)" – and the recruitment of "unplanned spoken language," is to draw on unplanned, unthinking, or careless language-use "for the rich resources it has, even for careful writing."[53]

Language is a live entity; it speaks to us even as we speak it.[54] Writing can become part of (or more a part of) our academic backgrounds if we begin with a style that is close to language as we quite literally live and breathe it; if, that is, we begin close to home (with "unschooled" language) and are *led out* (*educated*) from there. Writing, as Janet Emig says, isn't simply "talk recorded" (though perhaps we'd want to say "isn't always, necessarily spontaneous talk recorded").[55] Not only are they different media with different contexts of production, they may also be the functions of different cognitive capacities.[56] Regardless of the biological or neurochemical differences between speech and writing, the gap between being able to say it and being able to write it is a common experience (whether from the side of the teacher or aspirant writer). The suggestion that we bring writing a little closer to home does not ignore the differences between speech and writing. It is, firstly, offered as a pedagogic device, a way of reducing the alienness of (especially academic) writing, so that writing can get started, so that a little thought can be teased out of the flow of thinking. Secondly, though it's right to say that writing is not simply speech, and certainly not thought, recorded or transcribed, still writing may draw on various linguistic resources; and perhaps in doing so – in becoming a little more carnivalesque, more openly heteroglossic – academic writing might be reinvigorated (for both students and professionals).[57]

The Politics of Language and (Good, Bad, and Ugly) Academic Writing

It's a sociolinguistic given that there's no one standard, universal English, only varieties of more or less stable Englishes: introductory and survey works tell us that varieties of English are constantly emerging through processes of creolization and *x*-isation;[58] a 2021 report on the emergence of European English as a stable variety noted that there are more second- or additional-language speakers of English worldwide than there are first-language speakers;[59] literary-journalistic and academic accounts of Black American English repeatedly demonstrate its stability *as* a distinct form of English, rich in expressive and communicative power (not a type of "broken" English);[60] for more than a half-century, sociolinguistics has tracked synchronic and diachronic variations in English along identitarian axes.[61] Sometimes, prescriptive defences of "standard" or "White Mainstream" English are made in the name of clarity.[62] But as numerous sociolinguists have shown, non-prestige varieties of English are often sufficiently stable that marginalizing them on the grounds of some communicative deficiency is either incoherent or disingenuous: to do this is to recast symptoms as causes, to explain the effects of sociohistorical power imbalances as linguistically internal deficiency.[63]

The claim that spoken English is both various (there are many different styles) and variable (those styles are forever moving and changing) is hardly original; nor should it be controversial. Yet references to, or presumptions of, a universal standard English persist: one journalist recently referred to "our universal language," the principles of which, he complained, were threatened by some English universities' decisions to stop assessing students' standard written English.[64] Prescriptive talk of "standard English" can easily shade into equally prescriptive talk of "academic English" and-or "academic standards." But if correct writing is, as Elbow says, no one's mother tongue, then academic writing certainly isn't. *Couldn't* be. Indeed, it's tempting to think that it's because so-called academic conventions and standards seem to forbid so many traits of familiar, casual, spoken language that students may feel they're having to unlearn one set of linguistic behaviours at the same time as they are having to learn a new set.[65]

Just as the variety of standard spoken Englishes is not news, nor is the claim that "academic English" is not one thing but many. Elaine Maimon, writing in 1979, makes the obvious point that different academic disciplines produce their own sets of writerly conventions. However, she suggests, while the "special conventions of different disciplines are rarely explained to students," the technical conventions of standard written English are often overemphasized. "Too often," Maimon writes, "talking about commas becomes a safe substitute for *teaching and demonstrating how writers behave.*"[66] There's a good deal to wrestle with in these few words. Were it a pedagogical commonplace to discuss what it means to think or behave like a writer, and what it means to be writing "in" or "from" particular traditions and-or disciplines, we'd likely get on fine without all the familiar though poorly conceptualized talk of "academic standards." Just what those standards are and where they're to be found is anyone's guess. Certainly, what makes for "good" and "bad" academic writing is up for debate.

In several contributions to Jonathan Culler and Kevin Lamb's *Just Being Difficult?*, "bad" academic writing is ironized and celebrated as writing against the institutional or disciplinary grain, as writing that is innovative and fruitfully disruptive in its difficulty.[67] Badness is vaunted as that which stylistically, and therefore cultural-politically, rocks the boat. But the defences of complexity in *Just Being Difficult?* presume that the writing being defended was composed by a sure hand. This means that the debates over the goodness or badness of writers and their work can be played out in terms of responsibility: is what this writing does permissible; should the writer have known better?

To recall Chapter 3's discussion of Chaplin: does the writer know what game they're supposed to be playing, and therefore which rules they are or aren't following? Here, badness is never supposed to be a product of writers not knowing what they're doing: the bad writing under scrutiny, it's assumed, makes some kind of a stand against received standards of decorum and good behaviour; is hyperaware that its unapologetic self-reflexiveness and syntactic tortuousness are a sort of intellectual gobbing in public. Writerly control is never explicitly a going concern, and therefore never addressed directly; but there are, I'd suggest, two sources of its presumption in the bad writers considered in *Just Being Difficult?*: one is internal, the quality of the writing itself, particularly the tendency towards grammatical conventionalism; the other is external, the contexts in which the writing circulates.

Externally, academic publication situates the writer as a professional, someone writing not to answer and satisfy some formal assignment and its assessment criteria, but because they have a (supposedly new) contribution to make to their field. The professional academic is one who has licence to speak but also bears full responsibility for what they say. This permits certain risks, but also leaves those situated as professionals and experts open to the fallout of those risks.

Internally, all the examples of "bad" writing considered in *Just Being Difficult?* are grammatically conservative or conventional. Take the following sentence written by Judith Butler:

> The move from a structuralist account in which capital is understood to structure social relations in relatively homogeneous ways, to a view of hegemony in which power relations are subject to repetition, convergence, and rearticulation, brought the question of temporality into the thinking of structure, and marked a shift from a form of Althusserian theory that takes structural totalities as theoretical objects to one in which the insights into the contingent possibilities of structure inaugurate a renewed conception of hegemony bound up with the contingent sites and strategies of the rearticulation of power.[68]

Such difficulty as there may be is *not* at the grammatical-syntactic level (though it's possible that a sentence of this length risks disorienting the reader). The problem is one of reference and extension, or possible lack of them, and this problem inheres in the unusual combination of semantic lexical items (mainly the adjectives and nouns): what *is* the structural homology of social relations? What are the precise dynamics of, and where are we to find, those convergences of power-relations of which Butler writes? Problems of extension and reference are philosophically technical, likely of interest only to those interested in hard problems of logic, language, and mind.[69] The short version: if we aren't sure to what "social relations" and "homology" point, then we don't know how to picture or interpret what is said; we don't know what Butler means to mean, cannot orient ourselves in relation to her writing.

Butler's sentence was made famous for winning the 1998 round of the Bad Writing Contest, run by the journal *Philosophy and Literature*. Editor Dennis Dutton mocked Butler and others whom he considered merely "kitsch theorists" of "mimic[king] the effects of rigor and profundity without actually doing serious intellectual work." "To ask what [Butler's sentence] means is to miss the point," he wrote. "This sentence beats readers into submission and instructs them that they are in the presence of a great and deep mind. Actual communication has nothing to do with it."[70] Culler defends Butler and her sentence, arguing that it cannot be understood pulled from the context in which it was written. The sentence, Culler claims, is perfectly sensible, so long as one understands the ideas and arguments of which it is the synthesis and culmination. For that, one needs to have read far more than this sentence alone. Dutton distinguishes between contemporary theorists, whom he accuses of hiding intellectual vapidity behind impenetrable prose, and the "real" philosophers who are difficult only because "they are honestly grappling with the most complex and difficult problems the human mind can encounter." Culler responds, simply and correctly, that in critiquing the political and discursive constructions and workings of gender, Butler *is* dealing with complex matters.[71]

Scraps over Butler's sentence, then, and others similarly "difficult," are fought on the overlapping grounds of good and bad taste and faith, not on grammatical stability. The "real" issue seems to be, with Maimon's comment on writerly behaviours in mind, whether or not Butler is behaving well. And here, there seems to be consensus: she's not. Some celebrate her for this, while others castigate her – but either disposition is only possible because we impute control (or ability) and commitment (or intention), and therefore both responsibility *and* agency, to professional academics in ways we tend not to in our students: when the latter's "bad" writing gives us teacher-readers a hard time, it's easy to assume that they don't yet know how to say what they're trying (or "need") to say.[72] And one marker of writerly control will, as Maimon recognizes, be the grammatical security – or conventionalism – of the work: conventionalism equals correctness equals control. There's something to this; but what this equation leaves out is that it's perfectly possible to say very little accurately (conventionally), and equally possible to say a great deal scrappily.

In her work on composition and writing teaching, Patricia Bizzell attempts to dispel the myth that "academic correctness" was stable until the incursion of postmodernism and cultural theory in the '80s and '90s. Rather, she claims, academic writing, like natural language itself, has always been mutable. In the late '90s, Bizzell herself tried to launch a new phase in basic writing instruction, "in which the unitary nature of traditional academic discourse as a target for composition teaching [was] called into question, on the basis of the proliferation in contemporary academic writing of forms that do not follow traditional criteria."[73] In terms of writerly behaviours, it's of little help to refer students to academic standards and appropriateness. Many of the commonplace values of "traditional" academic writing – technicality, formality, disinterestedness – are stylistic correlates of an aspiration to generality, an aspiration modelled on certain ideas of "hard" scientific research and its dissemination, and rooted in the idea that knowledge proper is contextless. But as I argued in Chapter 4, and as critical philosophies of race, feminism, gender, sexuality, and anthropology have been at pains to show, there are no unframed forms of knowledge: the epistemic precedes the epistemological.[74]

We teachers need to recognize that we're not teaching our students universal academic standards: there are relatively few of these. What we're asking of our students is that they demonstrate they can meet a particular brief (and possibly that they can adapt their writing to styles that suit us, for reasons of disciplinarity or expediency or taste). Some teachers will be more, some less, prescriptive. This doesn't matter very much, so long as the rules of the game are laid bare and students know what they're in for; so long as teachers are clear about the discursive practices with which we ourselves are aligned; and so long as teachers tread carefully the line between light-touch stylistic prescription and heavier-handed conceptual prescription, between guiding students on *how* they say and prescribing *what* they say.

That last point matters if we don't wish to teach solely to the test – a common complaint among educators – and if our assessments are not to be merely ego-driven. It strikes me that when university students ask for guidance on their assessments, often they're not really asking about assessment criteria; they're asking what they need to do to get a good mark from their teacher. To situate what students are writing *for* in a context broader than my own satisfaction, I need to convince my students that they aren't writing to one tutor cut off from any other context; but, rather, that they're writing to a particular discursive community of which I may be a part and in which the assignment is embedded. It therefore behoves me to say something to my students about my own relationship with, and to situate myself precisely in, that discursive community. This is a matter of how we teachers write ourselves and our practices *into* the classroom space – not as "disinterested" observers with gods'-eye-views, but as participants with vested interests and standpoints. We teachers are not gatekeepers of standards that have nothing to do with us; we're both playing and watching the game.

"Academic writing" is not a set of qualities or traits, it's a general term for a vast array of identities; and our identities, as Kwame Anthony Appiah has suggested, are constituted in a two-way movement: we must *identify as...*, and others must *recognize us as...*.[75] The "correctness" of academic writing isn't a matter of measurement; it's one of negotiation and judgement, of balancing the push of grammatical conservatism (as a means of communicability) and the pull of expression (the desire to say things the way you want to say them). Grammars have their norms and their limits; but the principle of grammatical *conservationism* (grammars have a breaking point) doesn't entail grammatical, and certainly not tonal, *conservatism* (conventions taken as correctness are never innocent). Nor are there any good reasons why language varieties which, viewed from the normative linguistic "centre," are standard but non-prestige should be excluded from all domains of academic writing.[76]

Standard English as Second Nature

Once more: we need not appeal to notions of "academic standards" if we're clear on the what (form), the why (purpose), and the who (imagined readers). But a problem for many teachers and academics is that we've had the *apparent* strictures of standard written English so firmly inculcated in us that they and it have become something like a second (linguistic) nature – one that has its affordances, to be sure, but also its limitations.

The philosophy of second nature, associated especially with McDowell and some of his interlocutors, is complex: rooted in the Kantian problem of how to "reconcile reason and nature," empiricism and rationalism, second-natural capacities are those that aren't raw givens (they're not simply and always-already "there" from the start), but which it is in our (first) nature to develop. It's by virtue of our second nature that we can form our habits of action, develop our non-reflective and automatic capacities. Because second nature is both a precondition and product of human being, we're able, through reflective effort, to change it.[77] Reading and writing "standard" English may not be second-natural in the way that, all things being equal, spoken language acquisition is; but for many of us – especially teachers, and even more especially those who are required to teach writing but may not consider ourselves writers[78] – it isn't far off. If I don't consider myself a writer, it's easy enough to develop a habit of reframing my judgements not as judgements, but as measures of standards and correctness to which (I think) I'm as beholden as are my students.

I don't exclude myself from the problem of habituated, second-nature commitment to "standard" English (the present book, for example, is, relatively speaking, linguistically conservative). Sometimes, it's hard to see past what's written to hear what's said, equally to read past grammatical and-or lexical convention to (likely intended) meaning. My distinction here between seeing and hearing isn't figurative. It was only when, during a lesson, I was able to read the words a student had written as they were reading those words aloud that I realized the gap (sometimes very wide) between what one sees written on the page and hears in speech. Here was a cogency of thought hidden from me by *my* second-natural commitments to *and* the student's relatively frequent minor lapses in so-called "standard" written English. Had I not heard the student's work, I would likely, just as Maimon suggests, have substituted a concern with the conventional placement of commas for discussion of meaning and style. It was far easier for me to engage with the student's ideas once *the linguistic expectations of my eye* weren't being repeatedly frustrated: the student's written "lapses" disrupted *my* ability to read fluently. In a sense, the student and I did not "speak" the same written dialects. Or perhaps we can say that I was as expert in as I was unconsciously hidebound by standard written English, while the student was, by comparison; a learner – albeit a fluent one – who was not yet fully immersed. Here, "correction" according to the norms of standard English spelling, punctuation, and grammar was relatively unproblematic: there was no attempt by the student to challenge such norms; moving the student to the normative "centre" was a matter of coaching them towards greater control over – and, yes, conformity with – the forms they intended to use. This was a traditional game they were willing to play: greater grammatical conventionalism would likely mean a closer meeting of readers' and writer's minds.

In another case, it was the report, mentioned above, on the emergence of European English as a "new standard" that led me to think carefully about the differences between unidiomatic and nonsensical English, which spurred me to read slow and allowed me to discover a great deal of insight in a student essay that was consistently unidiomatic – because English was an additional language for the student – yet never nonsensical, and only rarely ungrammatical. Theresa Lillis has documented examples of academics, writing in English as a second or additional language, who've been accused of intellectual deficiency on the basis of their English-medium work. She shows that the negative reactions to these academics' writing are grounded in highly personalized views on "appropriate" or "correct" academic style, while the judgement of intellectual deficiency is grounded in the idea that language "mirrors" thought.[79] On that model, imperfect language use equals imperfect thinking. In Part II, we rejected the view that knowledge resides "in" the head or mind in propositional form, waiting only to be amplified. If writing is, as I've insisted throughout this book, a form – one among others – that thought might take, then we need to give up the idea that there's a direct line from the words on the page to the thoughts "in" the writer's head. For writers whose first natural language isn't English, English-medium academic writing is a complex negotiation, not a case of putting one's thoughts into the words of a second or additional language (because, remember, nothing is put into words other than words)[80] according to a simple model of lexical and grammatical equivalences.[81] The negotiation is between writer, text, and context, a matter of having to work in a target or host language that is not one's own, and having at the same time to anticipate (or guess at) and adapt to the demands of a genre that seems to be tightly bound by rules that are not always explicit nor even consistent (the "rules" vary according to academic institution, learned society, publishing venue, and so on). If academic writing consists not in prescribed qualities but is, rather, a set of always shifting identities, then the English-medium writer who is fluent, grammatical, yet unidiomatic is in the position of having to learn not "only" a language, in an easily isolable sense, but (what is much more like taking on a "real" language) an entire culture.

If, as I agree it is, the mirror model of thought and language is wrong, then "intellectual capacity" is the wrong currency in which to cash out one's objections to another's work – wrong not because such a move is unkind (it is), but because it fails to acknowledge the responsibility of the reader, who may have some negotiating of their own to do: how to decide between meaningless and merely unidiomatic writing, between complexity, clumsiness, and obscurantism? The lines between these are finer than we might think. In the case of the nonidiomatic and insightful student, my and my co-tutor's final view was that the nonidiomaticity of the writing was more our (the teacher-readers') problem than the writer's: occasionally, communication failed (here and there we really weren't sure what the student was claiming); more often, what had been written simply wasn't what we were expecting, and this made our going slow in a period of institutionally imposed administrative-time poverty.

Two last examples.

Recently, a student used an assigned essay on education and social class to ask why their style of expression was being stifled by the demands of academic writing. There were two prongs to the complaint: the student objected to what they saw as academic writing's prescriptivist conservatism, its insistence on grammatical hypercorrectness; they also objected to being told to "evidence" their claims regarding the educational lives of working-class persons when they themself had lived and continued to live the very life they were writing about. The student raised an important question: to what extent were we demanding that certain things be said in a certain way (or not said at all), and to what extent were we trying to help the student better articulate things deeply felt but only half said? Months later, and unrelated to this first example, student Abbigail O'Gilvie commented on a particular assignment and the flexibility of the assignment brief: "I enjoyed writing this piece because I was able to write from the first person, and was able to say things I believe, things that I wanted to say."

To set limits first to *how we say* is to set limits to *what can be said and thought at all*, and to do that is to use – consciously or no – the language of academic standards and correctness to squeeze certain perspectives, experiences, and cultural identities out of the classroom. In a fascinating piece on style as a method of analysis, Phil Ford considers the tension between academic musicology and music criticism – a tension and distinction not unlike the critic/scholarship problem considered in the last chapter. Writing about the formal features of this or that piece of music seems to demand an apparently dispassionate, technical, and general language. But if, Ford writes, it's affect that the critic is concerned with, then style isn't an optional extra laid over content; it *is* content, and it *is* method: "attention to style and voice really can allow an analyst to go (boldly, even) where no musicologist has gone before."[82] In a very different context, examining racist social and intellectual structures, Charles Mills has critiqued academic philosophy's tendency, in the name of objectivity and generality, to abstract away from the realities of structural inequality and lived racialized experience. Presumption of academic standards' cultural neutrality, of their contextlessness, can, if we're not careful, hide from teachers and students alike the often un(re)marked cultural and identitarian specificities of "normal" academic discourse and practice.[83]

The Finite Elasticity of Language

Language is *not* infinitely elastic; at some point, language fails, communication breaks down. I'm not suggesting otherwise. But framing what is good/bad, effective/ineffective in terms of standard or academic English, as if either were a clear and distinct idea, is of little help – in part because what's permissible and what we can get away with in language are constantly up for grabs. "This is not standard English," "this is not appropriate academic English," other like comments – these are shorthands for sets of particular, intersecting linguistic matters (some textual, others contextual). Left unqualified, such comments fail to distinguish between grammatical soundness (or conventionalism) and logical coherence, or between grammaticality and idiomaticity. All of these, as I hope the cases above demonstrate, need to be considered if we're to help students, in the spirit of Zinsser, claim *their writing as theirs* (whatever subject-area they might be working in).

I'm not arguing that there's no practical advantage to gaining greater control over grammatical convention; nor that the student work I've mentioned couldn't have been made better in easily identifiable ways. I *am* suggesting that the advantages that standard written English might confer, and the *pressure* to conform to certain styles of languaging,[84] are neither politically nor ethically neutral and that they may involve losses (of students' sense of self, of having a voice) as well as gains (widespread communicability; acceptance into this or that discursive community).

I'm suggesting, too, that the line between helping students find what it is they want to say and setting limits to what they're permitted to think may be – like those readerly lines of negotiation mentioned above – finer than we realize.

Some readers might take this chapter as anything-goes advocacy. Worse, as a refusal to teach. Worse still, as a meritocratic justification of inequality: those who can write well will; those who can't won't. These are not my arguments or suggestions. But if learning to write, in the spirit of WAC, is learning to follow the rules of particular disciplinary language games, then there is no single academic writing game, just as there is no single standard spoken English: to speak of the rules or conventions of academic writing is about as precise as speaking of the rules of sport; or, if that is too high a level of generality, then perhaps the rules of athletics or of ballgames or of strength sports. Overlap is not symmetry; and bare similarity is neither here nor there, as all things are or can be made alike in some respect. The idea of a universal standard – either of English or of academic writing – is, first, a politically dubious fallacy; second, an unhelpful teaching tool. That English-medium student essay that was at times insightful, often unidiomatic, only occasionally ungrammatical was a problem for both the student and for me and my co-tutor. Certain qualities of her writing impeded her ability to communicate and mine to understand. Of course, writing can be improved. But thinking locally, contextually, in terms of what the writer and their writing are trying to do, what the purpose of the writing is, who the imagined reader is, which traditions they are writing in or from – thinking and conversing along such lines will likely address many of the issues intended by appeals to standard written and-or academic English. Perhaps, too, thinking and conversing in this way will encourage us to question – not necessarily to give up – our deep-rooted, sometimes unreflective, commitments to certain linguistic norms and sources of linguistic influence. For Bizzell, widening the scope of academic writing – its norms, forms, and sources – is not about "lowering standards," nor about making academic discourse somehow more comfortable. It *is* about playing with and in language drawn from a range of sources, so that new ideas might be voiced; it's about unsettling and renewing academic writing, which runs the risk of hardening from the generic (genres are living traditions; there are no genreless texts) to the simply formulaic.[85]

Writing is not the only way in which learning might be made manifest; but it is an exemplary and educationally significant way. It illustrates the ways in which background familiarity enables Thought to emerge from the tide of thinking, and it of course looms large in formal education. In writing I can become other with myself; acts, moments of self-learning are externalized, given form; in writing, I am in dialogue with – among others – me. That we teachers cannot instruct others to become writers hardly matters in general educational terms. What we can do is create routine and encourage discipline with relatively little stylistic prescription, so that students might re-cognize their own linguistic expertise, their own backgrounds against which Thought might take shape. Like Zinsser and other WAC advocates and writing scholars, and like the handful of students who've told me they too feel this way, I often discover what I think in the act of writing. Often, it's not until writing begins that Thought emerges.

Conclusion: Writing as a Kind of Philosophy

In *Writing to Learn*, Zinsser remembers being given a copy of *On Philosophical Style* by the book's author Brand Blanshard, who, drawing on William James, pithily defines philosophy as "'a peculiarly stubborn effort to think clearly,' to find out by thinking what is true."[86] Blanshard's starting point is the importance, and frequent lack, of clarity in philosophical writing. He begins with the difficulties Kant and Hegel have presented – not for non-specialist but expert readers. One explanation of the difficulty of a great deal of philosophy is that it is, in fact, garbage: bad writing on boondoggle topics. Another is that reading philosophy is difficult because doing philosophy is difficult. Blanshard agrees with neither. Great philosophers Kant and Hegel might have been; but greater still had they been better writers:

> Hard as philosophy is, there have been writers who have actually succeeded in making it intelligible and even exciting, not to the exceptionally gifted alone, but to a wide public. Socrates talked it, and Plato wrote it, in a way that some millions of readers have not been willing to forget. Bergson, without once descending to vulgarity, made it for a time one of the excitements of Paris. The British tradition in philosophy has been exceptionally fertile in writers with the gift of making crooked things straight. So if a philosophical writer cannot be followed, the difficulty of his subject can be pleaded only in mitigation of his offence, not in condonation of it. There are too many expert witnesses on the other side.[87]

Zinsser quotes this passage at the close of the third chapter of *Writing to Learn* (43). He takes comfort not only in Blanshard's strident attitude towards philosophical writing, but in its general relevance to writing and learning. A little later, in a move straight from the Blanshard playbook, Zinsser writes: "If you force yourself to think clearly you will write clearly. It's as simple as that."[88] As simple and as hard. And, we should add, the reverse is true: force yourself to write clearly and you may just find yourself thinking clearly. (This is implicit throughout *Writing to Learn*, but perhaps, if we're to hold Zinsser to the rules of his own game, we can say that he missed an easy trick here in not stating it.)

Writing, as both a mode of thinking and a form of thought, takes place in the seam between desire and necessity: the desire to say what we want to say the way we want to say it (because to say it any other way would be to say something else), and the need to make our ideas available to others. As Richard Rorty thinks it, philosophy is a kind of writing in the sense one gets from Wittgenstein and (especially) Derrida: hitching yourself to any disciplinary or discursive wagon is to join a certain language game.[89] Rorty divides philosophers into two groups: those who do and those who don't wish to have to write. Kant is the exemplar of the second group; Derrida of the first:

> Kantian philosophy, on Derrida's view, is a kind of writing which would like not to be a kind of writing. [...] Kantian philosophers would like not to write, but just to *show*. They would like the words they use to be so simple as to be presuppositionless. [...] So they cherish the thought that, at least in some countries, philosophy has no literary pretensions [....] Derrida's reply is that anybody can get by without literary pretensions – without writing – if

he is content simply to demonstrate how something falls into place in a previously established context. [...] The important thing to notice is that the difference between the two forms of activity [writing and not-writing] [...] *is determined by normality or abnormality.* Normality, in this sense, is accepting without question the stage-setting in the language which gives demonstration [...] its legitimacy. Revolutionary scientists need to write, as normal scientists do not. Revolutionary politicians need to write, as parliamentary politicians do not. Dialectical philosophers like Derrida need to write, as Kantian philosophers do not.[90]

Here, Rorty writes in the gap between writing to learn and learning to write: the dynamic, disruptive sense of *writing* that Rorty celebrates is imagined in terms of the traces of free, expressive, exploratory, even careless writing making its presence felt in the final form of the careful or transactional piece. Perhaps we can abbreviate this by saying that what Rorty imagines is the palpable trace of experimental learning in writing. Once again, the push and pull of disciplinary conformism and expression. And, once again, perhaps thinking in terms of context (the what, the why, and the whom) will help us navigate both.

If philosophy, on Rorty's suggestion, is a kind of writing; and if writing, on the insistence of Zinsser and other WAC-olytes, is a mode of learning and, as I've been urging, a form of thought; and if, finally, philosophy, on Blanshard's echoing of James, is no more than "a peculiarly stubborn effort to think clearly" – if all these ifs are the case, then writing is, in very many situations, a kind of philosophy. Classrooms, then, should be philosophical spaces, in a weak sense: philosophy understood as an inquiring and critical stance or attitude. The classroom should be weakly philosophical inasmuch as we want it to create space – a little breathing room – for thought to emerge from the flicker of a lightbulb.

Notes

1 See, for example, Brian Dillon, *Essayism* (London: Fitzcarraldo Editions, 2017).
2 See Susan H. McLeod and Margot Soven (eds), *Writing Across the Curriculum: A Guide to Developing Programs* (1992; e-book; WAC Clearing House, Colorado State University, 2000), available online, <https://wac.colostate.edu/books/landmarks/mcleod-soven/> (accessed 23 July 2021).
3 It takes four years to achieve an honours degree (it usually takes three years to complete an honours degree in the UK, apart from in Scotland, where, as in North America, it takes four.
4 McLeod, "Introduction," *Writing Across the Curriculum* (4).
5 *Ibid.* (3). See the discussion of the conversational model or figure in Chapter 4 of this book.
6 Williams Zinsser, *Writing to Learn* (London: Harper Perennial, 1989), p.20. One is reminded of the embedded anecdote in E.M. Forster's *Aspects of the Novel*, in which an old woman declares, "How can I tell what I think till I see what I say?" (Middlesex: Penguin, 1962, p.108).

7 MacLeod, "Introduction" (3).
8 Peter Elbow, *Vernacular Eloquence: What Speech Can Bring to Writing* (Oxford: Oxford University Press, 2012); see also *Writing Without Teachers*, 2nd Ed. (Oxford: Oxford University Press, 1998).
9 On this, see Robert Brandom, *Articulating Reasons: An Introduction to Inferentialism* (Cambridge, MA: Harvard University Press, 2000), and the discussion of him in Chapter 4 of this book.
10 Gary Thomas, *Education: A Very Short Introduction* (Oxford: Oxford University Press, 2013), pp.1, 1–2
11 *Ibid.* (2).
12 R.S. Peters, *Ethics and Education* (London: George Allen and Unwyn, 1966); Richard Rorty, "Education as Socialization and Individualization," in *Philosophy and Social Hope* (London: Penguin, 1999), pp.114–126.
13 William Blake, *All Religions are One*, in *Blake's Poetry and Designs*, 2nd Ed. (Mary Lynn Johnson and John E. Grant, eds.; London: Norton, 2008, pp.5–6), p.5; "The School Boy," in *Songs of Innocence and Of Experience* (Oxford: Oxford University Press, 1970), p.53.
14 The student is Lewis, whom you met in Chapter 1.
15 Maxine Greene, *Variations on a Blue Guitar: The Lincoln Center Institute Lectures on Aesthetic Education* (New York: Teachers College Press, 2001), pp.7,6.
16 Michael Fielding, "The Person-Centred School," *Forum* 42(2) (2000), pp.51–54 (54); Ivan Illich, *Deschooling Society* (1971; London: Marion Boyars, 2010).
17 Gert Biesta, *The Beautiful Risk of Education* (London: Paradigm, 2013), pp.1–9.
18 This phrase stolen shamelessly from Dan Rebellato's play, *Static: A Story of Love, Loss and Compilation Tapes* (London: Oberon 2008).
19 David Aldridge, "Reading, Engagement and Higher Education." *Higher Education Research and Development* 38(1) (2019, pp.38–50), p.44.
20 *Ibid.*, (44, 45; 45; 47, 44; 48).
21 See n.39 as well as those cited by Aldridge (*ibid.*). This is *not*, of course, to suggest that are no important differences between Aldridge and those others cited below.
22 Aldridge, "Reading, Engagement and Higher Education" (47).
23 *Ibid.*
24 Martin Heidegger, "The Origin of the Work of Art" [1960], *Poetry, Language, Thought*, trans. Albert Hofstadter (New York: Harper Colophon, 1975), pp.15–87.
25 Aldridge (*ibid.*).
26 On strong and weak concepts of education, and a defence of the latter over the former, see Biesta, *Beautiful Risk*.
27 Philosophy of Education Society of Great Britain (London) (28 April 2021). My thanks to Prof. Paul Standish and the organizers for the invitation and to those who offered questions and comments. My thanks in particular to David Aldridge, who attended the talk and whose responses made it clear that I'd misread parts of his piece on engagement.
28 See the Jonathan Culler and Kevin Lamb (eds) collection *Just Being Difficult?: Academic Writing in the Public Arena* (Stanford, CA: Stanford University Press, 2003).
29 One would need, on this point, to find a way of adjudicating between (unavoidable?) complexity and (mere?) obscurantism. Jonathan Culler's contribution to *Just Being Difficult?*, "Bad Writing and Good Philosophy" (43–57), offers an example of this (he makes a case study of Judith Butler's writing and Denis Dutton's repudiation of it). Compare the various defences of complexity in *Just Being Difficult?* with Brand Blanshard's excoriation of philosophical obscurantism, *On Philosophical Style* (1954; South Bend, IND: St. Augustine's Press, 2009). No lesser philosophers than Kant and Hegel come in for a battering in Blanshard's short monograph.

30 Aldridge, "Three Epiphanic Fragments: Education and the Essay in Memory," *Educational Philosophy and Theory* 46(5) (2014), pp.512–526.
31 Aldridge, "Epiphanic Fragments," 513–516; Andrea English, "Transformation and Education: The Voice of the Learner in Peters' Concept of Teaching," *Journal of Philosophy of Education* 43(S1) (2010), pp.75–95.
32 Aldridge, "Epiphanic Fragments" (515).
33 That utopias are simultaneously good- non-places is down to etymological confusion. See Adam Roberts, *Science Fiction* (London: Routledge, 2000).
34 English, "Transformation" (88).
35 See John Dewey, *Art as Experience* (1934; New York: Perigee, 1980); *Experience and Education* (1938; New York: Touchstone-Simon and Schuster, 1997).
36 Kate Chopin, *The Awakening* in *The Awakening and Other Stories*, Pamela Knights (ed.) (London: Penguin, 2000), pp.15–16.
37 If kitsch is asking for tears without earning them, pedagogical kitsch would be asking for commitment or engagement without earning or allowing space for it. This is nicely ironized in an episode of the sitcom *Community*, in which a teacher, Professor Whitman, desperate to be seen as inspirational and who models himself on Robin Williams's character in *Dead Poets Society*, encourages students to tear up their textbooks and stand on the desks. The students, far from being inspired, invariably end up out of pocket and down a textbook and injured when their desks give way beneath them. Anthony Russo (dir.), "Introduction to Film," *Community* (Season 1, Episode 3, 2009).
38 On background see Hubert Dreyfus, "Heidegger's Critique of the Husserl/Searle Account of Intentionality," in *Skillful Coping: Essays on the Phenomenology of Everyday Perception and Action*, Mark A. Wrathall (ed.) (Oxford: Oxford University Press, 2014), pp.76–91.
39 As well as Aldridge's work, see, for example, my "On Tacit Knowledge for Philosophy of Education." *Studies in Philosophy and Education* 37(4) (2018), pp.347–365; Biesta, *Beautiful Risk*; Joseph Dunne *Back to the Rough Ground: Practical Judgement and the Lure of Technique* (Notre Dame, IND: Notre Dame University Press, 1993); Sharon Todd *Learning from the Other: Levinas, Psychoanalysis, and Ethical Possibilities in Education* (Albany, NY: State University of New York Press 2003); Nell Noddings, *Care: A Feminine Approach to Ethics and Moral Education* (Berkeley, CA: University of California Press, 2013); Eva Feder Kittay *Learning from My Daughter: The Value and Care of Disabled Minds* (Oxford: Oxford University Press, 2019). For overviews, respectively, of phenomenology, existentialism, and existential phenomenology as philosophical methods, see David R. Cerbone, "Phenomenological Method and the Achievement of Recognition: Who's Been Waiting for Phenomenology?" [Ch.15] and J. Reynolds and P. Stokes, "Existentialist Methodology and Perspective: Writing the First Person" [Ch.16], Giuseppina D'Oro and Søren Overgaard (eds), *The Cambridge Companion to Philosophical Methodology* (e-book; Cambridge: Cambridge University Press, 2017); Mark Wrathall "Existential Phenomenology" [Ch.3] Hubert Dreyfus and Wrathall (eds), *A Companion to Phenomenology and Existentialism* (e-book; Oxford: Blackwell, 2006).
40 Dreyfus, *Skillful Coping: Essays on the Phenomenology of Everyday Perception and Action*, Mark A. Wrathall (ed) (Oxford: Oxford University Press, 2014).
41 See Dreyfus's and McDowell's contributions to Joseph K. Schear (ed.), *Mind, Reason, and Being-In-The-World: The McDowell-Dreyfus Debate* (London: Routledge, 2013).
42 This is illustrated comically in the film *Old School* (Dir. Todd Phillips, 2003) when the "uneducated" Frank (played by Will Ferrell) has an inexplicable moment of revelation and trounces political pundit James Carville in a competitive school debate.

43 Our talk here of "background familiarity," then, is the habituating of oneself to a milieu or milieux. It doesn't conflict with the line of argument, regarding background, developed in Chapter 3.
44 On place and space, see Chapters 1 and 2, and Michel de Certeau, *The Practice of Everyday Life*, trans. Steven Randall (Berkeley: University of California Press, 1984).
45 All of these have happened to me more than once; most of them have contributed to the writing of this book. Archie Shepp and Jason Moran's 2021 album, *Let My People Go*, is to be thanked for Chapter 4 (possibly 3) being no worse than it is.
46 Hans Ulrich Gumbrecht, *Production of Presence: What Meaning Can't Convey* (Stanford: Stanford University Press, 2004), *In Praise of Athletic Beauty* (Cambridge, MA: Harvard University Press, 2006). Brandom, *Articulating Reasons*. For educational articulations of Brandom, see Jan Derry "Can Inferentialism Contribute to Social Epistemology?" *Journal of Philosophy of Education* 47(2) (2013), pp.222–235; Hanno Su and Johannes Bellmann, "Inferentialism at Work: The Significance of Social Epistemology in Theorising Education." *Journal of Philosophy of Education* 52(2) (2018), pp.320–245; Alessia Marabini and Luc Moretti, "Assessing Concept Possession as an Explicit and Social Practice." *Journal of Philosophy of Education* 51(4) (2017), pp.801–816; Samuel Taylor, Ruben Noorloos, R., and Arthur Bakker, "Mastering as an Inferentialist Alternative to the Acquisition and Participation Metaphors of Learning," *Journal of Philosophy of Education* 41(4) (2017), pp.769–784.
47 Again, Brandom, *Articulating Reasons*, and the discussion of his work in Chapter 4 of this book.
48 See Blanshard, *On Philosophical Style*.
49 Elbow, *Vernacular Eloquence* (3); see also Elbow *Writing Without Teachers*.
50 Elbow *Vernacular Eloquence* (4 and *passim*).
51 A comparison might be made here between Elbow's work and Nelson Goodman's *Languages of Art* (Indianapolis: Hackett, 1976). One thinks, too, of James Britton's phrase from *Language and Learning* (1970; London: Pelican, 1972): "talk is the sea on which all else floats."
52 Maurice Merleau-Ponty, *The Prose of the World*, trans. John O'Neill (Evanston: Northwestern University Press, 1973), p.60.
53 Elbow, *Vernacular Eloquence* (4).
54 Heidegger says this in "...Poetically Man Dwells..." (1954) and "Language" (1959), both in *Poetry, Language, Thought*. However, I prefer to take my lead from the likes of Cassirer (e.g. *An Essay on Man: An Introduction to a Philosophy of Human Culture* (1945; New Haven: Yale University Press, 1972); *Language and Myth* [first German ed. 1925], trans. Susan K. Langer (1946; New York: Dover, 1953) and Goodman (e.g. *Ways of Worldmaking* (Indianapolis: Hackett, 1978)).
55 Janet Emig, "Writing as a Mode of Learning," *College Composition and Communication* 28(2) (1977), pp.122–128.
56 See *ibid*.
57 Here I'm close to the ideas of Patricia Bizzell (e.g. "'Contact Zones' and English Studies," *College English* 56(2) (1994), pp.163–169; "Basic Writing and the Issue of Correctness, or, What to do with 'Mixed' Forms of Academic Discourse," *Journal of Basic Writing* 19(1) (2000), pp.4–12. Bakhtin's idea of the carnivalesque involves the breakdown of received rank and hierarchy, while literary language cannot *not* be heteroglossic – double- or multiply-voiced, comprised of numerous stratified and nested speech types and genres. Mikhail Bakhtin, *Rabelais and His World*, trans. Helene Iswolsky (1965; Bloomington, IN: Indiana University Press, 1984); *The Dialogic Imagination*, trans. Caryl Emerson and Michael Holquist (Austin, TX: University of Texas Press, 1981).

Thinking as a Kind of Writing, Writing as a Kind of Philosophy

Parts of this final chapter originally appeared in what was to have been a 2020 conference paper. That conference never happened, due to the Covid-19 pandemic (though a revised version of that paper was eventually given at an online seminar – see n.27 above). The original paper contained the following passage:

> To ground the above in an example: In the autumn of 2019, I used free- or quick-writing exercises, in the context of a philosophy of education module on an Education Studies degree. Philosophy as a subject-area is a late introduction to the degree, though not, as I and my co-tutor urge, a new activity (or, indeed, subject-matter). Year on year, we find that many students are concerned at the prospect of having to write in a philosophical mode. None of the students had ever attempted freewriting in a formal educational context before, though some reported, after the exercise, that this was in fact how they often developed their written work. The exercise was free, inasmuch as they were asked to write continuously and to neither censor nor edit themselves, for a period of between ten and fifteen minutes. It was structured, inasmuch as they were asked to write in response to one of a set of educational questions or problems. One student admitted she found the process unnerving, as she usually started with what authoritative others ("The Literature") say and not with what she thought (I suspect that students in this position don't yet know what they believe: this is not to say they necessarily lack knowledge (though they might), but, rather, that they may not yet have worked out to which statements regarding topic X they're committed and why). Others found the process liberating, precisely because they felt they were able to express and think for themselves: these students, I'd speculate, felt they'd been given license to take responsibility in ways often prevented by (their perceptions of) standard academic writing conventions, because here there was something – one's own thought – to take responsibility for.
>
> Regardless of how the students found the free writing experience, and irrespective of my guesses as to why they experienced it this way or that, most were able to meet the challenge of writing continuously, in silence, for the specified time; all were able to reflect on the experience, to put themselves between presence and meaning; all were willing to subject themselves to a discipline (free/writing) that was structured yet (beyond the injunctions to write in silence for a specified time) stylistically non-prescriptive; and with few stylistic restrictions, all, it seemed, were able to write in flow, fluidly.

The passage was followed by a note, acknowledging the disruption caused by the pandemic. The note concluded: "My aim now, with a return to campus-based teaching likely (though not certain), is to better integrate writing workshops into that and other modules' routines." I've removed the passage from the main text of this book, because, at the time of writing, we are back on campus, and I have been able to integrate writing workshops into certain of my classes. The impact of these workshops has yet to be seen, however. Certainly, responses have been mixed: no student has said they don't want focussed writing support; many have admitted to struggling with writing; and several students, across different year-groups and modules, have raised pertinent questions regarding the apparent strictures of academic style and convention. However, quickwrite tasks have been embraced by some, not by others. For various reasons, I am beginning to think that dedicated writing courses, *pace* WAC, may be a better model for teaching writing in academic contexts (teaching which would create space for conventions to be challenged).

All this, then, crammed into an endnote in a spirit of confessional honesty, but also in recognition that I'm not in a position to report on the relative success or failure of these modest philosophical, classroom experiments.

58 E.g. Peter Stockwell, *Sociolinguistics: A Resource Book for Students*, 2nd Ed. (London: Routledge, 2007).
59 Marko Modiano, "Is European English at the Heart of Unification?" *EL Gazette* 475 (April 2021), available online <https://www.elgazette.com/is-european-english-at-the-heart-of-unification/> (accessed 03 June 2021).
60 James Baldwin, "If Black English Isn't a Language, Then Tell Me, What Is?" *Collected Essays*, Toni Morrison (ed.) (New York: Library of America, 1998), pp.780–783; April Baker-Bell, *Linguistic Justice: Black Language, Literacy, Identity, and Pedagogy* (New York: Routledge, 2020).
61 As well as Baker-Bell's recent study of Black Language, see, e.g., Jennifer Coates and Pia Pichler (eds), *Language and Gender: A Reader*, 2nd Ed. (Oxford: Wiley Blackwell, 2011); Roxy Harris and Ben Rampton (eds), *The Language, Ethnicity and Race Reader* (London: Routledge, 2003); Annabelle Mooney *et al* (eds), *The Language, Society and Power Reader* (London: Routledge, 2011).
62 White Mainstream English is Baker-Bell's term (which she uses rather than Django Paris's "Dominant American English").
63 A classic example of this is William Labov's study of race and class, *Language in the Inner City: Studies in the Black English Vernacular* (Philadelphia: University of Pennsylvania Press, 1973).
64 John Humphrys, "What Grade A nonsense! JOHN HUMPHRYS hits out as universities say correct spelling and grammar may be seen as 'white, male and elite'," *Mail Online* (12 April 2021) <https://www.dailymail.co.uk/debate/article-9463611/JOHN-HUMPHRYS-hits-universities-say-correct-spelling-grammar-elite.html> (accessed 07 June 2021).
65 E.g. Bizzell and Elbow. A similar point was raised to me recently by students.
66 Elaine Maimon, "Talking to Strangers," *College Composition and Communication* 30(4) (1979), pp.364–369 (365, emphasis added).
67 Culler, *Just Being Difficult?*
68 Judith Butler, "Further Reflections on Conversations of Our Time," *Diacritics* 27(1) (1997), p.13. The sentence is reproduced in full in Culler's "Bad Writing and Good Philosophy," *Just Being Difficult?* (45).
69 A word has extension if there are objects in the world for which it stands, reference if the word points to or denotes something. The difference is exemplified by words such as "centaur" or "unicorn": such words have no (null) extension, because (according to most of the literature) they don't exist; and yet "unicorn" still refers to unicorns (or, perhaps, to some particular unicorn), "centaur" to centaurs (or, perhaps, to some particular centaur).
70 Dutton's comments are available from the cached version of his website (which became inactive after his death). See Dutton, "Language Crimes: A Lesson in How Not to Write, Courtesy of the Professoriate," originally in *The Wall Street Journal* (5 February 1999); available online, <http://webcache.googleusercontent.com/search?q=cache:uXRigi6NlIAJ:www.denisdutton.com/language_crimes.htm+&cd=3&hl=en&ct=clnk&gl=uk&client=firefox-b-d>; and, from the Cached version of <www.denisdutton.com>, "The Bad Writing Contest: Press Releases, 1996-1998," available online, <http://webcache.googleusercontent.com/search?q=cache:FoFLJ4GgyNMJ:www.denisdutton.com/bad_writing.htm+&cd=1&hl=en&ct=clnk&gl=uk&client=firefox-b-d> (accessed 07 July 2021).
71 Culler, "Bad Writing and Good Philosophy," *Just Being Difficult?* (43–57).
72 On imputing commitment, belief, and so on to others, and inferring it in or from them, see Brandom, *Articulating Reasons*, and Chapter 4 of this book.
73 Bizzell, "Basic Writing and the Issue of Correctness" (5).

74 See Chapter 4; Cassirer, *An Essay on Man*; Lorraine Code, *What Can She She Know? Feminist Theory and the Construction of Knowledge* (Ithaca, NY: Cornell University Press, 1991); Thomas S. Kuhn, *The Structure of Scientific Revolutions*, 2nd Ed. (1962; Chicago: University of Chicago Press, 1970); Charles W. Mills, *Blackness Visible: Essays on Philosophy and Race* [e-book] (Ithaca, NY: Cornell University Press, 2015).
75 Kwame Anthony Appiah, *The Ethics of Identity* (Princeton: Princeton University Press, 2005), pp.65–71, *passim*.
76 E.g. Baker-Bell, *Linguistic Justice*; Bizzell, "Basic Writing and the Issue of Correctness"; see also Alain Locke's philosophy of art and its relation to the *volk*, "The Ethics of Culture [1923]," in *The Philosophy of Alain Locke: Harlem Renaissance and Beyond*, Leonard Harris (ed.) [e-book] (Philadelphia: Temple University Press), "The New Negro," in *The New Negro: Voices of the Harlem Renaissance*, Locke (ed.), Arnold Rampersad (intro.) (New York: Touchstone-Simon and Schuster, 1997), pp.3–16.
77 Things get philosophically complicated, however, because the idea of second nature is made intelligible for some, contradictory for others, by its having these two aspects. I'd add to this the problem of how we fit first- and second-order languaging processes into the idea of second-nature: usually, we expect the first-order capacities of speaking and listening to develop without explicit instruction, while the second-order capacities of reading and writing must be taught formally. Yet we are not born already speaking and listening fluently; and we are clearly "wired" so that we can learn to read and write. See Georg W. Bertram, "Two Conceptions of Second Nature," *Open Philosophy* 3(1) (2020), pp.68–80 (DOI: <https://doi.org/10.1515/opphil-2020-0005>) (accessed 15 June 2021).
78 As a professor told Zinsser, regarding her institution's adoption of a WAC programme: "I wanted to teach a [writing] course because I write very badly myself – in high school I was terrorized by writing" (*Writing to Learn*, 45).
79 Theresa Lillis, "Economies of Signs in Academic Publication: The Case of English Medium 'National' Journals," *JAC* 32(3/4) (2012), pp.695–722. For a classic articulation of the idea that there is no language/world mirroring relationship, see Richard Rorty, *Philosophy and the Mirror of Nature*, 30th Anniversary Ed. (1979; Princeton: Princeton University Press, 1991).
80 See Chapter 3.
81 See Richard W. Brislin, Brent MacNab, and David Bechtold, "Translation," in Charles Donald Spielberger (ed.), *Encyclopedia of Applied Psychology* (Elsevier Science & Technology). E-book (accessed 01 November 2021) via Credo Reference (<http://0-search.credoreference.com.brum.beds.ac.uk/content/entry/estappliedpsyc/translation/0?institutionId=210>); Merrill Swain and Ping Deters, "'New' Mainstream SLA Theory: Expanded and Enriched," *The Modern Language Journal* 91 (2007), pp.820–836.
82 Phil Ford's "Style as Analysis" (ch.2 in Ciro Scotto, Kenneth Smith, and John Brackett (eds), *The Routledge Companion to Popular Music Analysis: Expanding Approaches* (e-book; New York: Routledge). See also n.36 in the previous chapter.
83 See Code, *What Can She Know?*, Mills, *Blackness Visible*, bell hooks and Cornel West, *Breaking Bread: Insurgent Black Intellectual Life* (New York: Routledge, 2017).
84 "Languaging" is used by Baker-Bell, as by other socio- and psycho-linguists, as way of indicating the dynamic, practical, embodied nature of linguistic expression. See also Richard Beach and David Bloome (eds) *Relations for Transforming the Literacy and Language Arts Classroom* (New York: Routledge, 2019).
85 See Bizzell, "Basic Writing and the Issue of Correctness," "'Contact Zones' and English Studies,"; on genre and the impossibility of genrelessness, see Jacques Derrida, "The Law of Genre," in *Acts of Literature*, Derek Attridge (ed.) (London: Routledge, 1992), pp.221–252. See also Gumbrecht *Production of Presence* and *In Praise of Athletic Beauty*.

86 Blanshard, *On Philosophical Style* (13). Blanshard slightly misquotes James, who, in *The Principles of Psychology*, Vol. I (New York: Henry Holt, 1918, p.145), writes that "Metaphysics means nothing but an unusually obstinate effort to think clearly."
87 Blanshard (5–6).
88 Zinsser, *Writing to Learn* (58).
89 Richard Rorty, "Philosophy as a Kind of Writing: An Essay on Derrida," *New Literary History*, 10(1) (1978), pp.141–160. Rorty's version of Derrida's maxim that there's nothing outside the text is much like my insistence in the previous chapter that there are no forms or modes of knowledge that are not bounded by disciplinary lines (the lines are there, though they may be more or less rigid).
90 Rorty, "Philosophy as a Kind of Writing" (156–157).

Index

academic conventions/standards 21, 76, 111, 125
academic correctness 127
academic writing 4, 10, 13, 24, 111, 124–133, 139
aesthetics/aesthetic experience 9, 12–14, 71, 75, 89, 103n23; aesthetic education 16; location of 93–98; of spectatorship 75–76
African/Britain parallelism 17
Aldridge, David 113–116, 121
Angus, Joseph 19
antiphony 65
Appiah, Kwame Anthony 65, 74, 128; *The Ethics of Identity* 84n14
articulation 46
artworks 13
automaticity 121
The Awakening (Chopin) 117–118

background 42–45, 119, 121; line between context and 45
Badenoch, Kemi 17
Baker-Bell, April 84n13, 140n62, 141n84
Baldwin, James 140n60
being a knower 33, 65–66
Benchmark Statements 21–23
Biesta, Gert 113
Bizzell, Patricia 127
Black histories 17–18
Black History Month 17–18
Blake, William 93, 112
book reviewing 100
Brandom, Robert 46, 50, 74, 79, 83n11, 122; conception of knowledge 46, 50, 64; inferentialism 64; linguistic philosophy 64–65; linguistic pragmatism 63–64; propositional content 63–65

Britishness 17
Buchmann, Erin 24
Bugs Bunny 55n18
Butler, Judith 126–127
Buurma, Rachel Sagner 6–7

Cassirer, Ernst 64
Cavell, Stanley 45
Certeau, Michel de 7–8, 24; *The Practice of Everyday Life* 23
Chaplin, Charlie 47–48, 126; *City Lights* 47, 49
Clay's Ark (Butler) 20
close reading 14, 88–90, 98
coach 49–50
codifiable knowledge 51
Colebrook, Claire 105n38
Collingwood, R.G. 14, 96–97, 105n35; *The Principles of Art* 95
Collins, Harry 49–51
colour recognition 40–41
Coltrane, John 35
common-sense knowledge 32, 67, 70
conceptual criterion 68–69
conceptuality 40–42, 45–46
conceptual knowledge 63
context 45
context-dependent knowledge 36, 38, 52, 61, 123
context-free knowledge 44
context-independent knowledge 36, 51–52
contextualism 90
contextualizing 13, 51–52, 63, 66, 75, 80, 94
contributory expertise 49–51
core knowledge 32, 54n4, 76
Cowan, Andrew 23

Index

Creative Writing 21–24, 52–53, 88, 101, 123; knowledge-richness as 62
creative writing 3–4, 12–14, 24, 53, 99; disciplinary borders of 23; place/space of 21–24; QAA Benchmark Statement for English 21
creativity *vs* schooling 112
criticism/scholarship debate 10, 12, 89–93
Culler, Jonathan 125, 127
cultural literacy 62–63, 76, 78, 90

Dasein 42–43
decolonization 5
Deleuze, Gilles 10n8, 25n4, 105n38
deschooled society 112
descriptions 67
disciplinarity 59, 61, 68, 71, 74, 91, 111–112, 128
disciplinary identity 79
disciplinary knowledge 9, 33, 60–62, 66–68, 70, 76
disciplines 23, 33, 74, 125; criterion-based definitions of 76; as practice 77–79
distant reading 14
Dreyfus, Hubert 39–40, 42, 46, 53, 57n47, 120, 123

Eaglestone, Robert 68, 76, 90–91, 94
education: as learning 114–119; phenomenological accounts of 120–121; transformative 115; *vs* schooling 111–114
educational epiphanies 115–116
Education Reform Act of 1988 77
Elbow, Peter 110, 123–125
Emig, Janet 124
Emma (Austen) 91
engaged/autonomous art debate 104n27, 104n34
engagement 114
engagement proper 113
English education 15–21, 77
English Language 21, 101; academic English 132–133; Black American English 124; European English 124; standard English 125, 132; White Mainstream English 140n62
English Literature 3, 5–6, 12, 14–15, 19, 21–23, 34, 62, 66, 68, 73, 76, 79–81, 88–91, 100, 114; definition 76; QAA Benchmark Statement for English 21
English Literature and Creative Writing curricula 66, 73, 81, 88
English Studies 100–101

entitlement 82n3
epiphanies 115–116
epistemic injustice 24
epistemological pluralism 66
Examined Life (film) 74
Executive Order 13950 18
existentialism 75
existential-phenomenology 113, 119–120
Experience 116–117
explicitation 50–51, 122
explicit knowledge 34–35

fictionality 89
Fielding, Michael 112
Fincher, David 76
first- and third-person awareness 39
Fisher, Mark 20
Fricker, Miranda 24

Gascoigne, Neil 36–39, 42–43, 47, 54n1, 83n11
Gibb, Nick 22–23
good education 22
Goodman, Nelson 47, 64
Greene, Maxine 119
Gumbrecht, Hans Ulrich 75, 122

habituation 119, 121
Hardwick, Elizabeth 100
Harlem Renaissance 86n49
Heart of Darkness (Conrad) 81
Heffernen, Laura 6–7
Hegel 134
Heidegger, Martin: *Being-in-the-World* 42, 45
Hickey, Dave 96–97
Hirsch, E. D. 32, 62, 76, 80; curriculum theory 62–63; epistemology and hermeneutics 63
historicity 63
hooks, bell 7
Hopkins, Neil 5
How to Teach... project 4
Hunter, Ian 16

Illich, Ivan 112
inferentialism 64
informal modes of knowing 67
intellectualism 56n41
interactional expertise 49–51
internal realism 56n34
I-perceive-a-table method 43

Jarvis, Tim 24
Joseph-Salisbury, Remi 18

Kant 47, 48, 134
knowing-that and knowing-how distinction 33–38, 60
knowledge 18–19, 22; based curriculum 32; classroom as a centre of 8; gap between scientific and literary knowledge 91–92; knowledge-that/knowledge-how distinction 33–38, 60; in National Curriculum document 31; political meaning between 31–32; politicization of 32; powerful 32; skills and 31–33; transmission 62; truth and 66; . see also specific entries
knowledge-richness 22, 59, 61–66, 78; as Creative Writing 62

Lamb, Kevin 125; *Just Being Difficult?* 125–126
language 48, 50, 69, 110, 124
Language Study 101
languaging 141n84
learning, existential-phenomenological accounts of 74, 115, 120–121
library card 76; *see also* Yoda
lightbulb moments 114–121
linguistic descriptions 46
linguistic philosophy 64–65
Literary Critic 79
literary criticism 6, 12–14, 20, 70, 79, 81, 88–90, 94, 99
literary history 12
Lowe, Robert 19

Maimon, Elaine 125
maps/mapping 8, 22–23
mass schooling 3
McDowell, John 39–41, 44–46, 61, 120; *Mind and World* 40
McLeod, Susan 76, 109
methodology 103n20
Mills, Charles 16
mindedness 39, 48
Mirror of Nature species of argument 95
modernity 18
modern literary education 16
moral and value judgement 91–92
Morrison, Toni 92–93, 103n16; *Beloved* 92–93
Muller, Johann 63, 69–71, 73, 75, 78, 80; meaning-makers 70–71

Murray, Heather 99
Myers, D. G. 14

National Association for the Teaching of English (NATE) 20
National Curriculum, England 31, 91–92
New Criticism 89
nonrational attachment 97
North, Joseph 90–91, 93
novice learning 57n47, 120
Nussbaum, Martha 74

objectivity 44; and subjectivity 71–73
Paradise Lost (Milton) 91–93
personal knowledge 9, 34, 47, 59, 66; skill and, difference between 60; theoretical knowledge and, difference between 49–50, 60
Peters, R. S. 112
Phelan, J.W. 89–90, 93, 102n7
philosophical writing 112, 115, 134
philosophies of identity 118–119
Philosophy and Literature 127
phlogistics 66
place/space 7–8; in creative writing practices 21–24
Polanyi, Michael 34
post-Romantic ideals 3, 15, 20
powerful knowledge 66–71, 77–78, 90; conceptual criterion 68–69; disciplinarity and 74; discursive practices 69; explanatory or predictive power of 69; notions of objectivity and subjectivity 71–73; perspective of a specialist 70; revisions 67–68; social-realist framework for curriculum design 67; *vs* disciplinary knowledge 67
practical coaching knowledge 49–50
practical knowledge 9, 36–39, 49
presence, notion of 75
Principle of Articulacy 36, 45–46
Principles of Codifiability and Inarticulacy 36
pro-criticism 88
productivity 70–71
propositional content 63–65, 71, 89
propositionality 46–48, 53, 60–61
propositional knowledge 33, 54n4, 61, 63, 74
Putnam, Hilary 33

Index

QAA Benchmark Statement for English 21

racial literacy 18
racism 16–17; *Race and Racism in English Secondary Schools* 18; structural 17
Rancière, Jacques 19
reading, critical 13–14, 98–100
recalibration 4
received knowledge 61
receptivity 70–71
repetitiousness 121
Richards, I. A. 14, 89, 98
Richmond, Lewis 5
Rodgers, Jimmie 45
Romantic aesthetic education 16
Rorty, Richard 3, 74, 99, 112, 134–135
Rose, Steven 66
Runnymede Trust 18
Ryle, Gilbert 33–35, 60; *The Concept of Mind* 47

schooled English 3, 8, 10n4, 12–16, 19–20, 24, 52–53, 73, 79, 81, 92, 94, 99–100
science education 77–78
scientific knowledge 50
self-unawareness 35
Seven (film) 76
Singer, Peter 74
slave period 17
Smeyers, Paul 115
socialization 113
space *see* place/space
specialist knowledge 50, 66
spontaneity 39–40
sports 75–76
state education in England 19
subject-centred inquiry 9
subject-matter 15, 20, 100, 113, 123
subject-specific knowledge 60, 62
surface/depth approaches to interpretation 89, 102n6
symbolic worlds and frames 48, 50–52, 57n42, 65

tacit knowledge 34–36, 45–49; definition 38
Tacit Knowledge (Gascoigne and Thornton) 36
taciturnity 38, 42
Taylor, Charles 48
The Teaching Archive (Buurma and Heffernen) 6, 24
text-centred criticism 94
textualism 61
theoretical knowledge 9, 37–38, 49
Thomas, Gary 111–112; *Education: A Very Short Introduction* 111
Thornton, Tim 36–39, 42–43, 47, 54n1, 83n11
training 121
transformative education 115
transformative learning 116–117
Trump, Donald 18

unconcealedness 114

value-free English Literature knowledge 91

walking 8
The Waste Land (Eliot) 96
White, John 7, 68, 76
Wittgenstein 43–45, 48, 52, 61, 74, 83n11; *Philosophical Investigations* 84n12
writing 133; academic 4, 10, 13, 24, 111, 124–133, 139; to learn 110–111, 123, 133; philosophical 112, 115, 134; practice 122–124; significance to learning 109; standard 129–132
Writing Across the Curriculum (WAC) 76, 109–111, 133, 135

Yandell, John 3, 19
Yes, and … game 114
Yoda 76; *see also* library card
Young, Michael 9, 63, 69–71, 73, 75, 78, 80; meaning-makers 70–71; powerful knowledge 9, 32, 60

Zinsser, William 110–111, 133–134